"This book has been long in within the Tibetan Buddhist wor thinkers. His interactions with J. Krishnamurti will remain one of the most prized encounters in the contemporary Indian spiritual and philosophical landscape. A must-read."

    The Venerable Tenzin Priyadarshi, Director, Ethics Initiative | MIT Media Lab, President and CEO, The Dalai Lama Center for Ethics and Transformative Values at MIT

"*Always Awakening* is much more than a 'good read,' beginning with an outstanding title that says a great deal. If one is willing to move slowly and reflectively, the dynamic interplay between the 'right and left' pages can be a form of dharma practice in itself. Rinpoche's point that Krishnamurti helped him understand Buddhadharma and Buddhadharma helped him understand Krishnamurti is very important. *Always Awakening* helped refine my understanding as well. Reading the book for a second time is a joy."

    Larry Rosenberg, Founder, Cambridge Insight Meditation Center, Massachusetts

"This is the most important book on Krishnamurti ever written and I have read them all. Reading slowly, listening quietly, I am finding jewels of insight on every page. I understand Krishnamurti more directly and the same can be said of my understanding of Buddhism."

    James Paul, Symphony Conductor; Former Chair, Krishnamurti Foundation of America Board of Trustees

"Immediately I see that *Always Awakening* is not a normal book, one to be read and thought about. It is an experience. After only a few pages I had to stop, meditate, and later continue. It is beautiful. A magnum opus (meaning 'great work,' referring to the largest or most renowned achievement by an artist)!"

    R. E. Mark Lee, Trustee Emeritus, Krishnamurti Foundations of America and India

"*Always Awakening* is a beautiful experience. There are times when it is possible to imagine that a conversation between a real-life Gautama Buddha and a real-life J. Krishnamurti might have sounded very much like the conversation between Samdhong Rinpoche and Michael Mendizza in this book. It is a dialogue of utter impeccability and integrity. Those wishing to listen to the voice of liberation can do no better than to have a ringside seat to this conversation."

    Mu Soeng, Resident Scholar at the Barre Center for Buddhist Studies, a former Zen monk, and author of *The Heart of the Universe: Exploring the Heart Sutra*, *Trust in Mind: The Rebellion of Chinese Zen*, and other books

"*Always Awakening* beautifully interweaves the exquisite harmony of Krishnamurti's mind and the deep affinity for illumination he shared with the Buddhist tradition."

Ram Dass, Teacher, Author of *Be Here Now* and other works

"*Always Awakening* renders me somewhat speechless! It confirms what I had felt after 12 years in Tibetan Buddhism — that there was no difference at the deep level between Tibetan Buddhism and Krishnamurti. I haven't finished absorbing the book; perhaps I never will. It has the effect of drawing apart a heavy curtain. *Always Awakening* is a fascinating, deeply significant study!"

David Skitt, Trustee, Krishnamurti Foundation Trust, United Kingdom; Editor of Krishnamurti Publications

"Professor Samdhong Rinpoche shows that Krishnamurti's teachings can resonate with others of the non-dual tradition. In other words, the principles that Krishnamurti was teaching can be found without ever having read Krishnamurti. *Always Awakening* reminds us that there are many ways in which timeless precepts can and have been presented. There's more than one way to cross the ocean using different means over time."

Robert Wolfe, Author of *Living Nonduality*

"*Always Awakening* is a treasure. Every sentence from Samdhong Rinpoche is enlightening. I have learned a great deal about Buddhism from his simple words. The mastery of including citations from many sources: Tibetan Buddhism, the Dalai Lama, companions of Krishnamurti, Annie Besant, David-Néel and others, alongside the teaching of Krishnamurti, makes the volume an important resource. The book is a service to us all."

Constance A. Jones, Professor, School of Consciousness and Transformation, California Institute of Integral Studies

"*Always Awakening* is a religious 'experience' more than reading a religious text, an experience that invites a leisurely but rigorous journey toward a deeper understanding of both Buddhism and Krishnamurti's insight. Turning the pages, one feels as if they have been invited to silently participate in a most intimate and wise conversation. *Always Awakening* is not a book to be read quickly, rather savored, slowly and thoughtfully. With luck, as described in the Introduction, you will catch wind of what Krishnamurti called 'the perfume of the teachings' or catch a glimpse of your own 'Buddha nature' along the way."

Meredy Benson Rice, MA, Education Leadership, Teacher's College, Columbia University; Former Head of the Oak Grove School

Always Awakening

Always Awakening

Buddha's Realization
Krishnamurti's Insight

Samdhong Rinpoche
with
Michael Mendizza

Foreword by His Holiness
The Dalai Lama

Always Awakening: Buddha's Realization Krishnamurti's Insight
by Samdhong Rinpoche with Michael Mendizza

Copyright © 2017 by Michael Mendizza

All rights reserved. No part of this book may be reproduced
or transmitted in any form or by any means, electronic or mechanical,
including photocopying, recording, or by any information storage
and retrieval system, without permission in writing from the publisher.

ISBN-13: 978-1-879118-04-1 (softcover)

ISBN-13: 978-1-879118-06-5 (hardcover)

Published by Mendizza & Associates
PO Box 1226, Solvang, CA 93464, USA
Email: michael@ttfuture.org

Designed by Margaret Kay Dodd
Studio K Communication Arts

Dedicated to Evelyne Blau
for her inspiration, creativity, support, and encouragement

Acknowledgments

Of course, this sharing would not be possible without the generous time and support of Professor Samdhong Rinpoche. Like a sharp knife, Margaret Kay Dodd has been relentless about grammar, proofing, editing, and layout. For over 20 years, Rebecca Reiland has transcribed our interviews, this being one of the most demanding. With this work and others, Mark Lee has always been encouraging and supportive. Thank you to Keith Buzzel, his wife, and colleagues for reviewing early drafts. And this is just the tip of the iceberg. My years with Krishnamurti, David Bohm, and Joseph Chilton Pearce, along with over 100 interviews, created the foundation for Always Awakening, *along with the care and support of my wife and children.*

CONTENTS

Foreword by His Holiness the Dalai Lama   11
Preface by Lee Nichol   12
Introduction   15

California, USA, 2008

The Self As We Know It   27
Misconception   31
Emptiness   33
Direct Perception   35
Enchantment   37
Language Divides   41
Use and Misuse of Imagination   45
What Is It That Reincarnates?   49
Different Realms, Dimensions, and Realities   51
The Source and Consequences of Greed   53

United Kingdom, 2012, Day One

The Self As Image   57
What's in a Name?   61
Relative and Absolute Realities   63
Tibetan Monastic Training: Understanding the Mind   65
Identification and Confusion   69
Karma Is Like a Hangover   69
Spiritual Kindergarten and Levels   73
With or Without Methods   81

United Kingdom, 2012, Day Two

The Self Is the Self   85
One Soul or Many   87
Masters or No Masters   91

Distortion, Converting the Unknown into the Known	93
Telepathy, Gestures, and Words	95
Resonate Subtle Consciousness	99
If You Understand Reality Completely, Everything Fits	101
Rituals, Krishnamurti, and the Theosophical Society	103
The Maitreya Prophesy, the Coming of the Future Buddha	105

United Kingdom, 2012, Day Three

Magic and Black Magic	109
If You Meet the Buddha on the Road, Kill Him	111
Transformation That Is Not Dependent on Knowledge or Time	115
Transcendent Insight	117
Changing World, Changing Traditions	121
The Monastic Experience	123
The Eight-Fold Path and Krishnamurti	125
Are the Masters Relevant?	127
Why Do You Remain a Buddhist?	127
Krishnamurti's Mission Is to Challenge	131
Confusion Leads to Inquiry	131
Has Tibet Gone Public with Its Secrets?	133

Dharamsala, India, 2014, Day One

What Is Consciousness?	137
Krishnamurti Did Not Conform to Any System	143
Begin with Emptiness	145
Grasping	147
Maya and the Power of Self-Deception	149
No Psychological Becoming	151
Negating Methods	151

Dharamsala, India, 2014, Day Two

Ritual Conditioning	155
The Method Is Not the End	157
Removing Misconceptions	157
Truth and the Absolute	159
Fragmentation Leads to Conflict	161
Two Types of Virtues	161
Samsara Is the Result of Ignorance	163
Ignorance Is the Ego: The Ego Is Ignorance	165

Dharamsala, India, 2014, Day Three

Happiness	167
Conditioning or Freedom	169
Two Realities: Absolute and Relative	169
Look at What We Are Doing	171
Compassion Combined with Energy	173
It Is So Damn Simple	175
Ultimately There Is No Path	177
Identity, Name, and Fame	179
Brain-Mind, Reincarnation, Past Lives	181
Mediums, Oracles, and Celestial Realms	183
The Theosophists' Idea of a Vehicle	189
The Most Effective Is Negation	193
Wisdom Cannot Be Achieved by a Partial Mind	195
Complete Attention Without a Center	199
Permanent Relief from Ignorance	205
The Western Concept of Soul	207
All Buddhas See the Same Truth	209

Dharamsala, India, 2014, Day Four

Krishnamurti Was Able to Stand on His Own	213
Krishnamurti Is Talking About the Human Mind	215
The Entire Process Becomes Distorted	217

The Ego Says, "I Have Done This"	219
Ignorance Cannot Be Removed by Ignorance	221
With or Without the Ego	223
Buddhists Believe That Thought and the Ego Are Always Combined	223
Bringing the Action of Enlightenment into the Relative World	225
Devotion and Belief or Wisdom	227
Negating the Basis of Our Inaction	229
The First Step Is the Last Step	233
The Individual Mind Is Part of a Universal Mind	233

Dharamsala, India, 2014, Day Five

The Maitreya Prophecy	237
So Many Mysteries	239
No One Can Understand What Was Going On with Krishnamurti	241
Can You Live with the Question?	243
Without Being Touched by Them Viscerally	247
What Will I Achieve?	249
Constant Challenge Is Krishnamurti's Real Contribution, His True Legacy	251
Exploitation of the Ego by the Ego Is the Root of All the Problems We Have Today	253
Krishnamurti's Consciousness Touched Everything	257
Thought Cannot Function Clearly When It Is Contaminated by the Ego	259
To Understand the Real Teaching, You Need to Transform Yourself	261

The Mystery	265
Epilog	273
Notes	277
Glossary	279
Appendix: Going Beyond Self As Image	285
About the Authors	293
Bibliography: Permissions and Sources	294
Photographic Credits	297

FOREWORD

In this book, *Always Awakening*, author, educator and documentary filmmaker Michael Mendizza records conversations he has held with Samdhong Rinpoche, stimulated to some extent by what he has understood Rinpoche's friend Krishnamurti to have said.

Although we met briefly in Madras in 1956 during my first visit to India I did not know Krishnamurti well, but mutual friends have confirmed to me the impression I gained at that meeting of the rigorous clarity of his mind. His statement, that it is the responsibility of each individual to bring about their own transformation, is reminiscent of the Buddha's advice, "You are your own master."

Samdhong Rinpoche, on the other hand, I know very well. He is a senior Buddhist monk and an erudite scholar, someone who has fully accomplished a traditional Tibetan Buddhist training. Besides this he has a well-versed knowledge of Sanskrit and Hindi, which affords him a fond and appreciative relationship with the broad range of Indian spiritual traditions and schools of thought.

A common interest all three of us share is the importance of education —and that it should be holistic, unbiased, founded on human values and affection.

Readers concerned with how individuals can transform themselves and so contribute to creating a happier, more peaceful world will find much to interest them here.

The Dalai Lama

PREFACE

The book you are holding, *Always Awakening*, will, if you allow it, present you with a plenitude of insight, inquiry, elegant logic, and the continual sparking of two minds passionately engaged. But most importantly, it will present you with ever-deepening paradoxes. These existential paradoxes are the real fruit of the logic, and the inquiry, and the insight. Any one of the paradoxes will, if you allow it, bring you to a point of feeling, "I don't know how to resolve this."

If your thinking says, "I don't know how to resolve this," then more likely than not, you will have the liberty to walk away from the challenge of the paradox. But if your thinking and your feeling—together, both of them—come to this point of "I don't know how," then the work of Krishnamurti, and the work of Buddhism, will have come alive within you.

On the face of it, there is little love lost between the work of Krishnamurti and the 2,500-year stream of Buddhism. Krishnamurti was graphically and persistently clear in his rejection of tradition. And every school of Buddhism has been equally clear about the value of tradition, with its practices, systems, and methods.

And yet, decades after leaving the Theosophical Society, Krishnamurti advised a young Desikachar to devote his life to the yogic teaching of his father Krishnamacharya, saying, "I want to make sure you learn everything from your father. His great wisdom must not die with him." Was this gesture from Krishnamurti only in regard to the teaching of physical asanas? Or was there something more implied? It may well be that Krishnamurti was indicating—albeit privately—a deep respect for those who he knew could uphold and embody a tradition, all the way down through its roots. If this is so, then we have here a splendid paradox, one worthy of both thought and feeling.

In a similar paradoxical vein, *Always Awakening* finds Samdhong Rinpoche negating many of the most hallowed practices and methods of traditional Buddhism, much in the spirit of Nagarjuna. And yet, Samdhong Rinpoche, like Nagarjuna, is by any measure one who reveres and upholds Buddhist tradition.

How is one to understand all this upside-down thinking?

* * *

I first met Michael Mendizza in 1980, in the Oak Grove in Ojai, where Krishnamurti was giving his public talks. After some amateur attempts in the 1970s to videotape the talks, Mendizza appeared, seemingly out of nowhere, offering to record the talks with professional equipment, at broadcast-level standards. The rest, as they say, is history. Virtually every video document of Krishnamurti produced in the USA from that time forward has been done by Mendizza.

The years between 1980 and 1986 gave Mendizza unique and extensive interaction with Krishnamurti. Now, thirty years later, Michael continues to mine his video archive and bring forth new facets of these seemingly inexhaustible teachings. Along the way, he has also, as a trustee of the Krishnamurti Foundation of America, lent his considerable management and entrepreneurial skills to the effort to keep Krishnamurti's work in the public eye.

Always Awakening offers a different side of Mendizza. Here we find not the film-maker, not the businessman, but the contemplative. The years of immersion with Krishnamurti have left their mark: Michael's passion for grasping the core of Krishnamurti's teaching is evident, and his interaction with Samdhong Rinpoche sparkles with clarity, depth, and wit. I daresay it was a stroke of genius for Mendizza to approach Samdong Rinpoche—a trustee of the Krishnamurti Foundation of India since the 1980s—and initiate these conversations. The two men play off one another in a way that is a joy to behold, tacking back and forth in ever-deepening currents. Underlying all of its remarkable content, *Always Awakening* demonstrates a true spirit of dialogue.

Very likely, some of Mendizza's penchant for such dialogue was fostered by his relationship with David Bohm. For many of those who inhabited the world of Krishnamurti in the 1970s and '80s, meeting and working with Bohm was an unanticipated opportunity for deepening inquiry and learning new aspects of dialogue. This was a remarkably rich and creative period, between Bohm and Krishnamurti, and between each of these men and the constellation of people who worked around and with them. A careful reading of *Always Awakening* indicates that Mendizza has "done his homework" from that time, and is contributing to the ongoing flowering of dialogue itself.

And what of all that upside-down thinking? Well, it is not for the faint-hearted. It is not for those who require black-and-white categories within which to live. It is not for those who hold unassailable worldviews (including any and all Krishnamurti fundamentalists, and any and all Buddhist fundamentalists).

But for those who have an appetite for the rigors of sustained spiritual inquiry, and the convolutions, permutations, and paradoxes therein, upside-down thinking can become a very good friend. A dangerous friend—but a trusty one. *Always Awakening* opens the door to such friendship—exhilarating, exhausting, confounding, and profoundly rewarding.

Lee Nichol
Albuquerque, New Mexico

Lee Nichol is editor of *The Essential David Bohm* and *On Dialogue*. He was a teacher at the Oak Grove School of the Krishnamurti Foundation in Ojai from 1981 to 1994, and an instructor at the Tibetan Nyingma Institute in Berkeley from 1998 to 2006.

INTRODUCTION

In the mid-1970s an obscure book, *The Secret Oral Teachings in Tibetan Buddhist Sects* by Alexandra David-Néel and Lama Yongden, landed in my lap, and so too did a paper bag with cassettes—eight talks given by J. Krishnamurti at the University of California San Diego. Both were compelling, challenging, yet completely different and strangely resonant in ways I did not understand. Some forty years later, *Always Awakening* is my answer to this riddle.

By 1977 I discovered that Krishnamurti was living and speaking part of the year in Ojai, California, two hours from my tiny beach apartment. By 1979 I had attended a number of talks, been invited to lunch at Krishnamurti's vintage ranch-style home, begun videotaping his annual talks in the Oak Grove, and was filming his major speaking engagements for the first of many productions in Canada, Switzerland, the United Kingdom, and India, a process that continued until his death in 1986.

At the very end of Krishnamurti's remarkable and equally mysterious life, those closest to him gathered to say goodbye, thus beginning a new chapter: documenting how people around the world had been touched by his presence and insights. Evelyne Blau, a trustee of the Krishnamurti Foundation of America and producer of the many projects we would eventually develop, appreciated that the oral histories of those close to or influenced by Krishnamurti were historical and critical if future generations were to have an undistorted record of the man and the message he so passionately shared.

Over one hundred personal oral histories have been recorded, including that of Samdhong Rinpoche, the highest-ranking Tibetan Buddhist scholar, first elected Kalon Tripa (Prime Minister) of the Central Tibetan Administration in Exile, and close associate of His Holiness the Dalai Lama, who had spent time in direct and personal dialogue with Krishnamurti over many years.

I knew none of this when we met for our first interview in 1987 near Deer Park, where 2,500 years earlier the Indian prince Gautama Siddhartha began his ministry. At that time Samdhong Rinpoche was serving as the Principal/Director of the Central Institute of Higher Tibetan Studies (Postgraduate Teachings and Research), Sarnath, Varanasi. From our first interview:

> *The Buddha and Krishnaji both tried to communicate the reality they perceived. But it is very difficult to describe the similarities or dissimilarities between these two personalities. They lived in different times, in different environments, and had different listeners. One thing we can say in definite terms is that the Buddha and Krishnamurti approached this challenge very differently.*
>
> *When Buddha teaches people, he comes down to the level of the listener, whereas Krishnaji doesn't come down to the level of the listener; he always speaks from his level. The Buddha deals with two levels: namely, the relative and the absolute. When Buddha speaks of the absolute, I personally do not find any difference with Krishnaji's teachings or the Buddha's teachings of* Prajnaparamita *or the absolute truth.*
>
> *When Buddha speaks of relative truth, he always compromises with the acceptance and notions and thoughts of people with whom he is speaking, but Krishnaji never compromises or accepts the conditions or the levels of his listeners.*
>
> *The other difference between them has to do with the preparation of the listeners. Krishnamurti is silent or doesn't speak about preparation, whereas the Buddha dealt a great deal with preparation of the person to reach the level of transformation. Both share a similar position that the moment of transformation or transmutation does not involve time, no graduation. It must be spontaneous and immediate. The perception is perception. There is no growing slowly, no graduation or becoming, anything like that. But Buddha dealt with the preparation of the person to reach up to that level with certain graduations and methods. Krishnaji never accepted these things.*

I admit being stunned then and now by the statement, "When Buddha speaks of the absolute, I personally do not find any difference with Krishnaji's teachings or the Buddha's teachings of *Prajnaparamita* or the absolute truth." To find no difference implies, at least to me, that the two teachers experienced the same absolute reality and quite naturally were using different words and metaphors to describe their shared insight with completely different audiences, worlds apart and separated by 2,500 years. Did Krishnamurti experience and share what is called the *Buddha Nature? Always Awakening* explores this question. From our interview in Dharamsala, India:

> *One thing no one can deny. Krishnamurti appeared in this world. He talked for sixty to seventy years and no one will be able to contradict his statements through logic or in any other way anything he has said. We may understand. We may not understand. But no one can prove them wrong. This fact is undeniable. This is the history. He was with us as one of the ordinary human beings. He walked around. He had happiness and sorrow. He had relationships, some good relationships, sometimes strained relationships. All the things that happen to ordinary human beings happened to him. His reactions may have been different but everything that happens to ordinary human beings happened to him. No one can stop what he has said. Not only said, but his words were recorded. A thousand years in the future people will witness the publications, and not only the publications but the visuals also. This is for the entire world. That is most important. No other teacher in human history has been so accurately documented.*

Over these many years, the notion that "we are not who or what we think we are" provided a strange bridge between Krishnamurti's so-called teachings and the very little I knew of Tibetan Buddhism. The whole question of enlightenment, self-realization, seeing the truth or the nature of illusion, along with the hundreds of hours of talks and dialogues I had experienced of Krishnamurti, seemed to focus on the images and beliefs we have of ourselves and others; in a word, *identity*.

If we are not who or what we think we are and this collection of images and beliefs creates our reality, then the world and all our relationships as we know them are built on a relatively false foundation. The relative reality the learned Rinpoche spoke about years earlier is relatively not true, relatively not sane, and this relatively insane reality is the source of our affairs and why our affairs, even with the best of intentions, so often appear like the Mad Hatter's Tea Party.

The Buddha's teachings describing the absolute and Krishnamurti's description of a silent mind point to a state of perception and implicit identity and therefore a relationship that is true, accurate, sane, and clear. I had collected a number of interviews exploring this in 2008 when Samdhong Rinpoche was invited to lecture at the University of California Santa Barbara. I asked if we could meet at Krishnamurti's home in Ojai for an interview. He graciously agreed. *Always Awakening* begins with this interview.

In 2012 Rinpoche and I were together for a week at the Krishnamurti Educational Center in the United Kingdom and we squeezed in three interviews. In 2014 I traveled to Dharamsala, India for a week, home of the Dalai Lama, Rinpoche, and the Tibetan Government in Exile, where we deepened and expanded our exploration together, now representing over sixteen hours.

The art and craft of film, drama or documentary is one of creating relationships. Having recorded well over three hundred interviews, one hundred plus with or about Krishnamurti, my approach begins with a theme that deepens, twists, and expands, given the flow of unfolding meaning. Preparation is key. Having traveled with Krishnamurti, filmed, recorded, and edited his talks and interviews for thirty-five years, the ground for our inquiry was well prepared. Missing, at least for me, was a basic understanding of Buddhism. I turned primarily to the writings of the Dalai Lama starting with his first major publication for the West, *The Opening of the Wisdom-Eye*, published in 1966. I followed this with six other books by the Dalai Lama, several dense academic works that were admittedly very difficult, books on Tibet, and generally anything that might seem to enrich the experience. I arrived in India with three one-inch binders overflowing with notes, questions, and references.

I share this to provide a context for both the meandering flow of the conversations on the right-hand pages, and the synergistic power of the quotes found on the left. In many cases the quotes on the left are the sources for the explorations on the right. I find the juxtapositions often generate an exponential effect in depth, context, and understanding.

Always Awakening is a collection of related themes: The self as we know it; Emptiness; What is it that reincarnates?; Different realms, dimensions and realities; Relative and absolute realities; With or without methods; The Maitreya prophecy; If you meet the Buddha on the road, kill him; Why do you remain a Buddhist?; What is consciousness?; Maya and the power of self-deception; No psychological becoming; Samsara is the result of ignorance; Ignorance is the ego; Mediums, oracles, and celestial realms; Ignorance cannot be removed by ignorance; Krishnamurti's legacy: Constant challenge; Exploitation of the ego by the ego; To understand the real teaching, you need to transform yourself; and more. All are metaphors pointing to something that cannot be put into words.

Always Awakening points to this unnamable. If I can be so presumptuous, the experience the book creates is not an accumulation of more information or a clever banter of comparisons; rather it is, hopefully, a catalyst for a penetrating insight into the simple but elusive common perception, source or essence of both Krishnamurti's and Buddhist teachings. Samdhong Rinpoche refers to this unnamable as our *Buddha Nature*. So does Sogyal Rinpoche, in *The Tibetan Book of Living and Dying*:

> *So whatever our lives are like, our Buddha Nature is always there. And it is always perfect. We say that not even the Buddhas can improve it in their infinite wisdom, nor can sentient beings spoil it in their seemingly infinite confusion. Our true nature could be compared to the sky, and the confusion of the ordinary mind to clouds. Some days the sky is completely obscured by clouds.*
>
> *We should always try and remember: the clouds are not the sky, and do* not *belong* to *it. They only hang there and pass by in their slightly ridiculous and non-dependent fashion. And they can never stain or mark the sky in any way.*
>
> *So where exactly is this Buddha Nature? It is in the sky-like nature of our mind. Utterly open, free, and limitless, it is fun, so simple and so natural that it can never be complicated, corrupted, or stained, so pure that it is beyond even the concept of purity and impurity. To talk of this nature of mind as sky-like, of course, is only a metaphor that helps us to begin to imagine its all-embracing boundlessness; for the Buddha Nature has a quality the sky cannot have—that of the radiant clarity of awareness. As it is said: "It is simply your flawless, present awareness, cognizant and empty, naked and awake."*

Renowned physicist David Bohm summarized our challenge: "We are faced with a breakdown of general social order and human values that threatens stability throughout the world. Existing knowledge cannot meet this challenge. Something much deeper is needed, a completely new approach. I am suggesting that the very means by which we try to solve our problems is the problem. The source of our problems is within the structure of thought itself."

A computer operating system that has preferences—likes and dislikes, anxiety, phobias, that is judgmental, paranoid, that conforms to the opinions of others, that is subject to fits of anger and rage, is greedy and narcissistic—how reliable is that, how sane? Quoting Krishnamurti, "How can you live a truly religious life when you are blind?" Is it possible to be compassionate or even clear, truthful, intelligent, accurate, and therefore reliable? Perhaps more kindly, Buddhists begin by saying we are ignorant of our own true nature.

Bohm noted that part of this ignorance is the way the operating system defends itself by pretending, concealing, and then trying to convince others that it is not ignorant, a symptom of the blindness Krishnamurti refers to. Krishnamurti and Buddhism address the nature of this blindness head-on.

Consciousness as we know it is the thought realm David is referring to. He, like Krishnamurti's and Buddha's teachings, realizes that a problem cannot be solved at the level of the problem. Something outside, something other, the unnamable, must intervene, like a bolt of lightning that illuminates, revealing that the imagined snake in the corner is only a coiled bit of rope. We are the snake and don't know it.

Alexandra David-Néel and Lama Yongden began *The Secret Oral Teachings in Tibetan Buddhist Sects* thus:

> *It is a long time since the idea of writing this book occurred to me. One fine summer afternoon I had explained my plan to a learned Tibetan who led a life of contemplation in a little house on the rocky side of a mountain. He was not encouraging.*
>
> *"Waste of time," he said. "The great majority of readers and hearers are the same all over the world. I have no doubt that the people in your country are like those I have met in China and India, and these later were just like Tibetans. If you speak to them of profound Truths they yawn, and, if they dare, they leave you, but if you tell the absurd fables, they are all eyes and ears. They wish the doctrines preached to them, whether religious, philosophical, or social, to be agreeable, to be consistent with their conceptions, to satisfy their inclinations; in fact that they find themselves in them, and that they feel themselves approved by them...*
>
> *"What, then, was that something that wanted to be agreeably caressed, satisfied? It was the collection of false notions, of unreasonable propensities, of feelings of a rudimentary sensuality, which are distinguished under the puppet named 'I'...*
>
> *"One may proclaim on the high road the Teachings considered secret; they will remain 'secret' for the individuals with dull minds who will hear what is said to them and will grasp nothing of it but the sound....*
>
> *"You have heard them. Do with them as you think fit. They are very simple, but, like a powerful battering ram, they run counter to the wall of false ideas rooted in the mind of man and the emotions which delight him, casting him into suffering... Try!"*

One fine summer afternoon sitting across the table, Krishnamurti leaned forward and asked about the documentary in progress: "Sir, I have only said one thing my entire life but I have said it a thousand ways," referring to his revolutionary declaration in 1929 that "there is no path to Truth," that no concept, idea or thought can hold or contain life, creation, which is spontaneously moving, changing, and transforming moment by moment.

Alan Watts, an early translator of Eastern thought, paraphrased this seminal insight by saying simply, "You can't catch the wind in a paper sack." I prefer, "with a sack over your head." Our identification with language, thought, concepts, memory and their implicit conditioning must end if we are to be aware, without choice, and therefore be influenced by what Krishnamurti and other traditions called *truth*, which is what we actually are. The most distilled description of this choiceless state is *Always Awakening*.

When asked, "But sir, what is your teaching?", Krishnamurti said, "There is no teaching. It's very simple. Where the 'I' is, 'that' is not." The "I" in this case represents our identification with memory, language, thought, in all its various forms. Then Krishnamurti questioned me, as the learned Tibetan had questioned Alexandra David-Néel a century earlier, "Do you think this will make any difference?" Without hesitation I replied, "Sir, I have no idea, but we need to try."

Krishnamurti often used "the perfume of the teachings" to redirect our attention to the unnamable dimension his thousand metaphors point to. The word, the concept, is not the perfume. With any luck you will catch wind of this perfume as you turn each page, slipping through the space, the silence, between one thought and the next, always awakening.

Michael Mendizza

Postscript: Notes on the Intent and the Experience

For nearly forty years I have experienced a curious resonance in what little I know about Tibetan Buddhism and Krishnamurti's insights. Every year of so I would revisit Alexandra David-Néel and Lama Yongden's little book, *The Secret Oral Teachings in Tibetan Buddhist Sects*, and discover there something I had missed. This curious resonance between Buddhist teachings and Krishnamurti was the driving force for my sustained inquiry with Samdhong Rinpoche.

I discovered in the process that a Buddha refers to an experience or a state of heart-mind, not a person or personality. I discovered that there is one enlightenment, not two or twenty, and that what one perceives in this enlightened state is common to all who realize it. The word not being the thing, as Krishnamurti said his entire mature life, the descriptions and observations, what we call *the teachings*, shared by Buddha are not that state any more than a road sign pointing to the Grand Canyon is the Grand Canyon. There is an unbridgeable gap between the two. The word must end before what the word describes can be experienced.

Another resonate theme is the absolute need to have a clear mind, a mind that is not polluted with prejudgments, tacit assumptions, beliefs, opinions, and all the emotions that are triggered by these mental phantoms. A great deal of what I discovered about Buddhist practices are various methods intended to draw attention to and bring about this critical-clarity prerequisite, while Krishnamurti simply stated it was prerequisite. Together these somewhat obvious discoveries changed, and fundamentally, my understanding of both Buddhism and Krishnamurti's insights. Further, this lucid quality of mind was there in every response Professor Samdhong made during our explorations. The experience of sitting together, marinating in Samdhong Rinpoche's steady clarity, had an impact on me and my state beyond the content being explored. In very palpable ways this steady, lucid clarity of mind touches the reader that taking the journey *Always Awakening* invites, and may be one of the more important treasures the journey provides.

The experience the book creates is meandering by design. There is no one point or climax. My thirty-plus years swimming in Krishnamurti's insights meeting Rinpoche's lifetimes of depth, experience and study is a rare encounter. Taking the time to wander together in today's split-second, fast-paced, just-the-headlines world is also rare. And the time I gave to prepare, the extensive readings from wide-ranging and diverse sources, brought even more depth to the experience. All this is embodied in the split-page format, our narrative on the right with provocative quotes on the left. The selection and juxtaposition of each quote is by no means random. The reader is forced to stop the narrative, to savor each quote. At the same time, digesting each quote has a way of deepening and expanding the narrative. Stopping and enjoying the view or the roses is not an option. In this way the form of the book is itself part of the deeper meaning or content you will find in *Always Awakening*. It is indeed much more than another good read.

When we say Buddha, we naturally think of the Indian prince
Gautama Siddhartha who reached enlightenment in the sixth century BC,
and who taught the spiritual path followed by millions
all over Asia, known today as Buddhism.
Buddha, however, has a much deeper meaning. It means
a person, any person, who has completely awakened from ignorance
and opened to his or her vast potential of wisdom.
A Buddha is one who has brought a final end to suffering and frustration,
and discovered a lasting and deathless happiness and peace.

Sogyal Rinpoche,
The Tibetan Book of Living and Dying

Samdhong Rinpoche with Jiddu Krishnamurti, Adyar Beach, 1970s

Agreement and *disagreement* are complicated words as we try to explore similarities and differences between Krishnamurti's and Buddhist teachings. Comparative study is valid only in fields like physical science or history. There is no comparative study in the spiritual field. Therefore we cannot compare the Buddha's teachings and Krishnamurti's teachings. We have to be very clear about this. Having said that, we are conditioned or trained in Buddhist philosophy, logic, metaphysics, and so forth. When we come to Krishnamurti, his message resonates with a person who has a Buddhist background. In a similar way, a person familiar with Krishnamurti's insights will find that his message complements Buddhist philosophy. Our efforts must be in this direction, not in finding similarities and dissimilarities. Not comparing. Not finding agreements and disagreements. Using Buddhist language, agreements and disagreements are all in the realm of relative truth, and there is no end. But the modern westerner has been trained in comparative study. That is a good academic exercise but it does not help in understanding Krishnamurti or in understanding Buddha.

Professor Samdhong Rinpoche

To suppose that things exist independently, have a "self-nature," is the atman-view and this in turn is ignorance. It is thus because of this atman-view that beings are wandering on in the realms of birth and death. The atman-view is then the root of samsara or the wandering-on. However, for one who is freed, such as an Arhat, this atman-view is destroyed (since he has penetrated to the truth of no-atman). It is only possible to eradicate this root of ignorance by the insight (vipasyana) called not-atman-knowledge (nairatmya-jnana) and by this alone. It is therefore essential that one develops the highest aspect of insight so as to see no-atman personally…

Generally, things such as a pot are regarded as though they existed independently. In reality, a pot is a result of the combination of a number of causes, such as clay, the potter, his effort, heat and so forth. That means that its existence is dependent upon many other factors different from the finished product called "pot" so that one may easily see that it has no independent existence…

All experienceable dharmas which make up the world we are aware of are of a like nature to the pot, requiring supporting conditions for their arising and existence. This aspect of existence is the most important proof that the nature of the dharmas is also one of "no-self-nature." This is in fact Absolute Truth. Although we may feel that dharmas (mental events) have a being or nature in themselves, Absolute Truth reveals them to be void of such a nature.

His Holiness the Dalai Lama, *The Opening of the Wisdom-Eye*

With His Holiness the Dalai Lama

California, USA, 2008

The Self As We Know It

M: *At the core of Krishnamurti's insights is what he calls* thought. *David Bohm, a theoretical physicist, clarified this by saying that most often Krishnamurti was referring to self-centered thought, the feelings and mental images we have about ourselves and others. Can you describe the source of this hallucination we have about a personal metaphysical identity, what we call "me"? Where does it come from and why is it so hard to see these images for what they actually are?*

S: According to Buddhism, there are four different philosophical traditions and among them there are so many subsets, subdivisions, each one talking about the self in a different way. Grossly we can classify them in two groups: one group conceives of the self existing as an independent entity that can be identified, and which comes from a previous life, awakens in this life, and goes to the next life in continuity. The other group says that the self is a projection of thought that is interdependently constructed, which exists but does not have an independent existence and, of course, degenerates, decays, and regenerates in permanent continuity. The stream of consciousness continues.

Both of these groups are saying that the "I" as we conceive it does not exist. The sense or actuality of "I" is different from our conception. Our conception perceives that there is an independent entity, unchanging, always existing, which experiences suffering, and also experiences happiness and pleasure, and the experiencer is perceived as being different from the experience. That is the illusion implicit in our concept of "I". This misconception needs to be corrected. Only then will we be able to perceive the "I" as it is.

M: *The image of a separate "me" that experiences is generated by the brain, particularly the systems that control language and what we call* thought. *Is there a "me" that is inseparable from the structures of language and thought?*

S: I think right at the beginning I must clarify that the "I", the self, the person, is not imaginary; it is true. We call it a relative truth. The person does exist. And this person not only exists, he is beginningless and endless, a continuity. And the nature of that self is a consciousness that is the nature of the mind. But we do not see it as it is. Our concept of "I" is

One's relationship with another is based on memory. Would you accept that? On the various images, pictures, conclusions I have drawn about you and you have drawn about me. The various images that I have about you, wife, husband, girl or boy or friend and so on, there is always image making.

This is simple, this is normal, this actually goes on. When one is married, or lives with a girl or a boy every incident, every word, every action creates an image. No? Are we clear on this point? Don't agree with me please I am not trying to persuade you to anything. But actually you can see it for yourself. A word is registered, if it is pleasant you purr. It is nice. If it is unpleasant, you will immediately shrink from it and that creates an image. The pleasure creates an image; the shrinking, the withdrawal creates an image. So, our actual relationship with each other is based on various subtle forms of pictures, images and conclusions. So when there is an image like that, she has and you have then in that there is division and then the whole conflict begins, right? Where there is division between two images, there must be conflict, right? The Jew, the Arab, the Hindu, the Muslim, the Christian, the Communist, it is the same phenomenon. It is a basic law, that where there is division between people there must be conflict. The man may say to the woman or the woman may say to the man "I love you," but basically, they are not related at all.

Then the factor arises, can all this image making, tradition and all that end, without a single conflict. You understand my question? Are you interested in this? What will you pay for it? That is all you can do. By paying something you think you will get it. Now, how can this mechanism of image making, not just image making, that is the desire for certainty, the tradition, the whole structure of that, can that end?

J. Krishnamurti, Brockwood Park, UK, 2nd Public Dialogue, 31 August 1978

entirely different from the real "I", the actuality. We do not see the real "I". What we conceive of as "I" is entirely different from what we think and therefore perceive.

We conceive of "I", for example, when somebody calls my name. My response is, "Oh, he is calling me." I am here and I immediately react to that name. If you look at your thought, it is conceiving an "I" that does not really exist but you assume, imagine, it exists. It is due to that illusion that we think that my "I" is entirely different from others. The perceived division between "me" and the other comes about because of that misconception.

We are saying this misconceived "I" does not exist as an independent entity or reality. That misconception needs to be negated. After negating the object of that misconception, only then will you be able to see the "I" as it is. The misconception is the real barrier for recognizing one's authentic self or recognizing the authentic other. If at this moment we are not able to see one's self as it is, then obviously we are not able to see others as they are. Both these misconceptions of *self* and *other* are projections of thought and are entirely different from what we are in reality. But it is very difficult to see that misconception. The misconception itself prevents us from seeing the misconception. You are not able to see your face without a mirror; similarly you are not able to see the misconception that misconceives you, that it entirely overpowers your consciousness and you are not able to see the actual face. Seeing the actual face demands clear observation, continuity of meditation or concentration, whatever you may call it. Through clear, consistent observation you are able to see the fact of this misconception. As soon as you see, observe, the misconception for what it is, it completely disappears.

When it disappears, then you will find a continuity of consciousness, which is an entity, which is the person who comes from the un-beginning of the previous life and goes on to enlightenment or salvation. Even after enlightenment, that consciousness will remain. You may call this *universal consciousness*, yet the stream of consciousness will remain. That never-beginning-or-ending consciousness is the real "I".

We don't really understand the nature of our thought process; we're not aware of how it works, how it is disrupting not only our society and our individual lives but also the way the brain and nervous system operate, making us unhealthy or perhaps even damaging the system. Krishnamurti recognizes that thought, rational, orderly, factual thought, such as in doing proper science, is valuable but the kind of thought that he has in mind is self-centered thought.

The ultimate purpose of K's work was stated very early in his life in his work, which was to free humanity from the destructive conditioning around this self-centered thought which is really an enslavement to absurdity, to destruction, to unhappiness, sorrow, and no other kind of freedom means anything unless we are free from that. Therefore, I think he felt that once man was free from that then the way would be open to creative unfoldment in all sorts of directions.

David Bohm, Interview with Michael Mendizza

C. W. Leadbeater, J. Krishnamurti, Nitya, Balfour Clark, 1910

Misconception

M: *Why is it so difficult to see this misconception? We could say that the misperception is the lens or paradigm through which we are looking. We are looking through a false perception trying to see the misperception. How do we break that?*

S: Yes, that is part of it. Krishnamurti called it *the conditioned mind*. We are so conditioned by this false perception. The Buddhists may call it *the diluted mind*, which has been perpetuated for centuries. It has been diluted for hundreds of thousands of years of births, and this conditioning is not easy to break. Because you are so conditioned by it, you never think it is necessary to look at it. Because you assume the misconception is the truth, you never feel the need to look at it. Even when you are told you must observe, you must look, and try to see the misconception at that moment, the conditioned mind creates another illusion and that is what you see. You are still swimming in the continuity of the delusion but think you are free from it.

We can use, as a metaphor, switching on a light in a dark room. When you switch on the light, there is no question of how the light appears or what the method was that generated the light. At that moment the darkness goes away. You can't ask where it went or how it went. These are invalid questions. The darkness is not there because of the light. Similarly, because of the seeing, the observation, then the illusion, the misconception, disappears.

Asking *how* is a natural question. The question *how* though, does not come from the clarity of the mind. The question *how* is part of our conditioning, part of our thought process. It always looks for a system, for a method, for an instrument through which the mind can be controlled. If you begin to really look carefully from the outside of this conditioning you will not ask how, because all the how's are within the limitation of the conditioning. Not asking how, but by being in a position separate from the conditioning, then you are able to look at the conditioned mind. At that moment there are no methods, no instruments. Krishnamurti describes this unconditioned state as *choiceless awareness*. Trying to look is part of the misconception that only sees itself, more of the same imagined to be different.

This question *how* is natural, how to look at it. I don't have an answer. You will have to try it. I don't know whether the word *try* is appropriate.

The tangible word is movement, say the Masters, not a collection of moving objects, but movement itself. There are no objects "in movements," it is the movement which constitutes the objects which appear to us: they are nothing but movement.

All objects perceptible to our senses, all phenomena of whatever kind and whatever aspect they may assume, are constituted by a rapid succession of instantaneous events.

Event here means "something which happens." These "somethings" arising instantaneously and in series, these rapid flashes of energy are sufficiently like one another during the series to remain imperceptible to us, then suddenly occurs, in this series of moments, a different moment which catches our attention and makes us think that a new object has appeared.

There are two theories and both consider the world as movement. One states that the course of this movement (which creates phenomena) is continuous, as the flow of a quiet river seems to us. The other declares that the movement is intermittent and advances by separate flashes of energy which follow each other at such small intervals that these intervals are almost non-existent.

As to the existence of matter which is motionless and homogeneous, this is flatly denied.

Alexandra David-Néel and Lama Yongden,
The Secret Oral Teachings in Tibetan Buddhist Sects

Meditation was pure delight, without a flutter of thought, with its endless subtleties; it was a movement that had no end and every movement of the brain was still, watching from emptiness. It was an emptiness that had known no knowing; it was emptiness that had known no space; it was empty of time. It was empty, past all seeing, knowing and being. In this emptiness there was fury; the fury of a storm, the fury of an exploding universe, the fury of creation which could never have any expression. It was the fury of all life, death and love. But yet, it was empty, a vast, boundless emptiness which nothing could ever fill, transform or cover up. Meditation was the ecstasy of this emptiness.

Krishnamurti's Notebook

You have the potential to look but it will depend on you, if and when that potential in you is awakened. I think you can do it. You can do it in the sense of understanding that what the thought process is telling you, your conception, the misconception of "I", the taught image of "I", is not in reality what I am. With this understanding or insight comes the realization that I need to find out who or what is the real me. To do this, I need to examine all the various ways this misconception is not what I really am. This intention itself has the ability to create an observation that reveals the false nature of the misconception. In this way I think you will be able to do it.

M: *There is the state of mind enchanted by this delusion, the misconception. That is a state. When that state stops, another state begins. The metaphor of light and dark implies this shift from one state of mind to another. Dark is a state. Light is a state. When one disappears, the other is. Methods from Krishnamurti's perspective are an extension of what we might call the endarkened state, which is one reason why Krishnamurti negates the use of methods. The content the brain produces may change but the state of brain-mind remains the same. An insight into the misconception demands a change in the state of the mind, not simply exchanging one bit of content for another. Silence, emptiness, is a different state than trying to use content to understand content. Emptiness is a different state and from that new state we look. I suggest this is a key to understanding Buddhist teachings and Krishnamurti's central insight. I understand that for the first five hundred years after Buddha's death he was represented by symbols of emptiness; an empty chair, footprints in the sand but no one there, and so on. What a great image that is. Rather than ponder how, which simply continues the noise, this image implies a direct experience of emptiness. Stop the noise and then look. Let's talk about emptiness.*

Emptiness

S: Yes, the Buddhist notion of emptiness is the simple negating of all the misconceptions of our mind. As long as our mind is conditioned, overpowered by misconceptions, there is no room for direct perception, to perceive things as they actually are. In our normal conditioned state we cannot differentiate between the images of misconceptions and the real existence of the world as it is.

K: To find out if there is something beyond this consciousness I must understand the content of this consciousness. The mind must go beyond itself.

A: *Are you saying, sir, that what we call consciousness is the very content of this consciousness, that the container and the contained are an indivisible thing? There is no entity to decide and will and juggle when the contents to be juggled are absent.*

K: That's right. My consciousness is the consciousness of the world. The consciousness of the world is me. Which is really a truth —you follow? Not just my invention or your acceptance of that invention, it is an absolute truth. The content of consciousness is consciousness. Without the content, there is no consciousness. Now, when we want to change the content we are juggling the...

A: *Yes. The content is juggling itself—because there is nobody outside of this content to do any juggling at all.*

K: At all—quite right.

A: *The juggler and the contents are one. And also the container and the contents are one. The world and the consciousness and the person, the entity who supposedly will change it, are all the same entity, masquerading, as it were, as three different roles.*

K: Putting on a mask, pretending. If that is so—which is so—then what is a human being to do to bring about a total emptying of the content of consciousness, so that this particular consciousness, which is the world, is me with all its miseries—how is that to undergo complete change? Not within the consciousness—how is that mind to empty itself of all its content?

A: *What is change, which will solve these three sets of problems that are really one?*

K: Wait, sir. Do I realise the thinker is part of this consciousness and is not a separate entity outside this consciousness. Do we realise that the observer, seeing the content, examining, analysing, looking at it all, is the content itself?

A: *Yes, sir.*

K: The observer is the content. Do I realise that? In that consciousness is all the content of human endeavour—mischief, human misery, human cruelty—all the human activities are within that consciousness. Man has brought about this entity which says, "I am separate from my consciousness." The thinker says, "My thoughts are different from me."

A: *Yes, he does.*

K: Is that so? Or, is it that the thinker is the thought? We are trying to point out that they are not separate, they are one. I observe that red eagle flying by, going by. When I observe that bird, am I observing with the image I have about that bird, or there is only mere observation? If there is an image—which is word, memory, and all the rest of it—then there is an observer watching the bird go by. If there is only observation then there is no observer.

J. Krishnamurti, *The Awakening of Intelligence*. 1st Dialogue with Alain Naudé, Malibu, California, 27 March 1971 *(Abridged)*

For example, we cannot negate completely the existence of "me". That would be nihilism. If there is no "me" then there will be nothing, and nothingness is not emptiness. The Buddhist idea of emptiness is not the negation of all of existence. All of existence does exist. Causality functions exactly as it needs to according to the laws of nature. But the conditioned mind, the diluted mind, always conceives the entirety of existence in a false way. So we have to negate all the misconceived things entirely. At that moment of negation you are not able to differentiate between what must be negated and what must not be negated. You will have to negate the structure that produces the misconceptions, not simply this or that misconception. For example, your clothes are spoiled by ink or dirt. You cannot wash only the dirt. You have to put the clothes into the water and wash them together. By washing, the dirt will go and the clean clothes will remain. So it is with the mind. After negating the existence of what has been misconceived, for a moment there will remain nothing. And that nothingness is the real source of creativity, creation of the entire universe. All the creativity, the causality, is able to function because there is space. There is emptiness of all misconceived things that exist independently. This is how Buddhism perceives emptiness.

M: *Emptiness is a mind that is free of the misconceptions created by thought and conditioning.*

S: Yes.

M: *I see you. "I" equals subject. "You" equals object. The whole structure of language reinforces the misconception.*

Direct Perception

S: Yes, but language is very useful. We cannot do away with language. Without language our relationship becomes very limited, but this is a different issue. According to Buddhist philosophy, language is a direct product of thought. Therefore, thought and language go together. They reinforce each other. The thought process creates language and language further stimulates the thought process. Not only that, but language exchanges and spreads the thought process between people. But thought does not touch reality. Thought always involves images created by the brain. For example, my "I" consciousness is not a thought; it is a direct

In Buddhism the term self has two meanings that must be differentiated in order to avoid confusion. One meaning of self is "person" or "living being." This is the being who loves and hates, who performs actions and accumulates good and bad karma, who experiences the fruits of those actions, who is reborn in cyclic existence, who cultivates spiritual paths, and so on.

The other meaning of self occurs in the term selflessness, where it refers to a falsely imagined, overconcretized status of existence called "inherent existence." The ignorance that adheres to such an exaggeration is indeed the source of ruination, the mother of all wrong attitudes; perhaps we could even say devilish. In observing the "I" that depends upon mental and physical attributes, this mind exaggerates it into being inherently existent, despite the fact that the mental and physical elements being observed do not contain any such exaggerated being.

What is the actual status of a sentient being? Just as a car exists in dependence upon its parts, such as wheels, axles, and so forth, so a sentient being is conventionally set up in dependence upon mind and body. There is no person to be found either separate from mind and body or within mind and body.

His Holiness the Dalai Lama,
How to See Yourself as You Really Are: A Practical Guide to Self-Knowledge

perception. My "I" consciousness is touched by the color white, and white reflects to my "I" consciousness that I perceive white as it is. But my "I" perception does not have the name *white*. It also does not have the image of white. There is only the direct experience of white in my "I" consciousness and that is the end of it. As soon as the white color enters my "I" consciousness, thought is engaged, which creates an image of white that is different from the direct experience of white. I may shut my eyes, ending the direct sensory experience of white, but thought will recognize the image of whiteness it has created.

M: *You are describing the difference between the sensory experience of seeing white and the image thought creates from that experience.*

S: Yes. I saw a white color. The eye was there, the white color was there, the activity of seeing was there, but when I shut my eyes what remains is the image thought created, not the actual experience. The eye is now shut, has no contact with the white color, but thought says yes, the white color is there, very bright or very dull. This world of inner images and language is very different from the world of reality. Then thought gives a name to this image and the name triggers the inner image of what thought has created. In this way the thought process is always creating language, and language also implies the thought process. In spite of its usefulness, language has to be suspended if you wish to see reality as it is.

Enchantment

M: *The images produced by thought and language are enchanting, almost like a spell, and we are not aware of this. We get caught in the show, not realizing that we are creating the show. Once caught, we don't treat the tool, thought-language, objectively as we do a tire or screwdriver. We need to have an insight, to use Krishnamurti's term, about the enchantment the thought-language process produces.*

S: Different people may experience the state of emptiness from different points of view but what is seen is the same. They all perceive truth as it is. But when it comes to explaining what was perceived using words, then there are vast differences. Some people talk about the soul, others talk about soullessness. These differences are all in the realm of language. Because of differences in the use of language, people's conception in their imagination becomes very different. However, when each sees the

Meditation is not controlling thought, or practicing some system or method, but freeing the mind, the brain, freeing the brain from its own conditioning. That's only the beginning of it. When there is that freedom, then we can inquire into what is a brain that is silent. Because it's only through great silence you learn, you observe, not when you're making a lot of noise.

To observe those hills, and these beautiful trees, to observe your wife and your children, or your husband and your relatives, whatever they are, to observe you must have space and there must be silence. But if you are chattering, gossiping, you know, you have no space or silence.

And we need space, not only physically, but much more psychologically. That space is denied when we are thinking about ourselves, so simple, right? Because when there is space, vast space psychologically, there's a great vitality, great energy. But when that space is limited to one's own little self, that vast energy is totally contained with its limitation. So that's why meditation is the ending of the self.

One can listen to all this; so one begins to realize when thought is quiet, watching, that there's something beyond all imagination, doubt, and seeking. And there is such a thing, at least for the speaker. But what the speaker says has no validity to another unless you listen, learn, watch, be totally free from all the anxieties of life. The ending of the self, the me, to be nothing, to have no image of any kind, no illusion, to be absolutely nothing. The tree is nothing to itself. It exists. And in its very existence it is the most beautiful thing. Like those hills, they exist. They don't become something. You understand? This is meditation. This is the ending of the search, and truth is.

J. Krishnamurti, Ojai, California, 4th Public Talk, 22 May 1983

truth, they see it equally. They see whatever it is. Therefore, we should not think there are a large number of different worldviews; there are a large number of explanations. The Christ, the Buddha, and other Rishis who have the ability to see reality as it is, all see the same thing. The differences exist only in the explanations, in the use of language.

The Buddha tried to explain to his disciples that the "I" or the universe does not exist as thought conceives it. Thought, language, and the images they produce are relative. That needs to be understood and the relative realm of reality needs to be seen for what it is and negated.

If you look at your thought, you always conceive of things existing independently. Thought has two limitations: first, thought does not differentiate between what is real and what is an image. We always think that the image thought creates is real. Second, thought cannot differentiate time. All the times in thought are mixed up. I saw the white color yesterday and the white color has gone, my consciousness of it has gone. All are in the past. But in thought it is still present, and my seeing last year, my seeing yesterday, my seeing today are all in the realm of thought; there's no differentiation. All are together. So thought has two limitations: mistaking the image as real, and mistaking that the past, present and future are all together. These are the two great limitations of thought. So the Buddha is saying that things do not exist as thought projects them. Then comes the question, does this mean that they don't exist? The Buddha says no, they do exist. Then how do they exist? The Buddha says they exist interdependently.

There is a basis by which a person can be designated. The body, the mind, speech, all come together and these distinguish this person from that person. To that designation we also add a name. The person exists in relation to all these together; the projection, the definition, the name, come together interdependently and that unity defines that person. But that person does not exist as an object independent of these forces. If it exists independently, when you search for it, you are not able to find it, to identify it. For example, there is a person named George, and we say, "Oh, there is George." But you will find the body of George and the body is not George. The mind of George is not George. Each part of George, the hand is not George, the head is not George, the foot is not George, and so on. By analytically trying to find George within the head,

Why, despite our deep desire to be happy, are we constantly confronted with suffering and pain instead?

From the Buddhist point of view, the reason is that we have certain fundamentally flawed ways of perceiving and relating to ourselves and to the world.

The first is to view things and events which are in reality impermanent and transient, as eternal, permanent and unchanging.

The second is to view things and events which are actually sources of dissatisfaction and suffering as pleasurable and as true sources of happiness.

The third false view is that we often tend to apprehend as pure and desirable things which are in reality impure.

And the fourth false view is our tendency to project a notion of real existence upon events and things which in reality lack any such autonomy.

Fundamentally flawed views of reality lead to certain false ways of relating to the world and to oneself, which in turn lead to confusion, misery and suffering.

Whatever brings disaster or harm should be called an enemy, so this means that the ultimate enemy is actually within ourselves.

If it is the case, as suggested by some ancient philosophers, that the pollutants lie in the very nature of consciousness itself, and are inseparable from it, then so long as consciousness exists these pollutants will exist as an essential characteristic of our mind.

    His Holiness the Dalai Lama, *Transforming the Mind (Abridged)*

you are not able to find him. You are not able to pinpoint George in any of the parts. Then where is George? George is obviously there, interdependently by all these things structured together, and on that structure the mind designates George.

There is another way to approach this. We have categories: big/small, long/short, bright/dull. *Big* exists in relation to *small*. If there is no *small*, *big* cannot exist. *Small* exists in relation to *big*. These are interdependent. If they are not interdependent, there must be a *big* that is big by its own nature, independent of *small*. That means inherently that an object is not big or small but it will become big by comparing it with small, and it becomes small by comparing it with what is bigger. This is how things exist interdependently, and that their existence, big or small, is relatively true. Of course it is not absolutely true, meaning *big* is not in relationship to *small*. That is how the whole universe functions. With emptiness, which is referred to as *the absolute*, no such relatives exist.

Language Divides

M: *That is it. We don't have to go any further. Nagarjuna says, "Past, present, and future are like bottom, middle, and top and one, two, three," which means the dividing line between them exists only in language. If life has no beginning or end, no before or after, which would be an absolute perception, how can it be centered in the present? Even the concept of* present *is a relative concept.*

S: Yes, exactly. The Buddha was asked many questions and by and large he answered the majority of them with very convincing and accurate answers. But there were, during his life, fourteen questions he did not answer through words because those questions referred to the absolute. If he had said something affirmative, something would be wrong. If he had said something negative, again something would be wrong, because language is limited. Language knows only alternatives. Beyond alternatives language cannot comprehend. So when you formulate questions — it may be from Buddhist teachings, Nagarjuna's words, Krishnamurti's words, or Gurdjieff's words — you take those words and formulate them into a question that involves alternatives, because questions can only be answered using alternatives.

We can say, "the absolute is one," or we can say, "the absolute is several," but in reality both are not correct. If you say that the absolute is one, it

Is there a way of living without conflict? I said there is, obviously. Which is to understand the division. To understand the conflict. To see how fragmented we are... Seeing the fragmentation, which brings about conflict, which brings about division, which brings about this constant battle, anxiety, strain, heart failure, you follow? So that's what's happening. To see it. To perceive it and that very perception brings an action which is totally different from the action of conflict. Because the action of conflict has its own energy, brings its own energy, which is divisive, which is destructive, violent. But the energy of perception and acting is entirely different. That energy is the energy of creation.

J. Krishnamurti, *A Wholly Different Way of Living*. 13th Dialogue with Allan W. Anderson

means that the absolute is in relation to something. *One* is only in relation to *two* or *three*. If there are not several, you cannot construct a single one. Then the tapestry of language ends, no word, no language. Silence is the answer. So therefore we have to understand the limitation of language. Language is limited because it is a product of thought, which is even more limited, which is always in parts, never the whole. Thought can never catch the whole; it can only catch the part.

Talking about the present is very difficult. Actually, it may not be an incorrect statement to say there is no present. There is a vast amount of past and there is also a vast amount of future, but where is the present? What your mind calls *the present* has already passed. If you look at the shortest unit of time, the shortest spell of time is not a subject or product of our thought because it is so subtle. The smallest particle of an atom is not perceivable by the naked eye. Perhaps it is with some instruments, but I don't think even today the best instruments of scientists can see the smallest particle because it is so small and so swift, always changing. Similarly, the present is so short and so swift, the ordinary human mind can never catch it.

Therefore, our concept of the present is always relative. For example, we say today is the present, yesterday was the past, and tomorrow is the future. We generally mean that the present is the whole twenty-four hours of today. Using that gross language may be all right, *today's present*. But more accurately, more precisely, we cannot live in the present; we cannot catch things in the present.

M: *The present is so quick, by the time we are consciously aware of something it has already passed.*

S: The present is the very shortest unit of time. From that state of silence you can look at the chattering of thought; then one begins to appreciate the limitations of thought, which by comparison are very cumbersome, inaccurate, relative.

M: *I don't know if one actually looks from silence. Looking would imply some act, non-silence. There is the state of silence and then thought happens, which is a completely different state, similar to what we said about light and darkness. Suddenly silence stops and another state begins. And we can be sensitive to the difference.*

With His Holiness the Dalai Lama, Main Temple, Theckchen Choeling, Dharamsala, 2007

His Holiness sets the stage for discovering the reality behind appearances. Our tacit acceptance of things as they seem is called ignorance, which is not just a lack of knowledge about how people and things actually exist but an active mistaking of their fundamental nature.

True self-knowledge involves exposing and facing misconceptions about ourselves. The aim here is to find out how we get ourselves into trouble, then learn how to intervene on the ground floor of our counterproductive ideas.

His central theme is that our skewed perceptions of body and mind lead to disastrous mistakes, ranging from lust at the one extreme to raging hatred at the other so that we are consistently being led into trouble as if pulled by a ring in our nose. By developing insight into this process, we can free ourselves, and those around us, from these endless scenarios of pain.

His Holiness guides readers through a variety of practical exercises to help us break down the illusions we have superimposed over and beyond what actually exists, and learn how to act in the world from a more realistic framework. This calls for valuing the interdependence of all things and appreciating the latticework of our relationships for the meaningful contribution it makes to our lives.

The book's third part describes how to harness the power of meditative concentration with insight to achieve immersion in our own ultimate nature… to develop in us a clear sense of what it means to exist without misconception.

And the way this profound state of being enhances love by revealing how unnecessary destructive emotions and suffering actually are.

> His Holiness the Dalai Lama,
> *How to See Yourself as You Really Are: A Practical Guide to Self-Knowledge (Abridged)*
> From the Foreword by Jeffery Hopkins, Translator

Use and Misuse of Imagination

S: Once you are in the state of silence, your mind is capable of experiencing that silence. Then when the thought process begins, you are aware of the difference and that awareness reveals the limitations of thought. This insight exposes imagination for what it is—mental images—and you are no longer overwhelmed by them. Imagination may be there, but you are aware that it is self-generated and you will not be carried away or lost in it.

M: *One is hallucination, delusion. I experience things that are not present to the senses, which is the definition of imagination, and attribute to these self-generated mental images the same reality as sense perception, which is irrational. And yet this same capacity to imagine, when used consciously, creatively, is extremely powerful. Reading with glimpses into the Tibetan tradition, which places me on shaky ground, there was mention of the intricacies of Buddhist metaphysics, which involve many practices that cultivate the creative use of imagination. These practices can be compared to going to a gymnasium and strengthening one's muscles. More specifically, these practices clear the imagination of the reflexive images created by thought so it can be used sanely, rationally, like a laser. Simply to say that imagination is hallucination is missing the point.*

S: As I mentioned, language is very important. Language is very creative. But language is also very limited. And the process of thought, which is inseparable from language, is equally important and equally limited. The most important part of the thought process is imagination. Imagination creates the arts, the architect, the poet, the teacher, which are so beautiful. All types of artistic expression, music, dance, emanate from imagination.

M: *Yes, war, violence, toxic chemicals, genocide, greed, comparison, racism, all emanate from the imagination.*

S: That is the negative part of imagination when it is used incorrectly. In Buddhist meditation systems there are three different kinds of meditation. One practice defines how one uses imagination, which we call *visualization*. Using only our thought process we visualize the entire construction of the mandala, the deities and enlightened beings. All these are visualized and within that visualization we do many meditations. That capacity for visualization comes from imagination. Without imagination you cannot visualize things. So in that way, the proper use of the limited

Tulpa, "to build" or "to construct," also translated as "magical emanation," a "conjured thing" and "phantom," is a concept in mysticism of a being or object that is created through sheer spiritual or mental discipline alone.

The term "thoughtform" is used as early as 1927 in Evans-Wentz' translation of *The Tibetan Book of the Dead*. John Myrdhin Reynolds, in a note to his English translation of the life story of Garab Dorje, defines a tulpa as "an emanation or a manifestation."

The term "tulpa" is used in the works of Alexandra David-Néel, a Belgian-French explorer, spiritualist and Buddhist, who observed these practices in 20th-century Tibet. Alexandra wrote that "an accomplished Bodhisattva is capable of effecting ten kinds of magic creations." Alexandra also wrote of the tulpa's ability to develop a mind of its own… Alexandra claimed to have created a tulpa in the image of a jolly Friar Tuck–like monk which later developed a life of its own and had to be destroyed. She raised the possibility that her experience was illusory: "I may have created my own hallucination."

Wikipedia: Definition of Tulpa

power of thought can be channeled in a very positive, healthy, whole direction. But visualization is not the end; rather it is a tool to transform visualization into a reality. That is also possible. So therefore, if we are aware of its limitations and aware how to use it properly, then imagination is one of the best tools for achieving silence.

M: *You say that it's not just to visualize, but is a step towards actually creating a reality?*

S: Yes, that's right.

M: *Reading various works, there was a description of* tulpa, *an imagined being, a magical creation generated by a powerful concentration of thought. What began as an inner visualization became so strong and externalized, others perceived the phantom as they would you or me. What began as imagination became a reality. That opens the door to all kinds of things. I asked physicist David Bohm, "Is there a difference between mind and matter?" He said, no. The only difference is in the way we are looking, our point of view. This ability to create a reality can be used for good or not. The whole stream of human consciousness, being an imaginative construct, is actively creating a reality every day. Can we say that part of your practice or meditation is to purify, to clarify, and create a more compassionate reality, a more sane reality?*

S: The positive state of mind can be purified and developed infinitely but the negative state of mind cannot be degenerated, diluted infinitely, only up to a certain point. The positive side of the mind is infinite. The negative side of the mind is finite. The negative can only go to a certain level, not beyond. Therefore, negative imagination cannot result in infinite negativity. Even the atomic bomb that can destroy the entire Earth is limited. When the mind develops the positive, it can become omniscient. It can know everything and perceive the entirety of existence. This is a fact. I believe we have misused the negative up to its limitations. But on the positive side, very few people have been or are able to develop the mind's full potential, though there are some people in the present world who have full usage of the mind's positive power of imagination. This we have to understand.

We have made life into a hideous thing. Life has become a battle, which is an obvious fact, constant fight, fight, fight. We have divorced that living from death. We separate death as something horrible, something to be frightened about. And to us this living, which is misery, we accept. If we didn't accept this existence as misery, then life and death are the same movement. Like love, death and living are one. One must totally die to know what love is. And to go into this question of what is death, what lies beyond death, whether there is reincarnation, whether there is resurrection; all that becomes rather meaningless if you do not know how to live. If you, the human being, knows how to live in this world, without conflict, then death has quite a different meaning.

Australian Broadcasting Company, Interview with J. Krishnamurti, 1970

What Is It That Reincarnates?

M: *In a strange way this brings up or spills over into the concept of reincarnation. What is it that reincarnates?*

S: The word *reincarnate* is not an appropriate word if we are going to be accurate, if we wish to explore this very subtle philosophy. But it has been used for a long time and now it has become a very common word. Why do I say this is not an appropriate word? Once incarnated, it will not be incarnated again. A better way of describing it would be to say *incarnation* and *after incarnation*. *After incarnation* means continuity. A person is born at a certain point of time, say 1910, and passes away in 1980. That person is born again in 1981. It goes on. It continues. It is not repetition but is a continuity.

M: *Why a continuity?*

S: This subtlest string of consciousness, which is the basic condition of a person, does not have any beginning. It does not have an end. That consciousness enters into a new body, and again gives birth to that stream of consciousness. The subtlest stream of consciousness is the real essence. It can never come to an end because the nature of consciousness has the potential to create its next reproduction. It creates anew each moment and destroys each moment. This process never ends, never ceases. Because there is no cause that can completely destroy that stream, it is continuous. It has its own potential to regenerate or recreate, so it continues. When this subtlest stream of consciousness enters into a body, it has a lot of baggage, conditioning, and limitations that come with that consciousness. That subtle consciousness is also capable of eliminating the baggage. When it is free of all conditioning, then it need not enter into a new body by compulsion, compulsion being the weight, what we call grasping, of this conditioning. Then it can remain without a body or it can enter into any body by choice, by its own will, not by compulsion. That is called *tulkul*, because the person is not in bondage, not in conditioning, yet takes a body for the sake of serving others. Without a body that consciousness cannot have contact with ordinary people. So in order to contact and serve ordinary people, it takes a body that has the capacity to be seen by everyone, can talk to everyone, but in spite of that, the consciousness is not in the bondage of conditioning or of the body.

Those who are ignorant of the Dharma and those who do not understand its depths, cherish doubts about rebirth, Punarbhava. They may suppose that the consciousness which in this life is partly dependent upon the physical body, is really totally derived from it, arising with it and therefore utterly ceasing with it.

They also assume that this present life has no connection to past existences. This is thought to be the truth because of another assumption: that because the events of this life are perceived and remembered, so those of past lives should also be perceived by means of the memory.

Further, they have not seen or experienced with their own eyes the existence of past or future lives. Thus they declare that at death the body reverts to the four great elementals while consciousness disappears as a rainbow in the sky. People of this sort have a view which is limited, for while they see the dependence of mental continuity upon the physical body, they do not understand that the mind can also be independent of a gross physical base.

It is not proper to think that there are no past and future lives just because one has not seen them. The non-perception of something does not prove its non-existence. This is well illustrated in the present time when, with the aid of modern instruments, many facts are known and many things seen which were unknown to our forefathers. Now, the existence of past lives has been confirmed by those practicing collectedness (samadhi). They, having become absorbed in high levels of mind-concentration when the mind is very subtle, and able to perceive very subtle objects, have experienced their previous births. Some mediators of great experience have recalled, even in great detail, many previous lives.

His Holiness the Dalai Lama, *The Opening of the Wisdom-Eye*

Different Realms, Dimensions, and Realities

M: *Implied are different realms, dimensions, and realities. A stream of consciousness that is not in a body must exist in a reality independent of this one.*

S: Yes, definitely.

M: *We now have different realities for different beings?*

S: Yes. We are in bondage, conditioned, and therefore see a limited reality. When our mind is deconditioned, free of conditioning, free of bondage, then the entire universe is before it. Then it sees the entirety, and that reality is different, not the small reality but the possible open reality.

M: *In the West we have the concept of ghosts, somebody who lived and is now dead, and some people see that person physically after they have passed. I know several people who have experienced this, including Krishnamurti.*

S: Yes, there are a number of bodies that are not similar to our bodies. The particles, the construction of those bodies, are usually invisible but can be visible on certain occasions. In Buddhism we call these invisibly bodied persons *gyuma*, which means *bodiless*, because they do not have a gross body that can be touched. Subtle body entities can pass through walls without difficulty. They need not come through a door or opening because their bodies are so subtle, a wave or frequency. Those we call intermediaries or ghosts. This is a reality. It happens. And for people who have strong attachments for something, that intermediate spirit may come back and do something. This happens everywhere.

M: *Regarding reincarnation, the Dalai Lama is the 14th reincarnation of a purified stream. You yourself are said to be the 5th reincarnation of Samdhong. Or, like me, are you compulsively drawn back again by your conditioning? Did you choose to come back to serve?*

S: Yes, definitely, His Holiness the 14th Dalai Lama, has consciously chosen to come back to look after the Tibetan people. As for me, it is an accident. People think I'm a reincarnation of my past, but sometimes there are karmic connections, influences, that can also place one in the line. Therefore, people place me as the 5th Samdhong, but I am not the reincarnation of the 4th Samdhong, though I might have had some close relationship with the 4th and therefore I take the place of the 5th.

M: *In quantum mechanics there's the field theory that talks about fields, which is similar to what you are calling a subtle stream of consciousness.*

Above: Principal Lhawang Paljor with students, Central School for Tibetans, Darjeeling, 1964

Right: With His Eminence the Zong Rinpoche, former Principal of the Central Institute of Higher Tibetan Studies, 1971

S: Right.

M: *There are many ways that we, physical human beings, access various fields.*

S: Yes.

The Source and Consequences of Greed

M: *These fields express in and through us all the time. Rather than this being an extraordinary event or altered state, I'm suggesting that it happens all the time. This ever-changing flow of interdependent influences is a very different way of experiencing myself. So let's go back to the beginning. Krishnamurti said, because we don't know ourselves, we are destroying each other and the planet. Do you feel that the survival of our species depends on each individual waking up to a different worldview, and this implies a fundamentally different identity?*

S: I don't think the survival of our species depends on awakening and knowing ourselves. Perhaps this may not be possible. If you become aware of yourself, who you are, then you may not remain within the community of unenlightened individuals. So many people realized this and stepped out. Of course they can come back and help unenlightened people, but for the survival of our species we definitely need to know our real needs and the evil of greed and desire. This much is necessary, otherwise we will not survive. We may not be able to keep the planet Earth livable. The consequences of our greed and desire may become quite obvious in the very near future, even in today's economic crisis. In developing countries, we do not know where it will lead. Even if the economic crisis were not there, our misuse of resources has damaged the environment, and if the environmental degradation is not stopped, the planet Earth may not sustain us anymore. So we need to awaken to such an extent that we know what our needs are and give up our addiction to greed. Only then will the species be able to survive.

M: *What is the source of greed?*

S: The source of greed is the misconception of "I", not knowing who I am and what I am, so therefore greed comes. Greed can be exploited very easily through comparison and competition. The market economy knows this very well; it makes everybody compare and compete. This is one of the reasons why we don't know who or what we are. Right from the beginning you are taught not to look at yourself but to look at others

J. Krishnamurti, Castle Eerde, 1920s

The negation of thought is attention, as the negation of thought is love. If you are seeking the highest, you will not find it; it must come to you, if you are lucky—and luck is the open window of your heart, not of thought.

J. Krishnamurti, *The Only Revolution*

and compare yourself with them. The whole of our education is in that direction. Teachers punish you, comparing you with others. Teachers watch you, parents watch you, and compare you with others. You are being conditioned to identify who you are by comparison and competition, which increases and exploits your greed. That is a fact, obvious when you stop and look.

M: *It's part of the social-cultural structure.*

S: It's part of the whole structure. But you are capable of coming out of that structure if you wish to. We are not helpless. We can step out. But the social structure tries to make you feel that you are helpless. This is the structure throughout the world, the corporate world. You are made to feel that you are a small creature and you are caught by that identity, that you are helpless. That may not be true but we think it is and so it is.

M: *There is a certain exploitation woven into our identity.*

S: That is our weakness.

M: *Imagine not having that image, that social identity that binds us. There would be nothing to compare. What is compared is the social image. The culture cannot control us without the image. That is the function of the social image: behavior modification and conformity. In moments when that image is not active, the limitations imposed by culture are suspended.*

S: Yes. Then, of course, you are free.

What we are trying in all these discussions and talks here is to see if we can not radically bring about a transformation of the mind. Not accept things as they are; nor revolt against it. Revolt does not answer a thing. But to understand it, to go into it, to examine it, give your heart and your mind with everything you have to find out a way of living differently.

But that depends on you and not somebody else. Because in this there is no teacher, no pupil, no leader, no guru, no master, no savior. You yourself are the teacher, the pupil, you are the master, the guru, you are everything. When you put that question, because you are serious, because you are intent, then you are aware of the whole process of the observer. Which means that you are totally attentive, completely attentive. And in that attention there is no border created by the center. And when there is complete attention there is no observer. The observer comes into being only when, in that look, there is inattention which is distraction.

We have put away the observer and therefore there is attention which may last a second; that is good enough. Don't be greedy to have more. In that greed to have more, you have already created the center, and then you are caught.

In that attention there is no seeking at all. And therefore there is no effort. And the mind becomes extraordinarily alert, active, silent. Such a mind is the religious mind. And such a mind has an activity totally different, at a different dimension which thought can never possibly reach.

The Collected Works of J. Krishnamurti. PBS Broadcast, Ojai, California, 1966

United Kingdom, 2012, Day One

The Self As Image

M: *I made the general observation that the role of mental images and the self as we think of it, being one such image, is at the heart of Krishnamurti's core insight. Your thoughts?*

S: This is a very pervasive and complex question. When we say *image*, there are many different layers and categories of images that we create. Unless we clarify them, just generalizing images alone may create confusion. Krishnamurti was referring to the limitation and also the trickiness of the thought process. Buddhism also talks about the thought process, thought as a concept, and direct perception, which are two different levels of mind that are always operating.

In consciousness, which is a continuum, momentarily changing but a continuum, if someone is a believer in a previous life and rebirth, in that case the stream of inner consciousness, the subtle consciousness, has no beginning, no end. It is always streaming. But when that subtle consciousness takes a body and then operates through the physical body, the whole mind operation divides into two compartments: one is on the level of perception, and the other is on the level of thought.

M: *When you say* perception, *do you mean seeing, sensory perception?*

S: Yes. Not only sensory, even mental perception is also there. Buddhists divide the perceptive mind into five senses: what we refer to as the sensory mind, sight, sound, touch, and so forth, and one inner mind. Take, for example, eye-consciousness. Through the eye organ we perceive color, a blue color. How does the eye-consciousness see the blue color? The blue color stimulates the physical eye organ and transmits that color to the visual centers in the brain, what we call *eye-consciousness*, which sees the blue color. There is no distortion of the blue color. The inner image of the blue created by the brain is an accurate, resonating representation of how the blue color exists outside. But eye-consciousness does not have knowledge of the name *blue*. The eye-consciousness does not make any value judgment; it is bright or it is light or it is beautiful or it is ugly, none of that sort of thing, only direct contact. Nothing more, nothing less. That is direct perception.

Thought is not separate from perception. In fact, thought also is not separate from feeling because thought can induce feelings. The thought that somebody treated me badly can induce anger or thoughts can induce feelings from memory. In order to understand this further we should make a distinction between thinking and thought. Thought is the past participle of something that has been done. Thought is the activity of the past and the present. Thought is the past.

We can understand thought as a conditioned reflex. We could take the example of Pavlov and his dog. The dog has a natural reflex. When it sees food it salivates when it's hungry. If you ring a bell many times every time it sees food, it will then salivate when you ring the bell. Perhaps ringing the bell is associated to the memory of perceiving the food and then salivation occurs. Eventually it skips the stage of perceiving the food so you'll get a conditioned reflex. I say thought works like a conditioned reflex. When you think something, when you have thought something, it leaves something in the memory and that something reacts according to the situation by our association.

Whatever you learn goes into the past and becomes thought. As the reflex gets more and more automatic, it becomes more thought and less and less intelligent, less and less adapted to the particular situation. We tend to fall back into automatic reflexes. Everything we see in the whole world, our whole world of society, was first thought about. Its form and function were determined by thoughts. All the houses and cities and factories and farms and airplanes are profoundly affected by thought. They're really an extension of thought. It's all part of the system. There's one system. It doesn't stop inside a human being. It goes from one person to another, all through society, all through history, all over the world.

Just as these patterns seem to be repeating themselves inside of each of us, there is a corresponding repetition of our outer patterns as well. It seems that today's young people are interacting more with information and technology than human beings or with nature, and I think that this might be compounding these reflexes.

Thought affects reality as well as creating a virtual reality. The important point is not whether it's virtual or real, but whether we distinguish between the effects which originate independently of thought and those which have been produced, at least in part, by thought. We have to keep track of that. Currently, thought does not do that. It never evolved to do that. That is its basic mistake.

Physicist David Bohm, Interview with Michael Mendizza

M: *Is that the sixth sense?*

S: No, the sixth sense is behind these five senses. The exterior color is transitory. It changes each moment. The eye-consciousness is also transitory, changing, but each moment they are both in the present. The color is in the present and the eye-consciousness is in the present. But the eye-consciousness does not see yesterday's blue or a blue to come. Whatever blue is in the present, only that is seen. Nothing else. So the transitory, changing nature of the blue color and the transitory changing nature of the perception of blue, the eye-consciousness, always go together.

Now what happens when the eye consciousness in touch with the blue color is gone? What remains is an image, a kind of picture in memory. Memory is a thought that has many dimensions. It carries the image of blue, which has nothing to do with the actual blue color. At the same time, thought says that this is blue, and if the person has developed the capacity for language, he will give that memory a name. Recall that we discussed that thought has two primary limitations. Its images are not in the present, and thought does not distinguish time. Thought does not know the blue has passed, that the memory is not the actual blue at that moment. It can be yesterday's blue. You saw the blue color yesterday, you had a memory today, and thought says how beautiful this was, how bright this was, or how dull this was, how ugly this was. All these are operating on the thought level.

So thought is only touching the image, not the real substance, the actual. Because of this, thought is not accurate. It messes up many things. First, thought messes up, fails to discriminate between the image and the actual reality. Thought cannot differentiate between the past, the present, and the future. And similarly to the image, thought adds a name and value judgment, liking or disliking. Therefore thought is limited, imprecise, and contradictory. It is easily confused and does not know it. The Buddhists say this is the beginning of all the problems, and Krishnamurti also says that thought is the cause of all our conflicts, whatever they may be.

All that we have been thinking, the rituals, the symbols in a church, all the temples and so on, they are all put there by thought. Thought has invented these things. You can't deny that. Is thought sacred? Or is thought a material process, memory, the result of experience, knowledge stored up in the brain cells? Thought has invented all these things called sacred. It invented the savior, invented the temples and the contents of the temples. So thought in itself is not sacred. When thought invents God, God is not sacred. So the question arises then, what is sacred? That can only be understood or lived or happen when there's complete freedom from fear, from sorrow, and the sense of love and compassion with their own intelligence. Then, when the mind is utterly still, that which is sacred can take place.

J. Krishnamurti, Interview with Michael Mendizza

What's in a Name?

M: *The* Tao Te Ching *was written around the sixth century BC by Lao Tzu. Six hundred BC is a long time ago. And the very first stanza states: "The name that can be named is not the eternal name. The named is the beginning of ten thousand things."*

S: Yes, that's right.

M: *Everything follows from that verse. As you say, this sloppy, imprecise nature of thought is the prime cause of messing everything up.*

S: Yes, the images we call *thought* never touch the actual reality. The name doesn't touch the reality. The image doesn't touch the reality. Memory doesn't touch the reality. And thought does not stop there. Actually, when you see the color through the perception, through the image, it creates a sensation, a feeling at the thought level. This feeling is not direct perception. Perception is the cause but the feeling—it is beautiful, how lovely, or it is ugly or it is nothing, neutral, not good, not bad—is different from direct perception. The feeling or judgment is part of the image created by thought.

M: *The memory of blue also creates a feeling but thought does not discriminate. It treats the memory-image and the memory-feeling as if it were a direct perception. The image is not treated as an image but as the truth.*

S: Thought does not discriminate between direct perception, memory-image, and memory-feeling. There's no discrimination between them. The feeling created by thought, by memory, generates emotions, positive and negative—desire, attachment, anger, hate, neglect, comparison. The judgment-feeling that is evoked by the memory-image is the source of all conflicts. When you come into contact with an object that is perceived at a sensory level and you make a mental image, that causes a feeling, the desire to have it again, that thought-feeling causes further attachment, the desire that I must achieve this. You have seen a beautiful car on the street. The sensory eye-consciousness just sees the reality and immediately sends the message to the thought realm. Thought makes a value judgment in the imagination as a picture, and then you become attached to that image and then arises the desire. And thought regenerates the image over and over again.

M: *And this is the named that causes ten thousand things.*

S: All this comes.

We need a quality, which I call proprioception, really self-perception. In the body this seems to be built in. If you move your hand, you know that you're moving it. Your intention or impulse to move is aware simultaneously with the movement. You can tell the difference between moving your hand and letting it drop using gravity to move it. If you couldn't tell that difference you wouldn't survive.

Thought apparently doesn't have this proprioception. We do things and all sorts of things occur, emotions occur and we don't see that our thinking has produced them. Nations are built. All of society is produced. Endless consequences are produced and the next thought abstracts them as independent. That's an inappropriate abstraction. Later it makes the wrong abstraction of the unity in order to compensate. It goes on and on. The question is, why shouldn't thought be proprioceptive? It's part of the body process too. It's a more subtle set of reflexes. There was no reason why it should not have developed proprioceptively.

The point is, if there's an emotion that's inappropriate, it's no use directing attention at the emotional center, which is only an image of the memory. The response has to be directed at the thought process itself. Proprioception depends on an attitude of learning, of being aware of the impulse to move and the results reflected back at the same time, without having to think about it. In proprioception, you're not aware of a separate observer who's observing. The awareness is there without thinking there's a self who's observing. Once you begin to think of a self who is learning, you have introduced a division. You have introduced this confusion between the result of thought and the process of thought. Therefore, you're not able to learn because you can't keep straight what is independent reality and what is not.

Physicist David Bohm, Interview with Michael Mendizza

Relative and Absolute Realities

M: *You described the relative and the absolute when we first met in 1979.*

S: Yes.

M: *Is direct perception, the sensation of blue without thought and memory, the absolute? Is the thought* blue *and the image-feeling it produces the relative?*

S: If we talk about the relative and the absolute, then both of these are relative. The real blue is in the relative realm and the thought images are also in the relative realm. We have a technical term for the differences. The first, the real blue, we call *the positive-relative realm*. And the second, the thought-feeling-image, we call *the false-relative realm*.

M: *Why do you call it positive?*

S: We call it positive because it is real. It is not an image or imagined. It is real, truth. Why is it in the relative realm? Because the blue as blue does not exist by its own inherent truth. It rises interdependently and exists interdependently and relatively. It is not completely independent. The negation of the independent existence of blue is the absolute truth.

M: *Say that once again.*

S: Negation of the perception that blue exists separately from all other things, independently, that its nature is not dependent on other forces, that is the falsehood. When that falsehood, our belief that the blue is independent, is applied to the "I", the "me", how I conceive of myself, that is the real ego. That is the falsehood. The assumption that the "I", the "me", the ego, exists as an independent entity, this is the cause of all the problems. So this thought, this assumption, this belief, has to be negated. The Buddha and Nagarjuna saw this deception directly, and Krishnamurti understood this directly too. The difference is that Krishnamurti described this deception in modern language. He did not use technical or philosophic terms. He spoke in plain English that anyone could understand. This is the only difference. Otherwise, all of them made similar efforts to negate the false impression that the ego exists independently, to negate the false belief that there is a thinker who exists independent of thought. The truth is that the thinker, the "I", the "me", the ego, has no independent existence.

M: *It is not an independent reality.*

S: Having said that, Buddhists distinguish between the operation of the mind at the level of perception-sensation and the level of thought-feeling,

I happen to have said many, many years ago that there's no path to truth. Truth, according to them, is a fixed point. And if it's a fixed point, you could have as many paths as you like. But if it is not a fixed point, it's a living thing, moving, movement in the sense not in the world of time, which is a different matter; naturally there's no path to it. But you see, we don't want such a dangerous outlook. We want everything fixed. We want every object to be final, which has continuity, a pattern, a mold, a framework which will help you to become more peaceful, more loving, more charitable, generous, and so on and so on. But in that pattern there are divisions—your pattern, my pattern, the Christian pattern, the Hindu pattern, the Buddhist. So patterns may be dangerous altogether, because they divide people. And religions have divided people. The Protestant, the Catholic, the Hindu, the Buddhist. They're all patterns, ways of thinking. They are rituals. They are beliefs. They are faith. They are saviors. To break away from all that requires intelligence, it requires investigation, study. Nobody is willing to do that.

To see that truth is a pathless land, you must have a free mind. Your mind must be inquiring, asking, doubting, and to doubt is the most dangerous thing for most people, to question whether the systems really do help, or have they become rackets. Whether the racket is introduced by Indians or by Westerners, it's still a racket. And when they offer systems and you accept them, you are enclosed, safe, protected, you feel that. And most people want to feel protected psychologically.

Institutions have never saved man, politically, religiously, never really freed man from his sorrow, pain and so on. We know that but systems have an extraordinary appeal to the thoughtless. And if anybody says there's no power in a system, an observation with great beauty and strength, you rejected it because you're accustomed to patterns, you feel safe, protected. At least you're certain in something that is uncertain.

J. Krishnamurti, Interview with Michael Mendizza

which is based on memory without really touching the external reality. In our day-to-day life, our mind is under the control of the thought process and this prevents us from seeing things as they are; to hear, to listen to a talk as it actually is, to smell, to taste, everything. Because thought accompanies, is attached to, the perception and the perception never gets free from the operation of thought.

M: *Thought always fills up the mind.*

S: Yes, it is always filling up the mind and we are not able to push away or stop the influence of thought on what we see and experience and let direct perception work, act. That's why Krishnaji says, "Can you listen? Can you see?" He often emphasizes seeing and listening directly. His vocabulary, however, uses ordinary English, which means that he does not use technical words. Anyone can understand him.

Tibetan Monastic Training: Understanding the Mind

M: *I have images of your monastic training, but again, I'm from Los Angeles, so what do I know about you or your training? It's so presumptuous. My understanding from what reading I've done is that these aspects of mind and consciousness we have been discussing have been refined to a very precise science.*

S: Yes, very detailed categories. We have a rich vocabulary and many detailed examinations and analytical ways of describing all these things.

M: *Is this throughout all Buddhism or is it uniquely Tibetan?*

S: No, there is nothing uniquely Tibetan. Tibetan Buddhism came entirely from the Indian tradition, particularly from Nalanda, Vikramshila and Takshila, the great centers of learning. Tibetan scholars have taken great care not to add anything that is not described by authentic Indian scholars. No one is authorized to comment on the Buddhist teachings. We rely basically on two great masters, Nagarjuna and Asanga. These two are considered to be the most accurate in describing or commenting on the Buddha's teachings.

Whatever commentary or interpretation or explanation is needed, we must find a specific reference from these two great masters. His Holiness the 14th Dalai Lama has identified seventeen great Indian scholars, whose commentaries are being thoroughly studied to make a complete, traditional way of interpreting Buddhism. For example, when Buddhism

With His Holiness the Dalai Lama on a visit to the Central School for Tibetans, Dalhousie, ca. 1968–69

Our highest duty as human beings is to search out a means whereby beings may be freed from all kinds of sufferings or unsatisfactory experience (duhkha).

Whether yourselves, myself, or beings in the animal-world, all wish alike for the increase of pleasure and the diminution of pain. The destruction of this duhkha can only be brought about by making an effort oneself. It is no use to have sublime aspirations but then to sit down and wait for their accomplishment, because this attitude, which is really laziness, will lead neither to the destruction of duhkha nor to the increase of happiness. It is necessary to stress that all the various aspects of duhkha do in fact arise from causes, thus making it possible to investigate this duhkha and to put an end to it.

By finding the root-causes of duhkha and then destroying them, human life can become happy and prosperous.

In order to achieve this, it is essential that we practice in our lives those causes producing happiness, while ceasing to operate those causes giving rise to duhkha.

His Holiness the Dalai Lama, *The Opening of The Wisdom-Eye*

came to China, China's written language was well developed. It is not parallel with Sanskrit. Buddhism came to Tibet much later. Buddhism reached China in the second century AD, and Buddhism reached Tibet in the seventh and eighth centuries AD. At that time Tibet did not have a developed written language. Its script was very primitive.

The written Tibetan language was developed in order to accurately translate the Buddhist canon. As a result, the Tibetan language is absolutely parallel with Sanskrit. Therefore, the largest and most accurate translations were done in the Tibetan language, which has the entire vocabulary of the original Sanskrit. Our translations are absolutely accurate. That is why, from the Tibetan version, we are able to reconstruct the lost Sanskrit texts. So nothing is unique in Tibet. Everything is in the Indian tradition.

M: *Again, forgive my not knowing. What is a Lama? They call you Rinpoche. What is a Rinpoche? Is a Rinpoche a Lama? What qualifies one to be a Lama?*

S: The expression or term *Lama* is similar to the Sanskrit word *Guru*. *Guru* translated into Tibetan becomes *Lama*. Later on, the word *Lama* by non-Tibetans was used for monks and teachers. That's all right. But a Lama is not necessarily a monk. *Lama* in the Sanskrit language stands for *teacher*. And the term *Rinpoche* is not a name, it is a title. In Sanskrit, if something is precious, the word used is *ratna*. *Ratna* means jewel, precious, and that word translated to the Tibetan language is *Rinpoche*, which is used for respected teachers and also for reincarnated Lamas. The word has become common.

Many Western scholars in the nineteenth and early twentieth centuries who could not understand Tibetan Buddhism in depth thought it meant something different. So they called it *Lamaism*, but there is no such thing. If you look in the Sanskrit traditions, you will find all these expressions there. So what we have been talking about is not something unique or special or something developed later by Tibetans. It's all based on the Indian tradition.

M: *Let me make a big jump. You mentioned reincarnation. Is a Rinpoche a reincarnated Lama or could be?*

S: Yes.

M: *Earlier you said that the color blue was interdependent.*

S: Yes, interdependent.

All counterproductive emotions are based on ignorance of the true nature of things. Practices that teach us how to overcome that ignorance undercut all afflictive emotions. The antidote to ignorance addresses all troubles. This is the extraordinary gift of insight.

Ignorance in this context is not just a lack of knowledge—it is an active misapprehension of the nature of things.

You have to recognize, at least in a rough way, what you are falsely superimposing on phenomena before you can understand the emptiness that exists in its stead. Understanding how you actually exist, who you really are without the overlay of false imagination, is the main topic of this book.

Ignorance, by relying on appearances, superimposes onto persons and things a sense of concreteness that, in fact, is not there. Ignorance would have us believe that these phenomena exist in some fundamental way. Through ignorance what we see around us seems to exist independently, without depending on other factors for its existence, but this is not the case. By giving people and things around us this exaggerated status, we are drawn into all sorts of overblown and ultimately hurtful emotions.

You need to appreciate the disparity between how you appear to your own mind and how you indeed exist.

Cruder conceptions of "I" and "mine" evoke grosser destructive emotions, such as arrogance and belligerence, making trouble for yourself, your community, and even your nation. These misconceptions need to be identified by watching your own mind.

If your mind is scattered, it is quite powerless. Distraction here and there opens the way for counterproductive emotions, leading to many kinds of trouble. Without clear, stable concentration, insight cannot know the true nature of phenomena in all its power. For example, to see a painting in the dark, you need a very bright lamp. Even when you have such a lamp, if it is flickering you cannot see the painting clearly and in detail. Also, if the lamp is steady but weak, you cannot see well either. You need both great clarity of mind and steadiness, both insight and focused concentration, like an oil lamp untouched by any breeze.

> His Holiness the Dalai Lama,
> *How to See Yourself as You Really Are: A Practical Guide to Self-Knowledge (Abridged)*

M: *One's perception of the color blue is not fixed; it is moving, changing, moment by moment. How do I then reconcile reincarnation? If something reincarnates, it must be steady, fixed. How can something that is not continuous reincarnate? I'm confused.*

Identification and Confusion

S: *Transitory-ness* is one of the basic principles of Buddhism. Buddhists do not believe there are any composed things that are unchanging or permanent. Whatever is created is created by causes. Those causes will change and decay, but change does not mean there is no continuity. As I mentioned, sensory consciousness, thought consciousness, meditative consciousness, whatever consciousness may be, all come from the subtle consciousness, which does not have a beginning, does not have an end, so therefore it takes a body and remains in that body for a certain period of time.

M: *And that consciousness gets confused by all the images.*

S: Yes, it gets completely confused. It becomes identified with this form or that and due to the confusion, it accumulates a lot of deeds, good merits or bad merits; we call it karmic force. When the body disintegrates, the subtle consciousness leaves every sensory organ. When the eye organ is damaged or dies, the eye-consciousness stops. But the inner subtle consciousness does not depend on a physical body. It can remain, ever-changing each moment, but it has continuity, like a river flowing. If you mark a point in a river, each moment new water passes by the point. Consciousness is like the water. Each moment, the old consciousness dies and a new consciousness takes its place.

Karma Is Like a Hangover

M: *You mentioned karma, the good deeds, the bad deeds, and so on. Pardon my metaphor, but karma is like a hangover. It's a residue.*

S: Residue, that's true.

M: *Is that hangover, that residue, attached somehow to this subtle continuity?*

S: Again, we are jumping to a different issue, but it has been raised. In the ordinary state, as I mentioned, thought gives birth to negative or positive emotions and these emotions cause further actions. For example,

What do you consider is life? Your life, what is your life? What is that life that you daily live? Dependence, attachment, pain, annoyance, anger, irritation, sorrow, you know all this, don't you? This is your daily life. Going to the temple and doing some kind of noise with the bell, and doing puja, doing yoga. That we say, that is our life. Then what do you mean by a religious life?

You tell me. What does religion mean to you? The word. The word religion means to gather all your energy. That is all it means. Do you understand sir? To gather all your energy to enquire, to find. Right? Not all the nonsense of temples and rituals, or all this either, sir, what you have put on your head. You see how you all agree?

The meaning of the word, that means gathering every particle of energy that you have, to enquire into what is truth and what is reality. To enquire into what is meditation, to enquire into why human beings live the way we are living, to enquire if there is an end to sorrow. To enquire into what is love. Whether one can live without any effort and control, all that is implied in that word.

A religious life implies being a light to yourself. Which means no outside authority. We are talking about having no spiritual authority. Including me, the speaker. Have you any authority, spiritual authority? You have had various gurus, Mr. Gandhi, and so on all the way from the sixth, fifth, fourth, third century down to the present. And where are you, having been led, for these thousands of years, where are you? Or do you want to be still led?

So I am asking, we are asking you courteously, if you have thrown away your traditions. Traditions being nationality, your castes, your beliefs, your rituals, going to the temples, all that. Have you thrown it away?

Listener: No, sir.

No? No. Then how can you find out what a religious life is when you are blind? So you want to find out what a religious life is and yet you won't leave your little enclosure. Right? You are tied to your tradition and you want to enquire into something that demands a mind that is capable, a heart that can really love. Without that freeing yourself from your tradition, your culture, your belief, how can you find out anything? You can repeat what the Gita said or the Upanishad or some other book. What value has it?

I was told the other day that some of the gurus now give lectures or talks on the Gita, is that right? And there are hundreds and thousands who go and listen to it. What value has it? What are we all playing at, sirs?

Apparently one doesn't see one's own tragedy, right, sir?

J. Krishnamurti, 3rd Public Dialogue, Chennai (Madras), 1979

a negative emotion or negative intention causes an action, which is expressed in three ways. The first is through the physical body. The second is vocal, through speech. And the third is through the mind. Action originating in the mind may not be expressed verbally or physically. Every thought that arises has its effect. Mostly when the action comes through the mind and the intention is strong, the desire is powerful, it will express vocally and physically. For example, when the negative emotions hate and anger arise in your mind, you are not able to control them. Due to the anger, you may wish to harm or kill some other living being. Then physically, by yourself or through others, you make an effort to kill and another's life comes to an end. You destroy that life, causing great misery and harm to another living being, which is a negative action that doesn't go away. It makes a residual imprint, like a drop of oil on a piece of paper, and remains there. An imprint is made on your subtle consciousness.

M: *And it doesn't have to be vocal or physical.*

S: It could just be mental.

M: *And you still get the drop on your subtle consciousness.*

S: Yes, you still get the drop.

M: *That's terrible.*

S: Yes. And similarly, if you have a compassionate mind and see a small insect or other living being whose life is in danger and you make an effort to save that life, then you earn great positive karmic force. That also doesn't go away. That imprint is made on your subtle consciousness. So your subtle consciousness has countless different collections of karmic forces that can only be completely removed if you awaken your wisdom, your inner intelligence, if you become realized and transform yourself. Until then all the karmic forces are there, action by action with their hangovers, their residue. And this pattern is escalated, momentarily, particularly at the time of your death when you pick up positive or negative karmic force depending on your mindset, and that carries over to the next birth, whether a good or bad one.

Even if it is good, you might experience sudden negative karmic force. You are reborn in a human form yet you are not a completely healthy person. There might be some disability or you are reborn into a very poor family, having no opportunity for education, and so on. Sometimes

> Much of our planning is like waiting to swim in a dry ravine
> Many of our activities are like housekeeping in a dream.
> Delirious with fever, one does not recognize the fever.
>
> Paltrul Rinpoche, *The Words of My Perfect Teacher*

If you do not have insight into the way you yourself and all things actually are, you cannot recognize and get rid of the obstacles to liberation from cyclic existence and, even more important, the obstructions to helping others.

You need to give up the false beliefs you are superimposing on the way things really are.

The supreme scholar practitioners of India—Nagarjuna, Aryadva, Chandrakirn, and Dharmakirti—understood that the truth cannot be realized without seeing that we superimpose on people and things a status of solidity and permanence that actually is not there. The emptiness of that false superimposition must be understood, and to do this they analyzed phenomena through scripture and through reasoning.

Although you might succeed in withdrawing your mind from disturbing objects, this does not constitute being absorbed in the truth. You have to actively realize that objects simply do not exist the way ignorance takes them to exist.

You have to put together that if objects really did exist in the way they seem to, the logical consequences would be impossible, and on this basis you can fully appreciate that phenomena do not exist this way. People and things may still seem to exist concretely and independently from their own side, but you will know that they do not. Gradually, this awareness will weaken your misconceptions and diminish the trouble they cause.

Accepting appearances as truth is the basic problem; the antidote is to come to realize the falsity of appearances through reasoning.

His Holiness the Dalai Lama,
How to See Yourself as You Really Are: A Practical Guide to Self-Knowledge (Abridged)

even a bad karmic force is combined with a good karmic force, being born in a very good family, for example, like a dog or cat in a rich family; they enjoy life without hunger or thirst and live a comfortable life. So, due to different kinds of karmic forces mixed together, there is a given result. This is the theory of karma and the theory of rebirth.

M: *What you're sharing is very basic.*

S: Basic fundamental Buddhist thoughts, yes, that's right.

Spiritual Kindergarten and Levels

M: *This explanation is the first level, spiritual kindergarten.*

S: Buddhist teachings are divided into various levels: the common, the average, and the most difficult to grasp. We discussed imagination, that the image has a number of different levels. Some image levels are described in *The Secret Oral Teachings in Tibetan Buddhist Sects* by Alexandra David-Néel. When engaging in Buddhist meditation, meditations can be roughly divided into three different categories. In the first, meditation takes the form of concentration. That means doing nothing but trying to concentrate, the practice of concentrating your entire mind on one particular object.

M: *When filming Krishnamurti in Madras (Chennai) in 1978 or 1979, he defined religion as "gathering every particle of energy and attention that you have to observe." Is this what you're saying?*

S: Yes, exactly, we call it *shamatha*, the power of concentration. People focus on one object, on the breath or sensation of the body, and so forth, whatever you might choose to encourage the power of concentration without any distraction. That is one kind of meditation. The other kind is cultivation of the mind. You are not meditating with *shamatha* concentration but to generate loving kindness, to generate *bodhichitta* or *bodhi mind*, to reduce negative feelings, negative emotions such as attachment, hate, anger, and so on, to bring the mind into the nature of compassion, love, kindness, affection, a warm heart, and others. For that, *shamatha* concentration doesn't work. You have to dialogue with your mind. You have to analyze all the things that cause negative emotions. You have to argue with your mind and in that way, the rational way, you negate negativity and harmful emotions.

At his residence, Theckchen Choeling, Dharamsala, 2014

It was a clear morning of winter, cold but bright, and there was not a cloud in the sky. As you watched the light of the early morning sun on the river, meditation was going on. The very light was part of that meditation when you looked at the bright dancing water in the quiet morning—not with a mind that was translating it into some meaning, but with eyes that saw the light and nothing else.

The light that the eyes see is not the light on the water; that light is so different, so vast that it cannot enter into the narrow field of the eye. That light, like sound, moved endlessly—outward and inward—like the tide of the sea. And if you kept very still, you went with it, not in imagination or sensuously; you went with it unknowingly, without the measure of time.

The beauty of that light, like love, is not to be touched, not to be put into a word. But there it was—in the shade, in the open, in the house, on the window across the way, and in the laughter of those children. Without that light, what you see is of so little importance, for the light is everything; and the light of meditation was on the water. It would be there in the evening again, during the night, and when the sun rose over the trees, making the river golden. Meditation is that light in the mind which lights the way for action, and without that light there is no love.

J. Krishnamurti, *The Only Revolution*

M: *Have a dialogue with oneself that asks, Why do I hate this person? Is he or she really the images and feelings I have created?*

S: That's right. You are purifying your mind slowly, reducing negative emotions and increasing, encouraging, and cultivating your mind in a positive way. This is the second kind of meditation. Here you are not concentrating but you are using contemplation to cultivate your mind, reducing any intention of violence or hate, and replacing negative intentions with love. You must have a compassionate mind. This kind of meditation is the cultivation of the mind. It is entirely different from practices that concentrate the mind.

Then there is another entirely different kind of meditation that is mostly found in the practice of *tantra*. Here the imagination is used in very positive ways. You may build up an image of a *mandala* or create an inner image of yourself as a deity. You surround yourself with powerful deities, all in your imagination. Imagination is imagination, but this is not reflexive imagination, the result of thought's mechanical and careless operation. You are using imagination creatively to make specific images, not images of disliking or liking a person. In this way you create an entirely different world within your imagination and an inner reality of all things being equal, all sentient beings being most dear, needing to be loved. You can do that because you have the capacity and the power to reach all sentient beings and to serve them, to take away their miseries and to give comfort, all in the imaginary world. By this practice we convert the disease into the medicine. The image that is the cause of all our problems can now be used to liberate yourself and others.

M: *In order for that meditation to occur, the first two are necessary.*

S: Yes, of course.

M: *First, you have to have the ability to focus.*

S: Without focus you cannot meditate.

M: *You are building the capacity to give attention so that attention is not scattered, diffused.*

S: Yes, that's right.

M: *Thought is reflexive. Without this ability to attend and to focus, the mechanical reflex generates images and we are carried away by them. The second level or form of meditation is to dissolve the sense of separation so you no longer create false images.*

The psychological content of consciousness of man is almost universal. The content of one's consciousness is greatly similar to all other consciousness of mankind. In that consciousness man suffers, goes through a great deal of agony, conflict and depression and elation. He has enumerable beliefs, a great many images about himself and about others. There is fear and the pursuit of pleasure. And there are the various types of religious divisions with their superstitions, illusions, saviors, and all that. That is the content of one's consciousness which is really the content of humanity. Because all humanity, whether it is in the East or West, in Africa, Russia, or wherever it is, human beings go through this crisis in consciousness.

We want order outside in the world, politically, religiously, economically, socially; we want order in our relationship with each other. We want some peace. We want some understanding. If the inward psychological state is not orderly, not conflicting, not contradicting, if that state in consciousness is quiet, steady, clear, then you can bring about order in the world.

What we are trying to do is try to bring order legislatively, nationally and so on, order out there in the world, which has been proved over and over again that it totally brings about disorder.

Without inward order in consciousness, which is in a mess, which is in a contradiction, without bringing about order inwardly, psychologically, you cannot possibly have order inwardly. And the crisis is there. We think the crisis is national, economic, social, and so on. The crisis is not out there! The crisis is really inward and we're unwilling to face that.

       J. Krishnamurti, Interview with Michael Mendizza

S: Right.

M: *When you move into this creative use of imagination, it's not what we call fantasy. What you are describing has the potential to be very powerful, to actually create a reality.*

S: It is not in the realm of fantasy. Fantasy is visualizing something that does not exist. For example, you visualize yourself as the Buddha Amitabha, who exists in reality. You are not the Buddha Amitabha. In the visualization you project yourself into the nature of the Buddha Amitabha, how the Buddha Amitabha looks with his thirty-two signs of great personality and eighty different beauties of the body, his clothes, and his surrounding lights; all this exists for the Buddha Amitabha. You are visualizing something that exists. And similarly, when you create a mandala of all the *kalachakra* deities, their surroundings and attributes do exist in accordance with the *kalachakra tantra*, and you are not visualizing anything more or less than what is described in the text. And this is done in great detail. There are very minute measurements for each hand or each face or even the eye and nose. All this is completely measured. Therefore, you are visualizing what is very clearly described and is believed to exist, but you have not yet achieved that state of being, though you visualize that you have. So this kind of visualization is not in the realm of fantasy because fantasy can be anything. But realization meditation is based on something that is described in the text.

M: *How does this third level benefit the person who is practicing? What capacity or strength or virtue does that meditation evoke?*

S: That is difficult to explain unless you have some basic knowledge of the practice of tantra, which talks about what you are going to achieve when you become the Buddha Nature. That end, that objective, is practiced while you are still on the path. For example, take a worldly metaphor. You are going to New York in a few days and to reach New York you have to take a long journey. It will take several hours of flying, and so on, but you are sitting here and visualizing that you have reached New York. You have visualized the streets and buildings and everything. You say to yourself, "I have already reached there." In this way, the purification of mind/body/speech and the world around your mind/body/speech is completely purified when you achieve the Buddha Nature. This is realized now. So that's why we say that the result takes into account the

R: Awareness, mindfulness, attention, how do you discriminate these three?

K: I would say awareness in which there is no choice, just to be aware. The moment when choice enters into awareness, there is no awareness.

R: Right.

K: And choice is measurement, division, and so on. So awareness is without choice, just to be aware. To say, "I don't like, I like this room," all that has ended.

R: Right.

K: Attention, to attend, in that attention there is no division.

R: Also that means no choice.

K: Attention implies no division, me attending. And so it has no division, therefore no measurement, and therefore no border.

K: One can be aware of what kind of dress you have. One may say, "I like it," or "I don't like it," so choice doesn't exist, you are aware of it, that's all. But attention, in that there is no attender, one who attends, and so no division.

R: But the Buddha's teaching is that in this practice of meditation there is no discrimination, there is no value judgement, there is no like or dislike, but you only see.

K: If you totally attend, with your ears, with your eyes, with your body, with your nerves, with all your mind, with your heart in the sense of affection, love, compassion, total attention, what takes place?

R: An absolute revolution, internal and complete revolution.

K: It has no quality, no center, and having no center, no border. This is an actuality, you can't just imagine this.

> J. Krishnamurti, *Can Humanity Change? J. Krishnamurti in Dialogue with Buddhists.* The Buddhist scholars included Dr. Rahula Walpola, Brockwood Park, UK, 1979

means. The end takes into account the means. You take a shortcut, meaning that by this kind of visualization, and not only visualization, this practice combines a great many merits and also the purification of the mind. Through these various ways, one achieves the end more quickly.

Apart from that, from this realization, another important technique is involved. You are using your entire biological body, the physical body, for purifying your mind. The common practice, called *paramitayana*, is the usual long way to achieve the Buddha Nature, where only the mind is involved in the meditation. The body and speech are not involved in this method or this path. And *tan* refers to the body; *tra* refers to using your body to go beyond your body.

The body has several components and the greatest is called *the breath* in English. But in Sanskrit and Tibetan it is called *prana*, meaning the essence of life. The essence of life is the force of moving, different from blood and other substances. The force of moving prana, *pranayama*, is an exercise of the breath or wind that circulates in your body. Prana is a vehicle for all body substances, such as the blood, which cannot circulate throughout your body if your body does not have the moving force of wind. For example, in a pipe there's a blockage; the water cannot flow and you have to remove the blockage. Similarly prana or wind goes into all parts of your nerves and throughout the body structure. Then blood or other substances, whatever the body needs, are able to circulate.

Wind is also the vehicle of thought. With the common path you don't have this method; you only have the practice of concentration, focusing your mind. While concentrating you can remove the influences of thought from your mind. The object of concentration becomes more and more clear, and then you can achieve direct perception. But when concentration stops, thought returns.

The tantric method is to negate the vehicle of thought. Thought is divided by tantra into eighty different natures, all with different kinds of winds. Each wind comes from a very specific place. By concentrating on that place and also removing the blockage of the nervous system, blocked places are opened. This way you can remove thought from the mind. For that purpose, you need to visualize all the winds and all the nerves and the body's system. Using visualization you can concentrate on a particular point and thereby help to control the wind when it goes in

What should be is a myth; it is the morality which thought and fancy have put together, and one must deny this morality—the social, the religious, and industrial. This denial is not of the intellect but is an actual slipping out of the pattern of that morality which is immoral.

So the question really is: Is it possible to step out of this pattern?…

Thought thinks that it can step out of the pattern, but if it does it will still be an act of thought, for thought has no reality and therefore it will create another illusion. Going beyond this pattern is not an act of thought. This must be clearly understood, otherwise you will be caught again in the prison of thought.

After all, the "you" is a bundle of memory, tradition, and the knowledge of a thousand yesterdays. So only with the ending of sorrow, for sorrow is the result of thought, can you step out of the world of war, hate, envy and violence. This act of stepping out is the religious life. This religious life has no belief whatsoever, for it has no tomorrow.

J. Krishnamurti, *The Only Revolution (Abridged)*

the wrong direction by bringing it back to the right direction. Then it will slow down and become still, and thereby all the images created by thought can be removed. This is a very different way. It cannot be explained in a short time or in a common language because it requires a great many technical terms.

M: *And at the third level, what I call creative imagination, you're using imagination as a creative force.*

S: Yes, that's right.

M: *To clean up the ink blots on your subtle consciousness, our karmic blotter.*

S: Yes.

M: *How does this sequence of practices relate to Krishnamurti? He achieved this and of course encourages us to do the same but without the formal or gradual steps.*

With or Without Methods

S: Yes. Krishnamurti does not refer to any graduation, any effort necessary to begin *here* to reach *there*. He negates all this. And I think he does so with a specific purpose. This is my understanding. You should not consider this an interpretation or commentary on Krishnamurti, but simply how I understand Krishnamurti when I listen to him.

M: *You must have talked to him about all this?*

S: Yes, many times. Krishnaji negates graduation, effort, and methods to shake us forcefully, because we are so deeply rooted in our conditioning and by that conditioning we convert all things, including spirituality and religion, into more conditioning. Unless and until we are shaken forcefully to awaken, we will convert what he tells us into an "ism" or another form of conditioning. All the methods, all the graduation, all the forces of meditation, reinforce our conditioning. To awaken us from that conditioning, he had to negate everything.

M: *This notion of translation or conversion is critical to understand. Here we have Krishnamurti in another realm, in another reality, and he's pointing, describing. And we listen and convert what he is saying back into our conditioning, and we do this over and over again. So we only hear ourselves and never really listen or hear what he's saying. This is not obvious but so very clear.*

S: Yes. This is why we, the few Buddhists who have listened to Krishnamurti, believe that he helped us a great deal in understanding the Buddha

ALWAYS AWAKENING

With the Abbot and scholars at the Atsagatsky Datsan Monastery, Buryatia, Russia, 2014

The thousand yesterdays cannot be made new; even a candle burns itself out. Everything must end for the new to be.

J. Krishnamurti, *The Only Revolution*

more clearly, to see and understand how we have diluted the understanding of Buddhist teachings. Krishnamurti made this clear by rejecting and negating all that our mind is holding on to.

M: *Even as a monk you're translating, converting, as you say. You're still in the same boat.*

S: The same boat, that's right. We also refer to Nagarjuna. Sometimes Nagarjuna is even more radical than Krishnamurti. He rejects the Buddha. He rejects the karmic causality system. He rejects everything but his rejection. And Krishnamurti's rejection, if you compare them closely, is very similar. After rejecting everything, then what remains?

M: *Because the concept of* karma *implies more conditioning?*

S: Sometimes, yes.

M: *Nagarjuna negated the Buddha and karma?*

S: Everything, yes, *nirvana*, everything. We are conditioned by all that, so they negate it all.

The problem with the self—there is an assumption or concept which, if it were real, would be extremely important, would be the highest value of all things. Just think of the word "self." The basic meaning is the quintessence, the essence of all essences and that would, of course, have supreme value. Now, if we assume there is a self, this stirs up the whole mind and brain inside so it feels, just from that assumption, that something is going on inside which corresponds to this assumed self and gives it an apparent reality. Once it has been assumed that this self is real and not merely an image, its attributed reality takes first priority and everything else comes second, so everything is distorted.

For example, if somebody tells you that the self is bad, this will create a disturbing feeling inside this image and therefore there will be a very powerful move to change that, to falsify, to say instead that you are good, as an example; this sort of distortion becomes universal.

The main point is that we don't really understand the nature of our thought process; we're not aware of how it works and it's really disrupting not only our society and our individual lives, but also the way the brain and nervous system operate, making us unhealthy or perhaps even in some way damaging the system.

Krishnamurti recognizes that thought, rational, orderly, factual thought, such as in doing proper science, is valuable but the kind of thought that he has in mind is self-centered thought. At first sight one might wonder why self-centered thought is so bad. If the self were really there, then perhaps it would correct to center on the self because the self would be so important, but if the self is a kind of illusion, at least the self as we know it, then to center our thought on something illusory which is assumed to have supreme importance is going to disrupt the whole process, and it will not only make thought about yourself wrong, it will make thought about everything wrong, so that thought becomes a dangerous and destructive instrument all around.

Physicist David Bohm, Interview with Michael Mendizza

United Kingdom, 2012, Day Two

The Self Is the Self

M: *When we talk about self or when we talk about "me", are there different "me"'s in your system?*

S: There are no different kinds of self. Self is the self. But there are so many different ways of grasping the self, how we conceive of the self. That's why there are hundreds of different philosophical Eastern schools in India. The basic difference between them is how they describe the self, selflessness. The self and selflessness point to or represent the same thing. What we usually conceive of or what our thought imagines about the self does not really exist. The actual self is entirely different from what we imagine it to be. We think of the self as a person. The self does not exist in a chair or in a camera. Non-living things do not have a self. We generally conceive of all living things having a self. And that self, if you are a believer in reincarnation, birth and rebirth, you identify as an individual, a person. But who or what will take the next life? Who are you? What we generally call a person, a self, is absolutely misconceived, misunderstood. No one knows who I am.

We can describe it like this. Somebody uses abusive words and you get angry. You lose your temper. At that moment you have a very strong feeling about "I", "me", that he or she abused me. I cannot tolerate it. The "I" that reacts to the abuse does not know who I really am, but there is a very strong feeling about this. That's one way of looking at it. The other way of looking at it is when all of a sudden somebody asks you, "Who are you?" At that moment the imaginary reaction is, "I am Rinpoche" or "I am Michael," the name. But the name is not what I am. The name is just a name, a symbol.

In the Tibetan tradition, the children are given a name a few months or perhaps a year after birth. In the West, where you are given a name at birth, your parents have chosen a name but the name is not you. The name can be changed. Many different people have identical names, George or Michael. There is not only one George. There is not only one Michael. But if somebody suddenly asks, "Who are you?" you reply, "I am George," or "I am Sunam," "I am Tushe." At that moment the grasping of

Every action, either physical or mental, every movement occurring either on the plane of gross matter or on the plane of the mind, causes an emission of energy. To use the established expression, it produces a "seed."

This seed, in the same way as all material seeds, tends—given favourable circumstances —to produce a being of the same species as that of the parent who has transmitted the seed. The seed of an oak tends to produce an oak. The seed of an animal, dog or bird, tends to produce a dog or a bird.

Likewise, the innumerable energy seeds launched into the universe by Desire, Aversion, Love, Hatred, and the actions caused by these feelings by attachment to individual existence with the material activity which it excites in order to preserve that individual existence to perpetuate it, to increase its power and enlarge its sphere of action, all these seeds tend to reproduce the counterparts of their parents, either psychic or material.

In order that the seed should be sown, it is in no way necessary that the feelings we experience should be materialized in action. The aspirations which we entertain without realizing them, those also which we restrain, our thoughts of whatever kind they may be, unceasingly give out seeds. Furthermore, the hidden activity, always at work in spite of ourselves in the subconscious part of our being, is one of the most powerful sources from which are thrown out these seeds.

It is necessary to go further, say the Secret Teachings; it is necessary to understand, to grasp, to see that there is not a blade of grass, not a grain of sand which is not a "sower" of seed by the activity of its physical life and by that of a psychic life, peculiar to its species, which we must in no way imagine as similar to our own.

There cannot happen the least movement—in this world which is movement—without this movement starting other movements, other manifestations of energy tending to repetitions, in dependence on "memories" (vasana) or, as the Tibetans call them, on propensities (pag chang). Each of our physical or mental movements is the fruit of causes coming from the whole universe and has its repercussions in the whole universe. Thus opens up the working, without beginning or end, of the activity which is the Universe.

> Alexandra David-Néel and Lama Yongden,
> *The Secret Oral Teachings in Tibetan Buddhist Sects*

the "I" does not differentiate the name as simply a symbol. We say, "I am Samdhong." This strong feeling does not differentiate between the symbol, the mental images we carry, and the subtle consciousness that has no beginning or end. It is all mixed up.

Somebody asks, "Are you George?" George is your name. Even when you die, the name will remain. I realize that George is my name but the name is not me. Then we ask, "Who am I?" But even when questioning that, there is a strong clinging to a firm belief that there is an independent entity held in the conception of your thought. That is to be negated. The Buddha negated it. Nagarjuna negated it. Krishnamurti negated it. As long as the mind grasps after, clings to, the false misconception that the mental image of an independent thinker is separate from thought, we cannot see ourselves as we really are. We see ourselves in a very mixed-up, wrong way. But still you feel, you hold on to, grasp very strongly, this image of the self.

After removing the false image completely, then what self remains is that transitory continuity of your inner subtle consciousness. At this moment, the inner subtle consciousness abides in the body, and at the time of death, it can divorce or separate from the body. The body might be healthy or weak but as soon as the inner subtle consciousness leaves the body, the body dies. It ceases to function. The entire functioning of the body is dependent on the subtle consciousness, which is a force that has the potential of knowing, thinking, visualizing. All the facilities come out of this. Some of the Western philosophies used to say, "I think, therefore I am." Now some philosophers say, "I am, therefore I think." These are some of the ways that are used to describe the false nature of the self as we generally think of it.

One Soul or Many

M: *Is your-self different from my-self? Or is there one self, one subtle energy that I individualize as "me", and you individualize as "you"?*

S: That is a very complex question with which the entire Indian tradition has been involved for thousands and thousands of years.

M: *Then it is a good question.*

S: Yes. And this question has divided the entire Indian thought into two

I have gone to the extent of saying that Krishnamurti is only a footnote on the Buddha's teaching. This was not said out of disrespect for Krishnamurti's teaching, but out of a feeling of the grandeur of the Buddha's teaching. When I was studying the Buddha's teaching and when I felt the potential of it, I felt it was tremendous. I felt that Krishnamurti had opened a window to it. I know several people who have gone through this exercise through Vedanta and through yoga and some through Buddhist yoga, and they have said that when you listen to Krishnamurti, a window opens, a clarity comes to your mind so that you see more in it than you could ever see yourself. Apart from that I think that Krishnaji has some very unique insights of his own which I have not come across in any scriptures which I have read—not in the Upanishads, not in the Gita, not in any of the Buddhist scriptures either. You come upon some statements which exist in the tantra, but then you never know the sequence of those. I have not been able to grasp the sequence of the tantra. So Krishnaji had said something original. I will give you only one instance. The entire teaching can be summed up in one word which is "attention." I would say that the teaching is that attention, as you know it, is totally enmeshed in your identification with the body and then spiritual life consists in fighting against this.

Now Krishnamurti says that this faculty of attention is not of the brain. Though it operates through the brain, it is not of the brain. And this faculty can see these biological reflexes; it can see what comes through the brain. So this attention is really a flash of the cosmic energy like, as it were, a high voltage current to which this low voltage current is tied.

> Padmanabhan Krishna, *A Jewel on a Silver Platter: Remembering Jiddu Krishnamurti*. An interview with Achyutji Patwardhan

mainstreams: one is *Ishwarvaadin*, and the other is *Unishwarvaadin*. *Ishwarvaadin* means *he who believes in a creator* and that we are all created by one creator. That in Sanskrit is called *Ishwar* or Almighty God, and the Almighty God by his will created all individuals and the entire universe, and so forth. The majority of Indian tradition belongs to this belief, except for three traditions: the Buddhists, the Jains, and the materialistic Charvaak. The Charvaak are no longer present today. Both the Jains and the Buddhists still exist. Jainism and Buddhism do not believe in a creator. All other non-Indian traditions, such as Christianity, Islam, and Zoroastrianism, believe in a creator. They talk a great deal about the soul in the individual, a living soul. So the self is, in reality, one, which is expressed as many different individuals. When you become free from your bondage, you merge back to the greater soul. They take the metaphor of a glass of water or water in a boat. They are limited. They are measurable. When the water is put back into the ocean, there's no difference. The water in the glass is indistinguishable from the larger ocean. They are the same. Similarly, when you are in your body you are in the bondage of ignorance, and when you become free from ignorance, you merge with one self or one soul. Each individual is created by the greater soul and when this individual dissolves, it goes back to the greater soul. Then there will be no suffering, no misery. This is one theory.

M: *Is this the Buddhist theory?*

S: No. This is the theory for those who believe in a creator. Buddhists and Jains do not believe in a creator. As I have said many times, individuals are not created by anybody but they do exist without beginning or end, and it is by this nature that there are so many selves, so many souls. Each self is different. Now, the word *different* must be used carefully. I am not you, you are not me, even if you achieve Buddhahood and I achieve Buddhahood. Both of us become the Buddha. Then there is no differentiation between your Buddha Nature and my Buddha Nature. *No differentiation* does not mean not having an identity. It means no greater or lesser, higher or lower. It means equality. All Buddhas are equal. Yet there is identity. They can be identified. The trace of the individual remains. So *your-self* and *my-self* are not expressions of *one self*. They are intrinsically different selves. There are countless selves that are called sentient beings, so there are unlimited sentient beings. They all have the potential of

J. Krishnamurti

When I began to think for myself, I found myself in revolt. I was not satisfied by any teachings, by any authority; I wanted to find out for myself what the World-Teacher meant to me and what the Truth was behind the form of the World-Teacher, what was meant by the taking of a vehicle, and what was meant by His manifestation in the world.

When I was a small boy, I used to see Shri Krishna as pictured by the Hindus. My mother used to talk to me about Shri Krishna; hence I created an image in my mind of Shri Krishna with the flute, with all the devotion, all the love and delight.

When I met Bishop Leadbeater and the Theosophical Society, I began to see the Master K.H.—in the form put before me, reality from their point of view—hence Master K.H. was the end. Later I began to see the Lord Maitreya. Now it is the Buddha, my Beloved.

You ask me what I mean by "the Beloved." To me it is all; it is Shri Krishna, it is the Master K.H., it is the Lord Maitreya, it is the Buddha, and yet it is beyond all these forms. My Beloved is the open skies, the flower, every human being.

Till I was one with my Beloved, I never spoke. I talked of vague generalities which everybody wanted. I never said, I am the World-Teacher; but now that I feel I am one with the Beloved, I say it—not to impress you, to convince you of my greatness, or the greatness of the World-Teacher, nor even of the beauty of life—but merely to awaken the desire in your own hearts and in your own minds to seek and discover the Truth for yourself. Hence I say that I am one with the Beloved—whether you interpret it as the Buddha, the Lord Maitreya, Shri Krishna, or any other name.

J. Krishnamurti, Castle Eerde, The Netherlands, 2 August 2 1927 *(Abridged)*

becoming the Buddha Nature, but they are all individuals, meaning they are different.

Different does not mean here something that may cause conflict or that may be treated as different. All sentient beings are equal in three ways: each wishes not to suffer; each wants happiness or pleasure; and each has the right or potential to get rid of the source of misery, achieve happiness, and even enlightenment, the Buddha Nature. In these three things all individuals are similar. They are not one, not the same, but they are equal. From that viewpoint, every sentient being is equal but different.

M: *In one you maintain some form of identity.*

S: Yes, maintain identity, that's right.

M: *In the other, that identity disappears and you go back to the one?*

S: Right.

M: *I appreciate how challenging these questions are and how difficult it is to answer them using common language. It feels that I am dragging you back to kindergarten.*

Masters or No Masters

M: *Regarding going beyond, Donald Ingram Smith was an Australian journalist who met Krishnamurti in the 1940s. Donald tells a story. They were driving and Donald said, "Krishnaji, I understand that you used to see the Masters. You saw them, you talked with them, is that true?" And Krishnaji said, "Yes, I did quite often." Krishnamurti went on to describe how one day he was talking to the Master and he said, "Sir, we've had these conversations for so many times. I want more. I want to shake your hand. I want to touch you." And Krishnaji got up and walked through the form, and when he turned around the image was gone. And he said, "And I've never seen it again."*

The reason I bring this up has to do with going beyond. Krishnamurti didn't say that he never experienced the energy, the pattern, or the meaning that form expressed. He didn't say that that energy disappeared. He said the image disappeared. My question is, did Krishnamurti go beyond the need to create an image? Does it make any sense as an expression of going beyond?

S: Any great personality who attains enlightenment without the assistance of another, or even one who is aided by another or is said to be used by another for certain purposes—these happenings will always remain a

Radhaji: It was perhaps a precognition, some kind of prescience, from the time of Madame Blavatsky, that the world conditions were going to change outwardly. Madame Blavatsky had even mentioned this kind of thing in her writings. Therefore the teacher had to be prepared to speak in a way that would be right for such a changing world.

P. Krishna: Yes, they said this manifestation was going to give a new interpretation to religion for the age of reason and science…

Radhaji: He himself [Krishnamurti] has accepted that the door is open for every person to become free. He was not a freak. To be free inwardly is to open up the wellspring of wisdom, so I think in his case there was no barrier for this to happen. The outer mind being a pure mind with almost no trace of selfishness, which is what Mr. Leadbeater noticed when he first saw his aura, created no blockage and the inner wisdom just came up when the time was ripe…

Madame Blavatsky said that she was doing whatever work she did under the inspiration or at the bidding of certain Masters of the Wisdom, and one of the prominent theosophists of that time, Mr. A. P. Sinnett, who was the editor of the *Pioneer* in Allahabad, which was a very influential paper at that time, received a number of letters from his Masters and they themselves have said something about what the Masters are. One is that they are completely unselfish. The qualification for becoming a Master, in one of those letters it is said, is the daily conquest of the self. In other words, to give up completely the idea of a separate self. In another letter, they say only your evolving spirituality can bring you near to us…

P. Krishna: Krishnaji has also talked about "the other." Mr. Mahesh Saxena, who was at one time the secretary of the Indian foundation, told me that he went to Krishnaji in the 1980s, probably 1983 or '84, and asked him a straight question as to whether he denies the existence of the Masters and Krishnaji said, "No, sir, I have never denied the Masters, but some of the theosophists brought what was sublime to the ridiculous and I denied the ridiculous…

Radhaji: On one occasion when he was speaking about this, he said to me also that the mistake that the theosophists did was to make "the Masters" into something personal and concrete. They are not that… Even Madame Blavatsky said the Master is a state of consciousness, not primarily the body.

Padmanabhan Krishna, *A Jewel on a Silver Platter: Remembering Jiddu Krishnamurti.*
Interview with Radha Burnier, former President of the Theosophical Society *(Abridged)*

mystery. It cannot be explained by ordinary people who have not reached the level of enlightenment of those who have. So it is useless to discuss it because whether Krishnaji met the Masters, Krishnaji did not meet the Masters, or the Masters taught him or did not teach him, all this is within our imagination or thought realm. What they have done or experienced, we cannot question or perceive or even conceive of in our thought realm. So it is better to leave it. I think Krishnamurti, in his later years, did not indulge in discussing these things. He neither denied them nor accepted them. Many times he said not to talk about all these foolish things. These things are not foolish but if we discuss them, they become foolish because our thought realm cannot touch what they may mean.

Distortion, Converting the Unknown into the Known

M: *We talked earlier about conversion, how the mind converts the unknown into the known. No matter what we do, we're going to convert a mystery into what we already know, and in that process distort, corrupt, it and not realize we are doing this.*

S: Yes, for example, the fish and other creatures living in water have never experienced how to walk on the solid earth. They might discuss what the earth would be like and how to walk on it, and so on, but this is a wish, a dream, for them. They can never understand it directly. So, in regard to the Masters, we are like the fish. Whatever the Masters may be is a mystery and should remain a mystery. We can say in the beginning Krishnamurti needed to find images of the Masters and then at some point he didn't need the images so they no longer appeared. These are all interpretations. It may be correct. It may not be correct. We cannot make any conclusions.

Your reference to *going beyond* does not apply in this matter. If Krishnamurti saw images or forms of the Masters and then he saw them no more, we cannot conclude that he went beyond the Masters. *Going beyond* means that you drop the limitation. Ordinary individuals have no capacity to drop the limitation of thought. Wherever you go, wherever you think, you are thought; it may operate in a realm of memory or imagination, fantasy. Whatever realm it may be operating in, there are limitations, and thought cannot go beyond those limitations. When the limitations end, the limitations are gone. Then you do not have a boundary, a limit, and

What is sacred? Where does sacredness lie? In that tree, or in that peasant woman carrying that heavy load? You invest sacredness, don't you, in things you consider holy, worthwhile, meaningful? But what value has the image, carved by the hand or by the mind? That woman, that tree, that bird, the living things, seem to have but a passing importance for you. You divide life into that which is sacred and that which is not, that which is immoral and that which is moral. This division begets misery and violence. Either everything is sacred, or nothing is sacred. Either what you say, your words, your thoughts, your chants, are serious, or they are there to beguile the mind into some kind of enchantment, which becomes illusion, and therefore not serious at all. There is something sacred, but it is not in the word, not in the statue or in the image that thought has built.

There is nothing sacred about tradition, however ancient or modern. The brain carries the memory of yesterday, which is tradition, and is frightened to let go, because it cannot face something new. Tradition becomes our security, and when the mind is secure it is in decay. One must take the journey unburdened, sweetly, without any effort, never stopping at any shrine, at any monument, or for any hero, social or religious—alone with beauty and love.

J. Krishnamurti, *The Only Revolution*

that is *to go beyond*. Even the concept of *going beyond* is an extension of language. *Beyond* refers to a relative reality. *Going* beyond implies negation of the relative reality. After that, beyond or not beyond, the realm and reality created by language no longer applies.

Someone was talking to me, saying that God is One, and he explained this in many ways and with lots of arguments. I jokingly told him, "That means your God is limited." He was surprised. "How?" he asked. *One* can exist only in comparison to *two* or more. If there is no *two*, the concept of *one* cannot exist. This is the limitation of thought and language. So we just say, *going beyond*. The appropriate way to describe this is to clear all limitations. That is what is meant by *going beyond*.

Telepathy, Gestures, and Words

M: *Krishnamurti's teachings are expressed in language, words. We can measure the words. We cannot measure what the words are pointing to. What the content points to is a state of the mind or brain that is free of the content created by words. The teachings or the essence of what Krishnamurti was pointing to is not verbal or written content but rather a state. Is there something parallel to this in your tradition, where one forgets about the content, the words, and cultivates the state? We seem to get lost in content.*

S: I agree with you. There was a dialogue between the Hindu God Brahma and the Buddha. Buddha achieved enlightenment, *Bodhi-Gaya*, on the full moon day of the *Vesakh* month and he perceived the truth. He did away with all limitations and all constraints, and for seven weeks he did not speak. Then the Gods became restless. They said, "He has achieved the Buddha Nature and is not teaching. We must go and encourage him to teach." So Indra and Brahma came to Buddha and offered a golden *chakra* and a conch shell, saying, "Now you are enlightened, you must teach." Buddha said, "Yes, I saw the truth but what I have seen cannot be described in words, with language. If I use language, it may create misunderstanding or misconception so it is very difficult to teach. I prefer to remain silent." Brahma said, "No, no, no. I agree, the truth cannot be described in words. But there are ways. You can use metaphors. The metaphors do not contain that meaning, but they can point in the right direction."

Is thought love? Does thought cultivate love? It is not pleasure, it is not desire, it is not remembrance, although they have their places. Then what is love? Is love jealousy? Is love a sense of possession, my wife, my husband, my girl—possession? Has love within it fear? It is none of these things; entirely wipe them all away, end them, putting them all in their right place—then love is.

Through negation the positive is—through negation; that is, is pleasure love? You examine pleasure and see it is not that—though pleasure has its place it is not that—so you negate that. You see it is not remembrance, though remembrance is necessary; so put remembrance in its right place, therefore you have negated remembrance as not being love. You have negated desire, though desire has a certain place. Therefore through negation the positive is. But we, on the contrary, posit the positive and then get caught in the negative. One must begin with doubt—completely doubting—then you end up with certainty. But if you start with certainty, then you end up in uncertainty and chaos. So in negation the positive is born.

J. Krishnamurti, *The Wholeness of Life*. 4th Public Talk, Saanen, Switzerland, 17 July 1977

M: *Point.*

S: Point, yes. And the second way is negation. *This is not true. That is not true.* By negating all the things that are false, what is true becomes clear. And the third way is by making gestures; your calmness, your facial expression of contentment. These also point. A finger can point to the moon and words can also point. "You must teach," said Brahma. This dialogue reflects what you are describing, that we are lost in content and miss the point, which is a state. Words, metaphors, are powerful tools. Therefore they had to use words. Krishnamurti reminds us, over and over again, that the word is not the thing. We are habitually grasping after words, the content. What he is pointing to is a state, which is not communicable in words. All his words and gestures point to that state.

M: *You brought up gestures, calmness, being a form of communication.*

S: Yes.

M: *If the relationship is good, the attuned gesture is all that is needed to communicate the meaning of the state.*

S: Yes. That's right.

M: *There is also telepathy.*

S: Yes.

M: *Even more subtle.*

S: Right.

M: *With attunement, that would be enough.*

S: Yes.

M: *So we begin with telepathy, formless meaning.*

S: Today we have a good metaphor, the tuning to a radio broadcast. Unless you are tuned to that broadcast, that frequency, you cannot hear. When you tune to that frequency, then you can hear. So we have to develop our frequency to catch Krishnamurti's teachings.

M: *If we are very refined in our attunement, we would not need words.*

S: Exactly.

M: *We would not need a video or a book. We would be attuned and that is it.*

S: Right.

M: *The success of the transmission is not Krishnamurti's responsibility. The responsibility is ours, to be attuned.*

Thoughts pour from the mind like water in a waterfall and it seems as though a veritable flood of thoughts arise. The truth is that the mind has always been in this state but never before was one aware of it, since one had never turned one's gaze within before. Now that the mind is turned inward because of the practice of mindfulness and clear comprehension, these thoughts become known.

From ignorance of Dharma there comes into existence the following succession of events: a continuous stream of enemies in ever-increasing numbers, the rivalry from achieving selfish aims, the effort to defeat others in this struggle while one triumphs as the conqueror. Those who view the world in this way try to make their own nation powerful and for this they equip their forces with the most deadly weapons, and then, no longer able to arrive at a peaceful settlement of disputes, prepare for terrible wars. Because of these uncontrolled stains in the hearts of individuals, the strong currents of lust, hatred, delusion, anger, greed, conceit, cruelty and violence, and so on, begin to rush along with full force like the roaring of mighty rivers carrying all before them. The result of all this, for beings who have no refuge, is that they are compelled against their wishes to exist amidst these torrents of dukkha; while, if only men had an understanding of Dharma and were guided by it, then this tumult of various sufferings would cease.

His Holiness the Dalai Lama, *The Opening of the Wisdom-Eye*

Truth is not in some far distant place; it is in the looking at what is. To see oneself as one is—in that awareness into which choice does not enter—is the beginning and end of all search.

J. Krishnamurti, *The Only Revolution*

S: Yes.

M: *The less attuned we are, the less subtle or grosser the transmission must be. Telepathy is too refined, too subtle. Grosser still are gestures. And the dullest, least refined, most indirect transmission is in words, symbols, and metaphors. When you consider the subtlety of what is being pointed to, states of mind and being, words are the worst.*

S: Words can be interpreted in many ways.

M: *Attunement is not.*

S: No, attunement is the most direct.

M: *Are there teachers in your tradition who only teach using telepathy, or only teach using gestures? Or does everyone use words today?*

S: When they use words, it is because of the limitations of the listener, not the speaker. Buddha, from the achievement of Buddhahood until his death, did not speak a single word. In the Mahaparinirvana Sutra it is said that he was absolutely silent. Words are the tools or inferments of unenlightened people. Enlightened people do not need words. Apart from that, in Tibet many mature disciples and enlightened teachers teach and receive many things without physically meeting. They live hundreds of miles apart and still communicate.

M: *May we apply this to Krishnamurti, his teachings, his life?*

S: Yes.

M: *Upon this foundation, we have three different ways of meeting Krishnamurti.*

S: Yes.

M: *We can meet Krishnamurti via attunement, telepathy or gestures; his physical presence; or through words.*

S: By reading books.

Resonate Subtle Consciousness

M: *Yes. Now this is a big jump. Krishnamurti's life, his living presence in the world, can be understood as the radio broadcast you were talking about. His presence radiated, broadcast, something.*

S: Yes.

M: *He was broadcasting this something his entire life. Is it still broadcasting, now, twenty-five years after his death?*

One must be free, to be completely a light to oneself—you understand? A light to oneself. And this light cannot be given by another, nor can you light it at the candle of another. If you light it at the candle of another it is just a candle, it can be blown out. But whereas if we could find out what it means to be a light to oneself, then that very investigation of it is part of meditation.

We are so accustomed, and our conditioning is, to accept authority. The authority of the priest, the authority of a book, the authority of a guru, the authority of someone who says he knows, and so on. In all spiritual matters, if one may use that word "spiritual," in all those matters there must be and there should be no authority whatsoever, because otherwise you can't be free, you can't be free to investigate, to find out for yourself what meditation means.

One must be very careful if you really want to go into this question of meditation, to be completely, wholly, inwardly free from all authority, from all comparison. I don't know if you can do it. Including that of the speaker—especially that of the speaker, that is me, because if you follow what he says it is finished. Therefore one must be extremely aware of the importance of authority in one direction, that is the doctor, the scientist, the man who…and all the rest of it; and understand the total unimportance of authority inwardly. Whether it is the authority of another, which is fairly easy to throw off, or whether it is the authority of your own experience, knowledge, conclusion, which becomes your authority, which then becomes your prejudice. So one must be equally free from the authority of another and also one must be free from conclusions, which become one's own authority from one's own experience.

There is no one to guide you, no one to tell you that you are progressing, no one to tell you that or to encourage you. You have to stand completely alone in meditation. You understand what it means? And this light to yourself can only come when you understand, or investigate into yourself what you are. That is self-awareness, to know what you are—not according to psychologists, not according to some philosophers, not according to the speaker, but to know, to be aware of your own nature, of your own structure, of your own thinking, feeling, find out the whole structure of it. Therefore self-knowing becomes extraordinarily important.

So to understand oneself there must be observation, and that observation can only take place now. And the now is not the movement of the past which observes the now. You see the difference? I can observe the now from the past, from my past conclusions, prejudices, hopes, fears, and all the rest of it. Which is an observation from the past of the present, and I think I am observing the now. But the observation of the now can only take place when there is no observer, who is the past.

> J. Krishnamurti, *Truth and Actuality*. Saanen, Switzerland,
> 7th Public Talk, 25th July 1976 *(Abridged)*

S: Yes, yes, very much yes. Buddha said that Buddha never dies and Buddha's teachings never come to an end. There may be a time in the future when no one listens to Krishnamurti. As long as people listen to him, read his words, watch him, Krishnamurti is always broadcasting. And even if there is no one listening, his broadcast is there. Whoever is attuned will receive the broadcast. It will never end.

If You Understand Reality Completely, Everything Fits

M: *Let's revisit the purpose of tantric visualizations. There are meditations where the student would encounter fire but not be burned. They could stop their breathing and not die, mental practices that went beyond physics. Mark Lee's wife, Asha, observed Krishnamurti in his room in the Rishi Valley and he stood between seven and eight feet tall, radiant, benevolent. If our reality is that fire burns, it will burn. If our reality is that fire will not burn, it won't. So there is something about the mental state we call reality that is causal. I am curious about your understanding of this casual aspect of reality and, as we discussed, the fact that one can cultivate the ability to move or participate in multiple realities, which implies redefining the laws of physics.*

S: I personally do not consider that anything is beyond reality. There is reality. If you understand reality completely, everything fits. The understanding of so-called modern physics is very small, very limited. Scientists do not have a holistic view or understanding of reality. What is science? Scientists have their ordinary sensory perceptions and instruments, and what their eyes can perceive with the help of enlarged glasses, which they may improve and gradually discover more stars, more planets, more subtle things. But these are still limited to their ordinary eyes, nothing more than that. Only by developing the capacity to see beyond the ordinary will you perceive reality in its entirety.

M: *There is one reality.*

S: Right.

M: *It is much bigger than what we perceive and call ordinary.*

S: Yes.

M: *As we expand our capacity, the borders of what we experience as reality expand.*

S: That's right.

"Housekeeping in a dream." We tell ourselves we want to spend time on the important things of life, but there never is any time. Even simply to get up in the morning, there is so much to do; open the window, make the bed, take a shower, brush your teeth, feed the dog and cat, do last night's washing up, discover you are out of sugar or coffee, go to buy them, make breakfast—the list is endless. Then there are the clothes to sort out, choose, iron and fold again. And what about your hair, or your makeup? Helpless, we watch our days fill up with telephone calls and petty projects, with so many responsibilities—or shouldn't we call them "irresponsibilities"?

Our lives seem to live us, to possess their own bizarre momentum, to carry us away; in the end we feel we have no choice or control over them. Of course we feel bad about this sometimes, we have nightmares and wake up in a sweat, wondering: "What am I doing with my life?" But our fears only last until breakfast time; out comes the briefcase, and we go back to where we started.

Sogyal Rinpoche, *The Tibetan Book of Living and Dying*

M: *The first book I believe the Dalai Lama wrote for the West was called The Opening of the Wisdom-Eye.*

S: That's right.

M: *As we open our wisdom eye, the boundaries of reality expand.*

S: Yes.

M: *From this expanded view, what we call miracles are not miracles.*

S: No, they are not miracles.

M: *They are simply the way reality is from an expanded or subtler point of view.*

S: That's right.

M: *Miracles are normal if you know how to look.*

S: Exactly. In the ordinary physical eye, there is so much difference in capacity. My teacher's teacher, one generation ahead of me, was a scholar called Denma Tongpon Rinpoche. He could recognize individuals traveling from the Drepung monastery to the Ramagang village, which is about eight kilometers away, whereas others could only see small forms moving. He would say, "Tashi is moving there" or "Sonam is moving there." He could recognize them. Out of one seed of wheat, with the help of a needle, he carved six different animals without the aid of a magnifying glass. That seed is now in a Beijing museum under a magnifying glass, and the animals are very clear. He had a special capacity of seeing. This is reality. Some human beings develop many kinds of capacities that others do not have. Those who do not cannot see or perceive or experience what is normal and natural for those more developed. A two-year-old knows nothing of the experience of a teenager. It is the same with us and Krishnamurti or the Masters or any realized being.

Rituals, Krishnamurti, and the Theosophical Society

S: Now, coming to rituals or apparent rituals that were done by the Theosophical Society and perhaps even rituals Krishnamurti used to do throughout his life, this again we cannot understand in its totality. If you like, accept it. If you do not, just forget about it. But one thing, a common reality, is that we must be grateful to the Theosophical Society, Annie Besant, C. W. Leadbeater, and the others who recognized Krishnamurti and took care of him. Later he left the society and declared he was

> There have been so many saviors, masters, gurus, political leaders and philosophers, and not one of them has saved you from your own misery and conflict. Perhaps there may be quite another approach to all our problems.
>
> J. Krishnamurti, *The Only Revolution*

Nitya and J. Krishnamurti

not a teacher, and so on. We need not indulge in what happened, why it happened. What Krishnamurti taught throughout his life is all that matters to us. That is the naked reality. We can listen to his voice and watch his image on the videos, and some of us heard his physical voice and experienced his physical presence. No one can deny this, nor is any of this a ritual. This is most important. There is no disputing the authenticity of it. Krishnamurti lived. He traveled the world. There is no disputing this. Krishnamurti gave his teachings his entire life. It benefited humanity immensely and is still benefiting it. This is the reality and does not contradict the ordinary way of seeing we call science. All the other phenomena that does not fit our ordinary way of seeing does not matter. One day it may fit or not fit. Fitting what is non-ordinary into the ordinary has no importance in understanding the teachings he gave or in understanding one's self.

M: *We are back to the conversion process we discussed earlier, the mind taking something that is non-ordinary, unknown, and converting it into what is already known.*

S: Yes.

The Maitreya Prophesy, the Coming of the Future Buddha

M: *There was a prophesy, the Maitreya image, myth. The story is Tibetan.*

S: Yes.

M: *I looked up the* Maitreya *and it is defined as* the future Buddha.

S: Shakyamuni Buddha, whose teaching is still alive, was, according to Buddhist mythology, the 4th Buddha. And the Maitreya Buddha is the coming Buddha, the 5th, and at this moment the Maitreya resides in Tushita, a heavenly place, and he is the *bodhisattava*, just one lifetime away from achieving Buddhahood. This is the mythology. Again, we need not give any attention to this. There may be the Maitreya or there may not be. It doesn't matter. Mythology is mythology. It is written there. We can believe it or reject it. Even if we believe it, there is no harm.

M: *Krishnamurti was said to be the vehicle for the Maitreya in this life.*

S: Yes, that is right.

M: *In the mid-1920s, prior to dissolving the Order of the Star, after his experience under the pepper tree, Krishnamurti was asked, "Are you the World Teacher,*

ALWAYS AWAKENING

What is the need of a guru? Does he know more than you do? And what does he know? If he says that he knows, he really doesn't know, and, besides, the word is not the actual state. Can anyone teach you that extraordinary state of mind? They may be able to describe it to you, awaken your interest, your desire to possess it, experience it—but they cannot give it to you. You have to walk by yourself, you have to take the journey alone, and on that journey you have to be your own teacher and pupil.

J. Krishnamurti, *The Only Revolution*

J. Krishnamurti, Arya Vihara, Ojai

the Maitreya?" The modern westernized word for the Maitreya was the World Teacher. *And Krishnamurti said, "Yes, I am."*

S: He never denied it.

M: *No, he did not. But he did say that what we think, the image we have of the Maitreya or World Teacher, is incorrect. Our concept is not accurate. He also denied that he was taken over or possessed by some outside force, which being a vehicle implied. He said there was no longer any separation. Can you comment on this? How does this fit into your traditional Buddhist training?*

S: For Buddhists, there is no problem. We can very easily accept Krishnamurti as the manifestation of the Maitreya in a human body. There are so many different manifestations. The very high spiritual people, so-called Masters, can manifest themselves in hundreds of thousands of bodies at one time. And they can also manifest in other individuals or use another individual's consciousness as a vehicle. All of this is possible. For Buddhists to think of Krishnamurti as the real manifestation of the Maitreya does not cause us a problem. It doesn't contradict the Buddhist way.

M: *Is the Maitreya alive in all of us? Is our expression of the Maitreya a matter of attunement?*

S: Yes, exactly.

M: *Can we say that Krishnamurti, by wherever processes he went through, was attuning?*

S: Yes.

M: *In his mind or experience, in his realty, there was no division in consciousness.*

S: Right, exactly. His last words before he passed were that a timeless wisdom had been passing through his body and for the next few hundred years this may not happen again. He also said at that time, "I am the Teacher." We, from our Buddhist background, understand this to mean that he was the Maitreya.

ALWAYS AWAKENING

In Buddhism, we combine single-pointed meditation with the practice of analytic meditation, which is known as vipasyana, penetrative insight. In this practice we apply reasoning. By recognizing the strengths and weaknesses of different types of emotions and thoughts, together with their advantages and disadvantages, we are able to enhance our positive states of mind which contribute towards a sense of serenity, tranquility, and contentment, and to reduce those attitudes and emotions that lead to suffering and dissatisfaction. Reasoning thus plays a helpful part in this process.

His Holiness the Dalai Lama, *Transforming the Mind*

Left: With His Holiness the Dalai Lama during his visit to Sarnath, Varanasi, ca. 1981–82

Below: With His Holiness the Dalai Lama during his visit to the Central School for Tibetans, Dalhousie, ca. 1968–69

United Kingdom, 2012, Day Three

Magic and Black Magic

M: *The capacity to imagine coupled with our staggering capacity for symbolic and metaphoric language enables human beings to enter into and change our own development perhaps as no other known species. The vast majority habituate to the prevailing culture and become that norm. Some realize that we have inherent within a tremendous opportunity to go beyond, to transcend the limitations and constraints implicit in being normal. Some develop, therefore, inner qualities of perception and insight far beyond the easily conditioned norm. You described three different types of practices or meditations that have this intent. We mentioned telepathy, not being burned by fire. The word used to describe these capacities, by those who have not developed them, is* magic. *Magic in the service of the non-enlightened ego becomes black magic. All esoteric traditions warn against this. What does your training say about this misuse of these capacities?*

S: I think they are quite different things, magic and occult powers. Magic or black magic is simply creating illusions in the mind of the watcher or seer. In reality there's nothing there, but the watcher can see horses or elephants or whatever it may be. In the Tibetan language, we call it *migthrul*. That means creating an illusion in the eye or in the ear. We call this *magic*. Occult powers are completely different and cannot be achieved without some spiritual background. The person may not be enlightened but a certain amount of spiritual background is necessary to achieve occult powers; telepathy, clairvoyance (from the French *clair*, meaning *clear*, and *voyance*, meaning *vision*), healing, and many others. Once someone has developed a real occult power, they realize there is no way to use it selfishly or in a wrong way. If used inappropriately, that power will simply disappear. It cannot remain. Magic may be used in many different ways and can be used as black magic to do harm; it may even come in a violent way. But occult power, by its nature, has to be used appropriately, for positive things, for helping others. I don't think there's any possibility of misuse.

M: *I find the distinction between the two very interesting. You talked about tantra and visualization. That power, that skill, capacity, can be used in this magical way.*

What is called "Buddhism" in the English-speaking West is called "Buddhadharma" in the old Indian monastic universities. It is a complex of doctrines and practices which derive their authority indirectly from the experiences of the masters of Buddhist doctrine and practice, and directly from the experience and teaching of the Buddha himself. Indeed, his teaching itself derives from his experience, particularly the experience known as his "enlightenment."

This experience is described in rather flowery terms in the Buddhacarita, a text which postdates the Buddha by 500 years, but is based on traditional teachings about his life. According to this text, Shakyamuni, the Buddha to be, renounced the householder's life at age 29 and set out on a religious quest that was marked by ascetic practices and mental disciplines which are generally known to us under the rubric "yoga." The text tells us that he attained mastery of two kinds of yogic concentration exercise under two different masters. Under the first master he attained a state of "nothing at all." Under the second master he attained a state of "neither perception nor non-perception." These were later known as the seventh and eighth dhyana(s) (concentrations), respectively. The mastery of these forms of concentration did not, however, satisfy Shakyamuni's religious quest, a significant point, for here he breaks with the tradition prevalent at his time which taught that the mastery of subtle states of concentration would liberate one from the sorrows of the world.

Next, he set out on a long fast (as a form of purification), but gave that up as merely weakening the mind. Finally, seating himself under what later came to be called the "bodhi tree," he vowed not to move from that spot until he had attained his goal. Shortly thereafter, Mara, a god who is the personification of lust and death, attempted to budge Shakyamuni from his seat, but touching the ground with one hand, Shakyamuni remained immoveable. In an interpretive sense, we may say that the meaning of this tale of the attack of Mara is that having vowed not to move until he attained freedom, Shakyamuni was immediately beset with impulses deriving from his own instincts to live, which were threatened by his vow of immovability. In touching the earth, he calls to witness the previous compassionate actions performed in his lives on earth which provided the strength (i.e., his store of merit) to resist his own desire for life.

It may be said that the entire subsequent history of the Buddhadharma is simply a progressive explanation, systematization, and interpretation of this experience.

We may interpret this enlightenment experience as a progressive unfoldment of a single truth about existence, whose implications are amplified over the course of the night. When the whole of this truth and all of its implications are not just comprehended, but directly perceived, the goal of the religious quest has been obtained. What is this one truth? Most simply put, it is causality and all its implications, but certainly not causality as we understand it.

David Ross Komito, *Nagarjuna's "Seventy Stanzas": A Buddhist Psychology of Emptiness (Abridged)*

S: Right.

M: *Spiritual practice or spiritual development is required for the occult.*

S: Yes.

M: *In my view, the essence of so-called spiritual powers comes with the dissolving of the self.*

S: Exactly. Yes, of course.

M: *You say, "of course," but for the rest of the world this is not at all obvious. It is refreshing to spend this time with you, to experience your thoughtfulness, the care and attention you give to each question. It reminds me of David Bohm. You knew David?*

S: Yes.

If You Meet the Buddha on the Road, Kill Him

M: *There's a Zen saying, "If you meet the Buddha on the road, kill him." How do we reconcile this with the respect and veneration given to the Dalai Lama or even yourself?*

S: "If you meet the Buddha on the road, kill him" refers to the level of the ultimate truth. On that level, everything is empty. If you see something, it means you're not seeing emptiness. Whatever you saw would be an image or projection of the ego. Without negating the ego, you cannot take refuge in the Buddha. So in this context, if you see Buddha, it means you have an idea about Buddha. You are seeing Buddha through your egotistical eyes. You are projecting your ego as Buddha. This must be negated. In the sense of negation, the word *kill* Is used. The killing is interpreted in many ways. To kill means to misuse. I'm killing time. And to kill is the taking of a life, killing a man or an insect. Killing also means to negate its existence. So in this sense, if you see Buddha, you are not meditating properly. If you see Buddha, you are just seeing through your ego and this must be negated. It must be killed. This is the Zen interpretation.

M: *I refer to His Holiness. Many people would say he's a holy person. He's like the Buddha. Should I not see him that way? How do I balance what we just talked about, and wanting to respect or honor the work he's done, who he is, his compassion, and so on?*

You can't be vulnerable without innocency, and though you have a thousand experiences, a thousand smiles and tears, if you don't die to them, how can the mind be innocent? It is only the innocent mind—in spite of its thousand experiences—that can see what truth is. And it is only truth that makes the mind vulnerable—that is, free.

You are quite young. Don't ever lose your innocency and the vulnerability that it brings. That is the only treasure that man can have, and must have.

J. Krishnamurti, *The Only Revolution*

With students from the Petoen School, Dharamsala, 2009

S: Yes. In the context of the Zen saying, "If you meet the Buddha on the road, kill him," what you are seeing is not the real Buddha. You are not able to see the selflessness or the nature of *shunyata*, the Buddha Nature. A Buddha is the embodiment of the reality or the embodiment of *Dharma* that is called *Dharmakaya*. If you are not seeing the *Dharmakaya* then you are seeing Buddha as a reflection or a projection of your own ego, and the respect you may feel is for something false. You are not seeing the Buddha Nature. You are in an illusion, seeing yourself in the form of Buddha. In that case, there's no respect. To see Buddha, you have to see the Buddha Nature. Buddha has said, not in the Zen philosophy, but with his own words, "Those who have seen the nature of interdependent-origination, they have seen me, and those who have not seen the nature of interdependent-origination, they have not seen me. They might have seen my gross form that we call Narupakia, but it does not mean they're seeing the Buddha." Without seeing *shunyata*, without seeing the interdependent-origination, without seeing the real nature of *Dharma*, you cannot see the Buddha. Seeing the Buddha depends on seeing the *Dharma*, seeing reality, the truth. In this way, seeing Buddha in reality means the negation of your own imagery, your ego picture in the form of Buddha. Only then can you see the Buddha Nature.

M: *You say the Buddha Nature.*

S: Yes.

M: *You are speaking of something other than the mental image, the form or personality.*

S: Yes, the nature.

M: *Krishnamurti referred to himself as* the speaker *to help draw attention to our strong tendency to falsely respect the image instead of, as you say, the nature. We can apply this same principle to what is called* the teachings. *The teachings are the nature, the state of perception being pointed to and lived, not what we think of as the teachings—the words, the books and videos.*

S: Right.

M: *Did you discuss with Krishnamurti what has been called* the process? *Krishnamurti did not seem to believe it was the* kundalini. *Are there parallel experiences in your tradition similar to the non-ordinary states that have been called* the process?

There is the silence between two noises, the silence between two notes and the widening silence in the interval between two thoughts. There is that peculiar, quiet, pervading silence that comes of an evening in the country; there is the silence through which you hear the bark of a dog in the distance or the whistle of a train as it comes up a steep grade; the silence in a house when everybody has gone to sleep, and its peculiar emphasis when you wake up in the middle of the night and listen to an owl hooting in the valley; and there is that silence before the owl's mate answers. There is the silence of an old deserted house, and the silence of a mountain; the silence between two human beings when they have seen the same thing, felt the same thing, and acted.

That night, particularly in that distant valley with the most ancient hills with their peculiar shaped boulders, the silence was as real as the wall you touched. And you looked out of the window at the brilliant stars. It was not a self-generated silence; it was not that the earth was quiet and the villagers were asleep, but it came from everywhere—from the distant stars, from those dark hills and from your own mind and heart. This silence seemed to cover everything from the tiniest grain of sand in the river-bed—which only knew running water when it rained—to the tall, spreading banyan tree and a slight breeze that was now beginning. There is the silence of the mind which is never touched by any noise, by any thought or by the passing wind of experience. It is this silence that is innocent, and so endless. When there is this silence of the mind, action springs from it, and this action does not cause confusion or misery.

The meditation of a mind that is utterly silent is the benediction that man is ever seeking. In this silence every quality of silence is. There is that strange silence that exists in a temple or in an empty church deep in the country, without the noise of tourists and worshippers; and the heavy silence that lies on water is part of that which is outside the silence of the mind.

The meditative mind contains all these varieties, changes and movements of silence. This silence of the mind is the true religious mind, and the silence of the gods is the silence of the earth. The meditative mind flows in this silence, and love is the way of this mind. In this silence there is bliss and laughter.

J. Krishnamurti, *The Only Revolution*

S: I never discussed with Krishnamurti anything about his own process or what is called *the process* in general, even if he mentioned kundalini, which is a typical way of practicing tantra. In Buddhism it is quite different. In the Hindu tradition, there are many ways of talking about kundalini but I never heard of or discussed kundalini with Krishnamurti.

Transformation That Is Not Dependent on Knowledge or Time

M: *Krishnamurti said it was the responsibility of each human being to bring about their own transformation, which is not dependent on knowledge or time. Are there any parallel instructions or practices in your tradition, what might be referred to as* the direct path, *and how is it possible to convey this from a teacher to a student?*

S: When Krishnamurti says you are responsible for your own transformation, that nobody can give you transformation, a Buddhist hearing this will remember that the Buddha also said that Buddha cannot give you transformation. Buddha cannot transfer his realization. Buddha cannot wash away an individual's demerits. Buddha can only give the direction towards achieving transformation. Transformation can only be achieved by one's self. Buddha can only talk about transformation knowing that talking about it is not the way to achieve it. After listening to Buddha, the seeker or listener may have the intention to search for the truth and discover transformation, but the effort would have to be made by one's self. The truth has to be discovered by each individual, whoever it may be. No one can search for the truth on behalf of someone else. This statement is similar to those made by Buddha and Krishnamurti. Regarding knowledge and time: the English word *knowledge* is used in many different ways, in different contexts, but Krishnamurti uses *knowledge* most often when he is referring to knowledge in the realm of thought, not in the realm of perception. Perception may be a form of knowledge, but perception in most cases is not what Krishnamurti is referring to as knowledge.

M: *We are distinguishing between knowledge as perception and knowledge in the form of thought or memory.*

S: Yes. In many other contexts, perception is referred to as knowledge; perception sees, knows, reality. Here it is important to understand that

The Tibetan Masters who pass on the traditional oral teachings repeat insistently the fact that these teachings are for the use of individuals in the rab category, that is to say endowed with superior and excellent intelligence, the "lotus whose flowers grow above the level of the water," according to the picturesque comparison quoted above.

The object of these teachings is not to amuse the simple-minded, those charitably called in the Tibetan Scriptures the "children"; it is meant for the strong to make them stronger, for the intelligent to make them more intelligent, for the shrewd to develop their shrewdness and to lead them to the possession of transcendent insight (lhag thong) which constitutes the real enlightenment.

The attainment of transcendent insight is the real object of the training advocated in the traditional Oral Teachings, which do not consist as so many imagine, in teaching certain things to the pupil, in revealing to him certain secrets, but rather in showing him the means to learn them and discover them for himself.

It is not enough to see with eyes which, according to the words used in Buddhist Texts, "are only covered with a thin film of dust," however thin this film may be; it is a question of removing the last trace of dust which interferes with sight.

Transcendent insight (lhag thong) literally means to see "more," to see "beyond," to see "extremely," "supremely." Thus, not only to see more than that which is seen by the mass of mankind who are crassly ignorant, but to see beyond the bounds limiting the vision of cultivated minds…

Alexandra David-Néel and Lama Yongden,
The Secret Oral Teachings in Tibetan Buddhist Sects (Abridged)

There is nothing permanent either on earth or in ourselves. Thought can give continuity to something it thinks about; it can give permanency to a word, to an idea, to a tradition. Thought thinks itself permanent, but is it permanent? Thought is the response of memory, and is that memory permanent? It can build an image and give to that image a continuity, a permanency, calling it Atman or whatever you like; it can remember the face of the husband or the wife and hold on to it. All this is the activity of thought which creates fear, and out of this fear there is the drive for permanency— the fear of not having a meal tomorrow, or shelter—the fear of death. This fear is the result of thought, and Brahman is the product of thought too.

J. Krishnamurti, *The Only Revolution*

Krishnamurti is referring to knowledge in the form or realm of thought. And similarly, Buddha says knowledge in the realm of thought cannot give you insight or bring transformation. In the Buddhist way, knowledge in the realm of thought, which is moving in the direction of truth, transforms into the nature of perception and this is transformation. That happens in time, but time has no control or influence in transformation, which is spontaneous. It is not gradual or partial. There are only two states: the awakened state and the unawakened state. There is no half-awakened or partially awakened state. Time has no role in the transmutation of an individual's mind. Time has nothing to do with it. Also, knowledge in the form of thought alone has nothing to do with it. The Buddhist teacher often uses the metaphor of darkness and light. The moment light appears is the same moment darkness disappears. No time is required. It is spontaneous. You cannot ask or question, where has the darkness gone? It simply does not exist where light is. Only the light exists. Awakening and transformation are quite similar.

Transcendent Insight

M: *The room is dark. That's one state. And you turn on the lights. That's another state. It's just like that. The lights can also go out again just as quickly. You can be enlightened or you can be en-darkened moment by moment. It happens all the time. There is another metaphor: a drop of water contains the same wetness as the whole ocean. Who cares if the wetness is in the ocean or in a glass of water? In terms of its nature, it is all the same wetness. In* The Secret Oral Teachings *by Alexandra David-Néel, she describes* transcendent insight; *in Tibetan,* lhagthong.

S: Yes, transcendent insight. We call it *Sherab kyi pharol tu chyinpa*.

M: *What is this transcendent insight and how is it expressed?*

S: We talked about going beyond or to transcend; these are the same thing. She refers to insight that does not have limitations and constraints, insight that becomes inseparable from truth. The seer, the seeing, what is to be seen, these three become three portions dissolved and emerge into the vastness, not divided, inseparable; that is called *pharol tu chyinpa*. The Sanskrit word is *paramita*. *Para* means *the end* or *the limit*. *Mita* means *beyond*, to go beyond that, beyond the limitation or beyond the boundary, beyond the measurement. It cannot be kept within limitations.

Then there is the very nature of mind, its innermost essence, which is absolutely and always untouched by change or death. At present it is hidden within our own mind, our sem [our ordinary mind], enveloped and obscured by the mental scurry of our thoughts and emotions. Just as clouds can be shifted by a strong gust of wind to reveal the shining sun and wide-open sky, so, under certain special circumstances, some inspiration may uncover for us glimpses of this nature of mind. These glimpses have many depths and degrees, but each of them will bring some light of understanding, meaning, and freedom. This is because the nature of mind is the very root itself of understanding. In Tibetan we call it Rigpa, a primordial, pure, pristine awareness that is at once intelligent, cognizant, radiant, and always awake.

Sogyal Rinpoche, *The Tibetan Book of Living and Dying*

At the Central School for Tibetans, Shimla, 1963

There's no boundary. There is no measurement, no limits. These are all gone. Then the insight becomes the immeasurable. Everyone, everything, is transcendent. *Transcendent insight* is a reference to the state of mind that is the real transformed mind. Or in other words, we can say we do away with all conditioning at the root, and then there is transcendence insight.

M: *I'm trying to embody what you are describing as an experience, something more direct than a concept. Normally when we look, perception seems to be focused, it has a direction. But perception without boundaries would not be focused; it would go in all directions. This is a very different state of mind.*

S: All directions, of course.

M: *Right now, because perception is focused, it seems to fan out in front of me or wherever my attention directs it. When I am focused in front, what is behind is more or less empty. If perception is not directed by attention, it would be quite different. Perception, mind, would go everywhere, in all directions. Can you describe this unlimited perception in your terms?*

S: Whenever your realization or your wisdom goes beyond limits and constraints, becomes transcendent, that means all your questions about direction, focusing, not focusing, attention, inattention, these distinctions do not exist in that realm. Those questions do not exist; they are always within the boundaries of thought. Thought knows only alternatives, either this or that, one or two, similar or dissimilar, good or bad. So these are always within the possibilities of choice. Choice means fragmentation, part and partial and many, and when you transcend them, all these questions are not there. So you can't even say it is *one* or it is *a part*. These divisions are no longer there. You have to transcend these limitations and then these questions have no relevance.

M: *Even oneness disappears.*

S: Yes, oneness disappears.

M: *We think* transcendence *means oneness. Even that disappears.*

S: That disappears. *One* is a comparison to *many*, so *oneness* is still partial.

M: *You brought up several words that are reminiscent of things that Krishnamurti spoke about often,* choice *and* choiceless awareness.

S: Yes.

If you are aware, aware, not say, "Well I am aware but I don't like that shirt, it is too blue," (Laughter) so I was told this morning! (Laughter) So are we aware in that sense, without choosing, a choiceless awareness? Then if you are so choicelessly aware, then you are attentive—you understand? Choiceless awareness means attention, not cultivated, saying, "I must attend." But becoming aware of the trees, the birds, the balloons going up the mountains, the light on the clouds, the evening, the moonlight and so on, watching, watching. Aware of all this and your reaction to all this, and by not responding, not choosing, I like this, I don't like that, it is mine, it is yours—you follow? Just to be aware. From this choiceless awareness there is attention, attending with your eyes, with your ears, with your nerves, with all your being.

Because I am attentive, there is no reaction. You understand? It is only when there is inattention, there is reaction.

So the quality of attention, and the quality of inattention, not attending, are two different things. Where there is inattention, there is choice, unawareness, lack of attention, then the recording process goes on, the old habit is established. But when there is attention, the old habit is broken.

J. Krishnamurti, Saanen, Switzerland, 22 July 1984, 1st Question & Answer

If the religious mind is to flower in anyone, then it can happen where the ground is carefully prepared and opportunities are provided without any expectations. He said that studying the Teachings would not provide it; that listening to him speak over and over and reading his books would not provide it; and that wanting and wishing for it would not work. The only way to realize that other state of mind, that other way of living, was through the hard work of attention and awareness constantly cleansing the mind. In this the ego and the self are seen for what they really are, constructs of thinking, with no intrinsic reality. Hence, to Narayan and the school heads present, he emphasized the importance of developing the senses of children. He said: 'Most of the mysteries of life, and opinions, beliefs, and ideas come from thought. The mind holds onto those because it creates them. But when the senses operate, particularly looking and listening, the mind has less to hold on to. Perception is clear and without something that memory can accumulate.

R. E. Mark Lee, *Knocking at the Open Door: My Years with J. Krishnamurti*

M: *Choiceless awareness is exactly what you described as transcendent insight.*
S: Yes.

M: *Mind without measure. Not measurable.*

S: This is a good expression, *mind without measure.* The insight that, when one transcends, there's no measure.

M: *When you take the concepts that Krishnamurti gave verbally, choiceless awareness, for example, and you get rid of the thought and experience, the concept as a state-of-being, everything changes.*
S: Yes.

M: *So often one does not get to the experience part. We remain in the thought realm, failing to go beyond thought and the body to experience what the concept points to.*
S: Yes, we remain in the thought.

Changing World, Changing Traditions

M: *Let's change directions. The world has changed. If you had a child, would you place him in a monastery as happened to you as a child? How would you awaken in your child the direct experience that we've been talking about?*

S: I do not know what kind of child I would have. I would look after the child until he or she could talk and think a little bit and do something for himself or herself. We would have to do everything in accordance with the free choice of the child. I would not insist that he or she become a monk or enter a monastery without the willingness of the child. Buddha put a limitation on taking small children into a monastery to become a novice. He said the person must be seven years of age, which is considered the age when a person can look after himself or herself and do things independently. Then the Buddha said, in addition to reaching seven years of age the child should be able to do something. For example, in the monastery when greens are separated to dry and crows come to eat them, the children should be able to drive away the crows. This example shows that there must be the capacity to do things, to act. I would act in accordance with this rule. Of course, we have to give an education and whatever else is required to develop the child into maturity, to cultivate the child's intelligence and power of discrimination. That much you must do. The rest the child must decide.

We know what we mean by tradition: custom, habit, has shaped the mind—that is a fact. And that tradition has established certain methods, certain specialized processes; it says you must meditate in this way. And organized thought, a method, has been established or is being established by people who think they know how to meditate and want to teach others. It is based on a tradition, or on their own experience; or they have borrowed it from others and put it together, and they want you to practice it in order to arrive at something which they call "peace," "God," "truth," "bliss," and all the rest of it.

Also, in a method, in a system, there is implied authority: "You know, I don't know. You have realized the self, whatever that may mean; and you are going to tell me what to do. I will get it." So there is established this thing called the guru: the authority, the enlightened, the self-realized, the man who knows, and you who do not know; and you want that, whatever that may mean. The guru looks fairly happy, fairly quiet, secluded, and he talks a great deal about self-realization and all that stuff. And you say, "How good it will be to have it!" You want it; you begin to practice, and he becomes your authority. So the method, the practice implies authority.

Now, what happens in an authority? You have not understood yourself, your life, your behavior; whether you have affection, love, sympathy, does not matter; you have not explored your extraordinary being yourself; you deny all that, and you follow somebody else. And by following somebody else, you have added an extraordinary layer of fear, because you might not follow according to the sanction of those people, and so on.

So practicing a method implies authority. Practicing a method implies a mechanical procedure; it becomes mechanical. It is not a living thing which you are examining, watching, exploring. You are merely practicing like a machine—you go to the office, there you do something; you get into a habit, and that habit carries on.

See the fact of it. When you see the fact of it, the impact of it, then your mind is no longer concerned with practice, no longer concerned with habit, no longer concerned with authority—spiritual authority—at all. Then you are concerned with exploration, investigation, understanding.

If you listen to this fact, then you will never go back to that. Then you become completely responsible for yourself. Therefore, you have no guru; you do not rely on anybody, including the speaker. You are then responsible for everything that you do.

The Collected Works of J. Krishnamurti. Bombay, India,
6th Public Talk, 28 February 1965 *(Abridged)*

M: *There are outward cultural symbols that represent the inward development of awareness and direct perception that we generally call spiritual. The uniform and robes of a monk are good examples. The outward symbols are fairly easy to recognize but the inner work, the care, discipline, and attention that the robes point to are not easily seen, certainly not by a seven-year-old. How do we expect people, especially at a young age, seven or ten or even twenty, to understand what it means inside rather than just adopt the outward appearances, conforming to cultural expectations?*

S: It is assumed that people willing to enter a monastery at a very young age have an intrinsic will in the mind to do so. But Buddha had to put a limitation. Unless and until you attain the age of twenty, you cannot be fully ordained. You can enter the monastery as a novice as early as age seven. After spending thirteen years in the monastery to get an education, to know the discipline and practice of Dharma, at the age of twenty you have a choice: to go back to the household or remain in the monastery. Remaining in the monastery means being a full-time seeker of the truth without the involvement of any social responsibility, depending on alms and thrown-away clothes to live a very simple, voluntary poor life so that you can use your entire time for seeking enlightenment, the truth. At the age of twenty, the education as a novice is sufficient to make a decision for one's self. That decision might be changed later on, but at twenty years of age, the decision cannot be considered immature. That is a good way to decide one's life.

The Monastic Experience

M: *Does it mean that you go to classes, read books, or that you serve an apprenticeship with a more experienced, wise person? Is it the classroom or a mentor that determines your path?*

S: Monastic rules dictate that two people are necessary when entering the monastery as a novice. The first we call *Upadhyaya*, which means "one who inducts you into monastic life." After asking many questions, he attends the monk congregation and says, "A person named so-and-so is willing to become a novice. I have questioned and found that he or she is qualified to enter the monastery." Based on the recommendation of the *Upadhyaya*, the congregation allows that person to become a novice.

Although humans can manage without religion, they cannot manage without inner values. So my argument for the independence of ethics from religion is quite simple. As I see it, spirituality has two dimensions. The first dimension, that of basic spiritual well-being—by which I mean inner mental and emotional strength and balance—does not depend on religion but comes from our innate human nature as beings with a natural disposition toward compassion, kindness, and caring for others. The second dimension is what may be considered religion-based spirituality, which is acquired from our upbringing and culture and is tied to particular beliefs and practices. The difference between the two is something like the difference between water and tea. Ethics and inner values without religious content are like water, something we need every day for health and survival. Ethics and inner values based in a religious context are more like tea. The tea we drink is mostly composed of water, but it also contains some other ingredients—tea leaves, spices, perhaps some sugar or, at least in Tibet, salt—and this makes it more nutritious and sustaining and something we want every day. But however the tea is prepared, the primary ingredient is always water. While we can live without tea, we can't live without water. Likewise we are born free of religion, but we are not born free of the need for compassion.

His Holiness the Dalai Lama, *Beyond Religion: Ethics for a Whole World*

With His Holiness the Dalai Lama at his residence, 2012

Another is called the *Acharya*, who is the constant teacher from the beginning. This teacher or mentor must give his guidance and permission for everything until the individual becomes a fully ordained monk. Even after twenty years of age and when the person is fully ordained, he is assigned to a particular teacher for another ten years. Only then is he is considered a permanent monk.

The Eight-Fold Path and Krishnamurti

M: *What's the main difference between the* eight-fold path, *the Buddhist's approach to teaching, and Krishnamurti's approach?*

S: As we discussed, Krishnamurti is not interested in any particular path or method. The *eight-fold path* is a careful composition of teachings, including order, conduct, discipline, and methods or practices for concentrating the mind. And part of the Buddhist teachings refers to realization, enlightenment itself. Krishnamurti talks about order, attention, right action, authority, conflict, and many other similar themes. If someone were to research Krishnamurti's talks, they might find references to all the elements and themes in the eight-fold path. I have not done this research, so therefore I cannot say.

And apart from that, remember, we cannot and should not make comparisons between the Buddhist teachings and Krishnamurti's teachings. Each is unique and complete, and at the same time, incomparable. Each was expressed to different listeners and the tapestry of listeners cannot be compared. Buddha appeared 2,500 years ago and Krishnamurti appeared in the twentieth century. There are 2,500 years of differences in attitudes, language, culture, and way of life. In this context, everything is radically different. So comparing will not lead to greater understanding. As we said, understanding Buddha's teachings will help in understanding Krishnamurti's teachings, and understanding Krishnamurti's teachings will help in understanding the Buddhist teachings.

What we are going to do this morning is to find out for ourselves…what happens to the mind when there is this extraordinary attention, when there is no center as the observer or as the censor.

We must begin with seeing "what is"… The "what is" is the past, is the present, and is the future. Do see that thing. So the "what is" is not static, it's a movement. And to keep with that movement, with the movement of "what is," you need to have a very clear mind, you need to have an unprejudiced, not a distorted mind.

To understand "what is" you need energy. Now, these fragmentations of which we are, are the division of these energies. I and the not I, anger and the not anger, violence and the not violence, they are all fragmentations of energy. And when one fragment assumes the authority over the other fragments, it is an energy that functions in fragments. Are we meeting each other—are we communicating? That means, communication means, learning together, working together, creating together, seeing together, understanding together, not just I speak and you listen, and say, well, intellectually I grasp it; that is not understanding. The whole thing is a movement in learning, and therefore in action.

So the mind sees that all fragmentations, as nation, not nation, my god, your god, my belief and your belief, is a fragmentation of energy—there is only energy and fragmentation. This energy is fragmented by thought. And thought is the way of conditioning.

So consciousness is the totality of these fragmentations of energy. And we said, this fragmentation of energy, one of those fragmentations is the observer, is the "me," is the monkey, that is incessantly active.

Bearing in mind, the description is not the described, that you are watching yourself, watching yourself through the words of the speaker. But the words are not the thing. Therefore, the speaker becomes of very little importance. What becomes important is your observation of yourself, how this energy has been fragmented—jealousy, non-jealousy, hate—you know.

Now to see that, which is "what is," can you see without the fragment, as the observer? Can the mind see these many fragmentations which make up the whole of consciousness, and these fragmentations are the fragmentations of energy—energy—can the mind see this without an observer who is part of the many fragments?

If the mind cannot see the many fragments without or through the eyes of another fragment, then you will never understand what is attention. Are we meeting each other?

We are asking, what is the quality of the mind that is highly attentive, in which there is no fragmentation… What is the quality of the mind?

J. Krishnamurti, *The Impossible Question*. Saanen, Switzerland, 8th Public Dialogue, 9 August 1970 *(Abridged)*

Are the Masters Relevant?

M: *Referring to the Masters, Krishnamurti was often asked the question, "Is it relevant?" He answered, no. What is relevant is understanding directly, as a living experience, what he was pointing to. I think this is what you're talking about.*

S: Yes.

M: *In terms of the purpose of both sets of teachings, comparisons are simply not appropriate.*

S: Drawing parallel lines or comparisons will not help anyone.

M: *Pretty clear!*

S: On the contrary, it might be confusing.

Why Do You Remain a Buddhist?

M: *Having met Krishnamurti and explored his insight, why do you remain a Buddhist, or has your contact with Krishnamurti altered what it means to be a Buddhist?*

S: This is a big question and also an important question. The few Buddhists who spent time with Krishnamurti understood what he said in the context of Buddhist philosophy. Whatever he said was digested by Buddhist conditioning, the Buddhist way of understanding. After listening to Krishnamurti for a number of years, my own understanding of Buddha and Nagarjuna has become much clearer, much more in depth. In terms of my spiritual journey, I did not come into contact with Krishnamurti hoping to find something different, a way other than Buddhism or to become a Krishnamurti follower and give up my Buddhist way of life. This was not my intention. Nor was it an objective of Krishnamurti's. He never asked anyone to be his follower. Of course, he categorically denied all so-called religions, Masters, gurus, all spiritual authorities. But he never asked anyone to give up his or her faith and convert to something else.

M: *Trading one belief for another is not transformation or realization. A deeper experience is having an insight into the true nature of our identity and into the nature of our beliefs.*

S: Yes, I understand. If by hearing Krishnamurti's teachings, we find the Buddha's teachings are not rational, not correct, not leading to truth—

As Einstein was to Newton, so Krishnaji was to us. He broke fresh ground. He saw that our behavior was childish; that we were destroying ourselves because we weren't able to see what we actually are, we weren't in control of our emotions; we were children with terrific facilities to destroy and hurt and damage, and he came along and he said, find out. "I will give you the tools to help you grow up to be responsible for your actions and your way of living," and that is exactly what he did. He said, "Your greed, your fears, your selfishness, your anger and aggression, all of these are stopping you from receiving this incredible world. So take a journey inside and find out about yourself and grow up. Stop being juvenile," which is really what we are.

He was the teachings, although I hesitate to use the word "teachings." It makes it finite and I think it was an on-going quest, adventure, and he personified this. He was the teachings if you must use that word. He lived it by the care and attention that he gave to everything and the depth of his passion and his affection and love for mankind. Yes, I think it did have an impact. You felt leavened by his presence. Everybody noticed him the moment he came in a room; you couldn't help it. He carried a quality with him that was rare and strong. People drew themselves together and tried to receive this seriousness and passion that he brought to life and that gave to life.

Dorothy Simmons, Former Head of School, Brockwood Park, UK

if this kind of realization comes to us — then I would not have any hesitation in giving up or reforming Buddhism. All Buddhists who are learning logic and philosophy would not hesitate to give it up if they really find something in those teachings that are false or untrue. But listening to Krishnaji has strengthened our understanding of Buddha and also clarified what one understands of Buddha and religion. This is what has taken place.

M: *Please forgive the personal questions but they're just for fun anyway. We discussed transcendent insight, which goes beyond intellectual understanding, goes beyond understanding being an idea or a concept. Transcendent insight implies a direct perception not bound or contained by the realm of words. Did meeting Krishnamurti, spending time with him, experiencing, as we said before, the telepathic nature of his presence, did that help you flip the switch?*

S: This is a very personal question and it is also implies the realm of spiritual realization, so I have to say very clearly and unambiguously that I am not a realized person. I have not achieved transcendent insight or choiceless awareness, however we might describe it. But we have moments of insight and also sudden direct understanding or knowledge of what insight is and how it is achieved. We get this from both Buddhist teachings and Krishnamurti's teachings. In his presence, taking part in dialogues, you experience certain qualities of mind, particularly the focus on the questions that he is exploring passionately. That kind of feeling, that kind of communication, this I cannot deny. I think that experience is common with people who had that communication with Krishnamurti. This experience is like a seed that has been sown in your own mind; when it ripens, you will get the insight. This is how the personal journey unfolds.

M: *Indeed. As we know, one doesn't flip the switch anyway.*

S: No. We just have a rough knowledge of where to look.

M: *Krishnamurti insisted that we be a light unto ourselves. Having spent most of your life gathering energy and attention, and dissolving, going beyond, the false identities we imagine about ourselves and others, that light is bright. For the majority of people hearing these words, with minds scattered and conditioned, be a light unto yourself is like handing them a tiny flashlight in a giant cave. How practical is being a light unto yourself, when that light is so scattered and dim? Is it serving or might it be equally confusing and harmful?*

The immeasurable cannot be sought by thought, for thought has always a measure.

Meditation is the total inaction which comes out of a mind that sees what is, without the entanglement of the past. This action is not a response to any challenge but is the action of the challenge itself, in which there is no duality. Meditation is the emptying of experience and is going on all the time, consciously or unconsciously, so it is not an action limited to a certain period during the day. It is a continuous action from morning till night—the watching without the watcher. Therefore there is no division between the daily life and meditation, the religious life and the secular life. The division comes only when the watcher is tied to time. In this division there is disarray, misery and confusion, which is the state of society.

So meditation is not individualistic, nor is it social; it transcends both and so includes both. This is love; the flowering of love is meditation.

J. Krishnamurti, *The Only Revolution*

Krishnamurti's Mission Is to Challenge

S: One can say that Krishnamurti's mission is to challenge us, to break up the conditioning we accept as normal and natural. This challenge may be confusing. It may not serve people immediately but it does not harm them. Listening to Krishnamurti may lead to doubts, to confusion and more doubts in their mind, but does it matter? Krishnamurti's seeds have been sown. This seed that challenges, that breaks up conditioning, is not harmful to anyone. The seed will at some time sprout as doubt, questioning, like a tiny blade of grass pushing through concrete. You benefit from it. This is another way of looking at it. If you ask many people they will clearly admit that they have not benefited from Krishnamurti's teachings. They say, "I could not understand him. He gave me nothing to do or not do." I overheard this from people but it doesn't mean it had a negative effect or harmed them. The seed is there.

M: *I experienced that for years. I understood intellectually certain phrases or paragraphs. But I was left confused. I did not understand the totality. This gave me a headache. You are saying that this confusion is actually the medicine at work. Let's open that up.*

Confusion Leads to Inquiry

S: Yes. Confusion leads to inquiry, makes it hard to find out. Confusion is the beginning of inquiry. Without confusion, doubt, you will believe that you have answers to every question, and your inquiry will be very superficial. It does not progress.

M: *Much of what we call* thinking *and* thought *implies having an answer. Often what we think is inquiry is not.*

S: Yes, it is not inquiry.

M: *I had open access to Krishnamurti for years. Questions would arise but I realized he had been answering the same superficial questions from the same audience for fifty or sixty years. Out of care and respect, I tried for years to come up with a question that was worthy of his time and failed. None were good enough. Real inquiry is a quality of mind, a state, not an intellectual chess move.*

S: Inquiry means two things. First, a realization of not seeing something. If you believe you have seen everything, then inquiry does not begin.

At the Mahabodhi Temple, Bodh Gaya, Bihar, 2006

All the canonical Sutras and Tantras which form the basis of Buddha-dharma in Tibet were taught by Lord Buddha in person. Tibetan scholars suffering many and various hardships on the way to Nepal and India, traveled there many times to get the correct manuscripts and traditions, and their comings and goings could be compared to a river always flowing between two countries. They studied and practiced Dharma under the guidance of the great and learned teachers whose scholarship was beyond question. They satisfied these teachers and the accomplished ones by serving them in every way, listened to their Dharma-teaching and translated this into the Tibetan language. On the basis of those teachings, Tibetan Buddhists listen to Dharma, think upon it and practice it. Apart from this authentic Dharma, there is no arbitrary teaching begun by lamas in Tibet.

His Holiness the Dalai Lama,
The Opening of the Wisdom-Eye (Abridged)

You must have a realization that I don't know. This creates a crack in the conditioning. Second, this realization brings a certain degree of energy. I might discover what is not seen and see it. If these two qualities are there, then inquiry begins. Not a hurriedness to find a conclusion, an answer, or disappointment in not finding an answer. With a relaxed and open attitude, the mind opens to new perceptions. If these two qualities are there, your inquiry begins.

M: *Doubt and inquiry are two sides of the same coin. I recall Buddha saying, and this is a famous quote, that doubt is the beginning of inquiry. Doubt what you imagine. Doubt what you revere. Doubt what people have told you. Doubt what you imagine has been revealed by saints or even God.*

S: Exactly. Yes.

M: *Doubt is a state and this state is inquiry.*

S: Yes. I agree.

M: *For centuries Tibet was hidden, isolated. Your culture has spent centuries looking at these deep inner questions, whereas much of the world hasn't touched the surface. Now with the Chinese invasion, the genocide of your culture, they're dismantling all aspects of this tradition.*

S: Yes.

Has Tibet Gone Public with Its Secrets?

M: *Native Americans and other traditions would hold things close, sacred, because the outer world didn't understand. They didn't want to share their so-called secrets, feeling they would be misunderstood. Do you feel that Tibet has gone public with your secrets? Have you opened up your treasure chest, all of your treasures, and are you giving them away to the world so your culture or your insight may be shared, preserved? What's happening to the depth of your tradition, given the circumstances of your country?*

S: Tibet remained completely aloof and had no connection with any other nation politically, socially, or economically. They remained isolated in the first place due to their geographical location. There was no easy access. Secondly, having no connection, there is a language barrier. All this contributed to Tibet remaining completely cut off from the rest of the world, which changed rapidly during the last two hundred or three hundred years. For these three hundred years, Tibet had no information

From the moment we began our conversations I was struck by his quality of attention. There was nothing contrived about it nor was it based on a muscular effort of the will to attend. It might be likened, on a different level, to the dynamic of balance as when one rides a bicycle, drives a car or simply walks. Unless there is a disturbance in the inner ear or other impediment, normal walking is unselfconscious yet not unconscious. Beyond strength and skill, it entails knack, which is a gift. Since most of us walk, there doesn't seem to be much, if anything, of a gift about it. Yet without knack, our walking would be unspontaneous, graceless, sheerly mechanical and wooden-puppet-like. Krishnamurti's listening was knackful. It had the simplicity and openness of a child with the alertness of a warrior. It combined the harmlessness of the dove with the wisdom of the serpent.

Allan W. Anderson, *Practical Wisdom: Reflections on the Teaching of J. Krishnamurti*

about what was taking place in the rest of the world. This created certain benefits and a lot of disadvantages. The advantage was to remain aloof. Tibet was able to preserve and promote the great Indian Buddhist tradition and all its knowledge in different sciences in a complete form. The authentic and complete form of Buddhism remained only in Tibet, not in any other Buddhist country. They have only branches, not the totality.

With the Chinese invasion, Buddhism and its knowledge inside Tibet was systematically dismantled and destroyed. Today it has almost disappeared. At the same time, Tibetan knowledge and tradition has been exposed to the rest of the world. We may view this as a coincidence or the result of karmic forces. During the 1950s and '60s there was a great curiosity about different ways of life, and Western civilization was going through the hippie culture. People were not satisfied with their own society and traditions, and it was during this period that we were forced out of Tibet.

Now, when we look back over the last fifty-three years, Buddhist teachings and traditions in Tibet have reached every corner of the world. This was not the result or achievement of our efforts. We have made no effort. Tibetan Buddhism has been widely received. Recently I was told that the Tibetan and Buddhist learning centers on all continents, which are officially listed, are around eight hundred, and there might be more. One thing we can definitely say is that the Chinese rulers might be able to destroy traditional Buddhism inside Tibet within their control, but there is now no way to completely destroy this tradition. It is sprouting fresh roots outside Tibet, particularly in Western countries. Everywhere I find people interested in learning Buddhism, Tibetan Buddhism. It may be in North America. It may be in African countries. Of course, in Asia there is a long-standing interest in Buddhism. It cannot be destroyed.

The content of consciousness is consciousness. Without the content is there consciousness? This is not an intellectual, or philosophical or rhetorical question, but a genuine, a valid question. The content of consciousness, of me, is my furniture, my goods, my behavior, my thoughts, my anxieties, my pursuits of sexual delights. You know? The content of my consciousness are all the things collected in it—verbal, non-verbal, ancient-tradition, the result of race, the family—do you follow—the whole of that is my consciousness. I am not different from my consciousness because my consciousness, the "me," is the content. Remove the content—there is no me. Remove my knowledge, the name, the thought, all the remembrances of the hurts, the anxiety, the sorrows of death and pleasure—empty all that, what is consciousness then?

Is there me in that emptiness? No, please don't agree or disagree, you don't know what it means. Is there a "me," which is my vanity, my jealousies, my extraordinary sense of loneliness, bitterness, cynicism, vanity that is my consciousness, that is my life, living, my gods, my shoddy little beliefs and opinions; take away all that—and death means that physically you understand death; the organism dies because it is used and misused, you know, driven and tortured—old age, disease, eating too much, you know how you eat—have you watched yourself? All that is me, that is the content of me. I am a Catholic, I am a Hindu, I'm a Buddhist, I'm a Communist, I am an atheist, I don't believe in anything—all that is mine, the consciousness. The content is consciousness.

All that is me and I don't like to think that me is so small, so I invent a super me, the higher me, the soul, the Atman—you know, the game that one plays. All that is still within the field of consciousness, and that is the content of consciousness.

So when I realize that, do you follow, when the mind realizes that, not just verbally, not accepting a description, which is silly, or the explanation of the description, but sees that, the whole of it, non-fragmentarily but it is totally attentive to all that, then in that attention the mind is empty of all that and that is death. Therefore there is something totally new, of a totally different dimension. But you can't come to it through prayer, through following some shoddy guru—you can't ever come to that. One can only come when you yourself are actively attentive totally, you totally perceive the unitary movement of life, the living, the love, death, all the agonies, miseries that one goes through as a whole movement, unitive perception. Then the mind empties itself of all its content. It is not afraid to be anything or to be nothing, then it hasn't got to invent a future life. Then it is incarnating each minute.

J. Krishnamurti, Brockwood Park, UK, 3rd Public Talk, 11 September 1971 *(Abridged)*

Dharamsala, India, 2014, Day One

What Is Consciousness?

M: *There are so many issues to explore. We use the word* consciousness. *What does that mean? Krishnamurti used the word* truth. *He had a very specific meaning for the word. Can you define what Krishnamurti means by* truth? *Is it the same or similar to the meaning Buddhists give to that word? We talked about beliefs. We have religious beliefs. We have beliefs about Jesus or the Maitreya. We have beliefs about reincarnation. What is the difference between truth and a belief? Is Buddhism a religion? The Dalai Lama said, "Buddhism is a very intellectual non-emotional religion." What's the difference between an emotional religion and an intellectual one? Let's start with the word* consciousness.

S: Actually, words themselves are empty. Human beings assign to them a meaning as a form of agreement. Once a word is assigned a particular meaning it becomes a convention and people understand it that way. In philosophy, the word and its meaning have to be very tightly related. We have to be very precise, unmistakably accurate. That accuracy, of course, is relative to the human mind that defined the word and its meaning. But words are necessary. Understanding this, in Buddhist terminology, we have three different words for consciousness. All three are synonymous; they carry a similar meaning. The first is *chitta*, which means, "that which can know." The second is *manas*, which is very near to the word *mind* in English, "that which has the capacity to think." And the third is *vigyan*, which means "to know directly, to perceive things, not only in the realm of thought, but that which can see, perceive, directly." All three refer to consciousness.

When Buddhists use each word, *consciousness* or *mind*, both are referring equally to that which is capable of seeing, perceiving, has the capacity of thinking, that which can know. Consciousness has three levels: the gross level, the subtle level, and the subtlest level. The first level is inseparable from the biological body: the physical organs of the eye, the ear, and so on. There are five different sensory forms of consciousness: the five senses, and the sixth belonging to *manovigyan*, the inner-sensory mind. If the organ is perfect, the organ consciousness is able to work perfectly. When you damage the body, the consciousness associated with that organ

With His Holiness the Dalai Lama at an inauguration, Kashag Office, Gangchen Kyishon, Central Tibetan Administration, 2010

What has to be understood is that theories and doctrines of all kinds are the fabrication of our mind. It is capable of fabricating some of them diametrically opposed to each other and one will be no truer nor less true than the other because they are all based on false perceptions or, at best, relative ones which are only of value for an observer constituted as we are, placed where we are, and such perceptions have no absolute reality.

Alexandra David-Néel and Lama Yongden,
The Secret Oral Teachings in Tibetan Buddhist Sects

malfunctions. One human being may see a wide range of colors; another may not see as many colors. Development is different from organ to organ. The sixth sensory consciousness is inseparable from the body. It does not have continuity beyond the body. When your body is damaged or ends, the function of the sixth sensory consciousness also comes to an end. That is on the gross level. And in the next life, when you have a different biological body, you will have a different kind of sensory consciousness in accordance with the organs of that body.

The next level is subtle consciousness, which has no beginning and no end. It is the source of all the functions of the different levels of consciousness. The body might have perfect organs but they are not functioning. They cannot see, they cannot hear, until subtle consciousness enters into the body.

M: *This subtle consciousness is the source, the energy, that animates?*

S: Yes, it is the source that animates. It enters the body. Then, in accordance with and dependent upon the body's capacity and the capacity of the organ, consciousness begins to function. It is open. That source has no beginning and no end. That is the Buddhist principal of how the unique individual develops, how one experiences and acts, how we accumulate karma, and how our experiences are the result of karma.

M: *What you are describing as* subtle consciousness *does not emerge from the sensory, from the gross physical?*

S: No, the gross physical emanates from the subtle. The subtle consciousness has continuity independent of the gross physical body. When subtle consciousness does not have the facility of the organs, the abilities of the instrument, subtle consciousness does not function. But subtle consciousness is also the knower, the thinker, and the perceiver. All the perceptions of the sensory mind are perceived because of the subtle consciousness. That is the source, the energy, and because of this energy, physical consciousness is possible.

Even in subtle consciousness there are two levels: one is the sensory mind we just described, and there is also that which has continuity beyond the physical, the source that animates the physical and continues from life to life. In addition, there is the subtlest consciousness that only functions when it leaves the body at the time of death and when taking

The minds of beings are, in reality, always void, being really not-self-nature. This natural voidness of the mind is variously called "the lineage of the self-existent," "the lineage of the Buddhas," "the seed of the Buddhas," or "the womb of the Tathagatas," this last name being found in many Mayayana scriptures. This Buddha lineage exists in the minds of all beings and it is for this reason that all beings are able (given suitable conditions) to attain to Buddhahood.

His Holiness the Dalai Lama, *The Opening of the Wisdom-Eye*

With his secretary, Dr. Tenzin Dhonyoe, 2014

a rebirth. Then the subtlest consciousness transits from one body to another, and at that time is conscious. Otherwise, it remains unconscious at the level of an ordinary person. Let's go into this.

When somebody achieves the Buddha Nature, there is no gross-level consciousness. There is no unconscious consciousness. Only what we call *always awakening consciousness*. Buddha is called *awakening* because his subtlest consciousness is permanently functioning. Then it becomes independent of the organs. It can manifest in anything. That is the Buddha mind.

This is the way Buddhists understand consciousness. Consciousness is the individual at the subtle level. And consciousness is the individual's functioning when he or she is alive. So consciousness can be physical and not physical. We use the word *energy*, but science is now using that word in so many different ways, so I object to that word. As I said, we need to be very precise, unmistakably accurate.

M: *Krishnamurti's use of the word* consciousness *is somewhat different. He says, "The content of consciousness is consciousness." Content implies autobiographical memory, which is only a small part of your system.*

S: I am describing what *consciousness* means in the Buddhist tradition. As I mentioned, consciousness is in two realms: unawakened consciousness and awakened consciousness. Ordinary people who have not liberated themselves, who are in the bondage of karma and *klesh*, do not see things as they exist. They only see things that do not exist and they project things onto it. That we call *aatmadharna*, holding onto the soul or holding onto the assumption that things exist by their own nature. All of this is based in the thought realm on mental images, and not only images. There is a general conception that what the mind or thought conceives, the image, exists due to its own inherent, independent nature. That is the delusion ordinary people are stuck in, what we call *samsara*, the repeating cycles of birth and death.

Once you realize things do not exist in this way, they have no independent existence, that all things arise interdependently, and what our thoughts grasp after or hold onto do not exist in the way we think, we have an insight into the nature of our basic ignorance. When we remove that basic ignorance, we remove the source of all misunderstanding and are free from the repeating cycles of birth and death that grasping after an illusion create. This is a systematic path that the Buddhists describe, but

J. Krishnamurti

Quietly, it came, so gently that one was not aware of it, so close to the earth, among the flowers. It was spreading, covering the earth and one was in it, not as an observer, but of it. There was no thought or feeling, the brain utterly quiet. Suddenly there was innocence so simple, so clear and delicate. It was a meadow of innocence past all pleasure and ache, beyond all torture of hope and despair. It was there and it made the mind, one's whole being, innocent, one was of it, past measure, past word, the mind transparent and the brain young without time.

Krishnamurti's Notebook

Krishnamurti does not go along this systematic path. He takes the whole realm of thought as one package and the awakened state as another package. In this way, his approach is very simplified. This makes our challenge of awakening understandable and communicable using modern language without philosophical jargon.

Krishnamurti Did Not Conform to Any System

M: *I asked what consciousness is and you broke it down into highly defined branches or levels. This is an example of what you call the Buddhist path—minute, analytical, defining—to eliminate any possibility of confusion. That's part of your tradition, using thought as a medicine or antidote to our misuse of thought. Krishnamurti did not conform to any system. He simply said, "We have thought; when thought is not, there something else is."*

S: Yes. As long as thought is operating, you cannot see the other. You cannot see what is not thought when your whole mind is filled with conditioned memories and these misconceptions are active. Unless you remove them, you cannot see the other. Even when you are talking about the other, you are again talking about image, which is thought. This is also said by Buddhists: as long as you are talking or thinking about the ultimate truth, at that moment you are not perceiving the ultimate truth. You are still caught in your own projections. Regarding this insight, Krishnamurti's and the Buddhists' perspective is very similar.

M: *Yes.*

S: We cannot make a fine distinction between Buddhism and Krishnamurti because the vocabulary, the way of teaching, the tradition and cultures are very different. Buddhist practitioners and scholars can understand Krishnamurti in the philosophical framework of Buddhist philosophy quite easily. I do not consider this an alteration or interpretation of Krishnamurti's teachings. But if we try to frame Krishnamurti's insights in Buddhist jargon, that will distort his teachings.

M: *Very well said.*

S: The Buddhist way of the training of the mind can take advantage of Krishnamurti's teachings to more clearly understand "K" and also to better understand Buddhism. But you cannot make them comparable with each other.

The mind is comparable with space; like space it has neither interior nor exterior; in its depths one finds nothing but the Void.

Ideas of continuity or discontinuity cannot be applied to the mind; it escapes them, just as in the case of space one cannot conceive it either as limited or as infinite.

It is impossible to discover a place where the mind is born, a place where it dwells afterwards, a place where it ceases to exist. Like space, the mind is void in the three times: past, present and future.

In space we see clouds arise and vanish, without being able to find a dwelling for them from where they emerge and to where they can go back to. In space we see the sun shine, the moon, the stars, the planets, but what is space itself?

The essence of space, its very nature space in itself, are beyond all words, all imagination. It is the same with the original mind, void of any essence or any qualities of its own—impossible to grasp.

The more compactly we furnish it with the help of theories, opinions, imaginations, the more all these, acting as bonds, tie us down and keep us prisoners.

The "going beyond," the "non-activity" are the means focus to attain mental freedom. In truth we have nothing to do; it is a question of "undoing," of clearing the ground of our mind, of making it, as much as possible, clean, void. The Void is here, for us always a synonym of liberation.

                    Alexandra David-Néel and Lama Yongden,
                    The Secret Oral Teachings in Tibetan Buddhist Sects (Abridged)

M: *However, they are pointing to similar things.*

S: Yes.

Begin with Emptiness

M: *A critical difference is embodied in Krishnamurti's statement, "There are no teachings." He said simply, "When the self is not, the other is." He is using the self as a unique expression of the content of consciousness. With this in mind, I suggest we need to begin with emptiness. We don't end with emptiness. We must begin with an understanding of emptiness to approach the Buddhist way and Krishnamurit's insights. If we start with an understanding of emptiness, we can explore both and not get confused in comparisons. Emptiness is a good place to begin.*

S: Yes. I agree. But emptiness in Buddhism is not as easy to communicate as Krishnamurti does, communicating his ideas simply and directly. The principle of emptiness is the negation of something. Emptiness means when you negate something, that negation makes a space in the mind. That is emptiness. But what is to be negated is difficult to pinpoint verbally. Once you recognize, identify, what is to be negated, then emptiness becomes very easy to understand.

I think Krishnamurti would say, negate the thought process or the content of consciousness, something as simple as that. But in the Buddhist world that is not sufficient, it will not work. We have to precisely identify the thing that needs to be negated. That is our way of conceiving the basic challenge, which is difficult to catch by our own mind. To catch one's own mind by one's own mind is very tricky.

M: *Not only tricky, but David Bohm and Krishnamurti suggested it can't be done. It's a delusion to believe that thought can self-correct. One needs to step out of the problem to see the problem as it is. Negation, and therefore emptiness, is this stepping out of the problem that reveals the problem as it is.*

S: So therefore, how we normally perceive or conceive this moment, that needs to be negated. And if that is negated, what will remain? That is the question. And what remains must be the real thing, otherwise you will fall into nihilism, nothingness.

M: *The term* void *is also used for* emptiness. *As a westerner,* emptiness *isn't as dark as* void. *Void is very dark. It is nihilistic. Void means nothing. But that isn't*

We crave pleasant sense experiences and grasp after their continuation, while we crave the cessation of painful sense experiences and grasp after their cessation. It was the Buddha's experience in the course of his enlightenment that all phenomena arise and cease, and so, of course, feelings must arise and cease. But we crave for the pleasant to remain and grasp after it even though it may begin to cease, and we crave for the unpleasant to cease and grasp after it, even though it may remain for longer than we wish. This cycle of grasping after the transitory is the nature of our existence, it is the limb of "becoming" (srid pa) and it depends upon craving for sense objects and the pleasures or pains associated with them, especially the grasping after objects and feelings appropriated to the notion "I," a concept which is the object of the sense organ known as "mind" (yid).

Life after life, as the Buddha saw on the night of his enlightenment, beings grasp after transitory satisfactions in an ignorant fashion. It is "grasping" that impels beings into the flux of rebirth, but this grasping itself ultimately depends upon "ignorance," which is an incorrect understanding of the actual nature of phenomena and the consequent attraction to or revulsion from these phenomena. Thus, the twelve limbs are often described as a wheel, with the limbs themselves comprising the rim and the "three poisons" of delusion (gri mug), attraction or lust (dod chags) and revulsion or hatred (zhe sdang) forming the hub of the wheel. The Buddha saw beings as endlessly cycling through this existence whose nature is described by the twelve limbs, moment by moment turning on the hub of the three poisons. This is the state of things, which he called "samsara" ('khor ba).

But the Buddha also saw that there was a way out of this cycle, a way to "get off the wheel," or stop its turning. Because each of the twelve limbs is a condition upon which the others depend; if any of these conditions could be destroyed, the entire cycle would cease. This cessation of the cycle is what he called "nirvana (mya ngan las 'das pa), and it can come about precisely because each of the twelve conditions arises in dependence upon the others: if one limb were to cease, so the whole interdependent chain would break.

The Buddha expressed this formally as the "Four Noble Truths," which was his perception on the night of his enlightenment that because the unpleasantness (sdug bsngal) of existence (the first truth) depends upon ignorant grasping (the second truth), so upon the cessation of this ignorant grasping, the unpleasantness would also cease (the third truth). He also saw how to bring this cessation about, which is, formally, the Buddhist path (the fourth truth), that is, what one can do to break the chain of the twelve limbs of dependent origination.

David Ross Komito, *Nagarjuna's "Seventy Stanzas": A Buddhist Psychology of Emptiness*

what is meant. We might look at emptiness or void as a verb rather than a noun. Emptiness means stopping something that allows something else that's already there to manifest, to express or be perceived. Emptiness implies ending, eliminating, mental-emotional noise or clutter so we can actually listen and see directly.

S: The *madhyamik* philosophers use a metaphor. A piece of rope is lying on the ground in the shape of a snake. The light is dim so you conceive the rope to be a snake, and due to that misconception, fear is created in your mind. Someone comes with a torch and the light reveals that it is not a snake but a piece of rope. At that moment no effort is needed to remove the fear; the fear goes away automatically. So what is to be removed is the grasping of the mind after the concept of snake as snake. A snake does not exist. The negation of "snake-ness," the projection of the concept on the object, that negation is emptiness.

Grasping

M: *Grasping is an important concept.*

S: Yes, the mind grasping after the concept or mental image of a snake.

M: *We're not just saying that this happens rarely because we misperceive the rope as the snake. We are saying that this is going on moment by moment. The mind is projecting images and chasing after, grasping, the image-reality that it is creating, like a dog chasing after its own tail.*

S: The entire *content of consciousness*, to use Krishnamurti's term, is that grasping. The entire image-making process that we misperceive as real and grasp after, this is always going on. So first you have to understand how thought is grasping. Then you must analyze if what is being grasped is true or false. That analytical search and not finding the object one is grasping after, that is the light that reveals the snake as actually a piece of rope. That insight is enlightenment, which applies to all life and not just the imagined snake. When the false grasping is removed, one sees how all things are interdependent, constructed through multiple causes. This becomes as obvious as the piece of rope on the floor. Until grasping after the images the mind projects is removed, there will always be disorder in one's self and in the world. You don't have to do anything to create order. When grasping is removed, order is automatically there.

M: *Which is common to Buddhism and to Krishnamurti.*

The Two Levels of Truth (Paramartha-Satya; Samorti-Satya)

All objects known to us (through the five senses plus mind, the sixth) are divided into two categories: Those which are relatively true (samvrti-satya) and those absolutely true (paramartha-satya).

Two levels or aspects of truth have been distinguished because they are quite different from one another. Any perceptible object which is true from the Absolute point of view, is bound to be viewed differently from the relative view-point. The conventional or relative truth of an object is its supposed existence while its existence from the Absolute point of view cannot therefore accord with this conventional truth. It is therefore said that these two levels of truth are mutually exclusive.

Absolute Truth is that which is realized by deep reasoning and contemplating the absolute or true nature of dharmas, while the dharmas which are given a name and cognized by the mind as such, are called relative truth. To understand this more clearly, let us take the help of etymology and examine the terms Paramartha-Satya and Samvriti-Satya. In the first of these, "parama" means "excellent, best, supreme, highest," while the word "artha" here signifies "that which it is able" (to know with the highest wisdom). It may also mean "that which can be examined by the highest wisdom." A knowable dharma such as this is called "paramartha" because it is the most excellent, indeed supreme, among all dharmas to be known. Literally, the word "satya" means "is-ness" or "things-as-they-are" and if we think carefully about it, to whatever "is-ness" applies, that cannot be otherwise and must therefore be permanent and hence is called Absolute Truth.

Samvriti-Satya means the view that grasps the truth of the real nature of the dharmas. It is called samvriti or relative because what is perceived from the angle of this truth is relatively true; or its meaning may be taken as "wrong, false" because the way that an object appears in the light of this truth is really distorted, there being no unity between the relative perception of the object and its essential nature. Although ultimately this "truth" is false yet the appearances created in a mind governed by relative truth are to that extent true, hence we say that it is "satya."

His Holiness the Dalai Lama, *The Opening of the Wisdom-Eye (Abridged)*

S: Right.

M: *This grasping is our life. It is the only reality people know.*

S: Yes.

M: *Having an insight into the false nature of this reality is the big step, and it is very difficult. Grasping is what we consider is real. We used the word* maya *earlier. Krishnamurti and David Bohm discussed what truth and reality are at length. In exploring the nature of reality, the word* maya *was discussed,* maya *being an illusion that looks like the truth. An illusion that is perceived as the truth is very powerful, given that we usually use the source of the illusion to try to see the illusion. When grasping, we really believe the coiled rope is a snake. This is what Krishnamurti calls* thought. *Your tradition uses analysis, debate, and argument to penetrate, to gain insight into the way thought tricks itself into believing the images it creates are real, that they represent an independent reality.*

S: Yes, dialectic debate.

M: *In the Dalai Lama's biography he described his training, having to debate the best scholars.*

S: Yes. We have to be very precise in the use of language, very precise with our ideas and all the categories and subcategories of logic.

M: *It's almost mathematical; one's logic needs to hold all the way through.*

S: Yes, like mathematics.

Maya and the Power of Self-Deception

M: *I would call that a method or discipline for training the mind. Krishnamurti, as you know, denied methods, that we can't get to the state we are calling* the absolute *using any methods. Let's explore that. The world is filled with methods and Krishnamurti is somewhat unique by insisting that we can't get where we want to go with methods. No paths. "Be a light unto yourself," he said. Only those things you discover for yourself matter. Don't believe in anything. And your tradition appears just the opposite. You have strict discipline and obedience to your teachers. You have to follow the rules. You have to do these things until finally you are liberated from all of that. And Krishnamurti says, "Do it now, sir." Skip the methods and simply be liberated from conditioning right now, this moment. How do we reconcile this apparent contradiction?*

S: I said years ago that Krishnamurti and Buddhists are talking about two truths: *Paramarthasatya*, the absolute truth, and *samvrittisatya*, the relative

The process of becoming is struggle, conflict, is it not? The clerk becoming the manager, the vicar becoming the bishop, the pupil becoming the Master—this psychological becoming is effort, conflict.

Living and becoming are two different states, are they not? Existence may entail effort; but we are considering the process of becoming, the psychological urge to be better, to become something, the struggle to change what is into its opposite. This psychological becoming may be the factor that makes everyday living painful, competitive, a vast conflict.

I am this, and I want to become that, and this becoming is a series of conflicts. When I have become that, there is still another that, and so on endlessly. This becoming is without end, and so conflict is without end.

The ideal is your own projection. See how the mind has played a trick upon itself. You are struggling after words, pursuing your own projection, your own shadow. You are violent, and you are struggling to become non-violent, the ideal; but the ideal is a projection of what is, only under a different name. This struggle is considered necessary, spiritual, evolutionary, and so on; but it is wholly within the cage of the mind and only leads to illusion.

When you are aware of this trick which you have played upon yourself, then the false as the false is seen. The struggle towards an illusion is the disintegrating factor. All conflict, all becoming is disintegration. When there is an awareness of this trick that the mind has played upon itself, then there is only what is. When the mind is stripped of all becoming, of all ideals, of all comparison and condemnation, when its own structure has collapsed, then the what is has undergone complete transformation.

In this transformation alone is there integration. Integration is not the action of will, it is not the process of becoming integrated. When disintegration is not, when there is no conflict, no struggle to become; only then is there the whole, the complete.

J. Krishnamurti, *Commentaries on Living, Series I (Abridged)*

truth or the concept of *maya*, something that appears true but is an illusion. It is not true to the awakened mind but it is true to the mind grasping after the illusion.

M: *That is the power of the deception, something false that we perceive as true.*

S: Yes. Buddhists talk about one thing at the relative level and when they talk about the absolute level, they often, like Krishnamurti, do not accept anything. They reject everything. To reach that level however, Buddhists do not reject the path, the levels, graduation, and growth. In Buddhism, as with Krishnamurti, at the level or moment of transmutation, insight or realization from the unawakened to the awakened state, there is also no graduation. Half-enlightened does not exist. One is unenlightened or enlightened, one or the other. But to reach that point or moment of transformation, Buddhists have to take many step-by-steps. I don't think we need to reconcile this, which is all in the realm of thought. We cannot fit Buddhism into Krishnamurti's way of teaching or fit Krishnamurti's way into Buddhism. We need to keep them separate.

No Psychological Becoming

M: *Let's remain with methods because it's a troubling area for many. Krishnamurti denies becoming psychologically. I'm going to become a better person. I'm going to become enlightened. He denies that. He says simply, it's now or never, this moment. You either are or you're not. There is no partial, which is a very tough standard. While all the paths say, it's okay, try a little harder, you'll be a little better tomorrow. Krishnamurti insists that tomorrow is now.*

S: He negates psychological time and progress.

Negating Methods

M: *But when we look at the mind being state-specific, there is no progress. One's state, as we talked about previously, is similar to a light being on or off in a room. If you are in darkness and turn on the light, where does the dark go? It is either dark or not. Krishnamurti, beginning in his early life, was very disciplined in what he ate, in his exercises. We can call this a method, but in terms of psychology or consciousness that is state-specific, these methods can be compared to preparing the soil. What emerges from that soil, which is a state, is not the soil.*

At his residence, Theckchen Choeling, Dharamsala, 2014

    Thought is a basic instrument of our life but for transformation, direct perception, thought has no role to play at all. Therefore, all kinds of thought have to be negated, according to Buddha, as well as according to Krishnaji. But for Buddhists, thought has been accepted, during some of the means or methods during preparation. Krishnaji doesn't accept or doesn't talk about preparation, so the idea of gradation of thought does not arise in his teachings.

    The Buddha and Krishnamurti both employed the method of negation, because the reality as perceived by them is incommunicable through language, through words, thought, or any means of communication. The only way left for them is to negate all the possible conceptions of thought or imagination or what we think or look for. This is not reality. In this way, the person comes closer and closer to reality. After negating everything, our habitual way of looking, the reality is clear.

        Samdhong Rinpoche, Sarnath, India,
        Interview with Evelyne Blau and Michael Mendizza, 1987

S: What I understand of Krishnamurti's negation of methods is our human weakness. We are not able to use methods and then leave them completely when we reach the destination. We get stuck in our methods. We remain forever conditioned by our use of methods. Buddha said somewhere, I do not remember his exact words but he used a metaphor: Dharma (methods, the path) is like a boat you use to cross the river. Unless you leave the boat you cannot reach the other shore. Or you cannot carry the boat on your head. If you get stuck in the method, believing, "This is my very precious practice, I must carry the boat always, by these methods we will save humanity," you remain, as we said, like a dog chasing its tail, believing falsely that we are making spiritual progress. All the methods used by various spiritual traditions have become a burden, a form of conditioning, and because of this, the person forgets the other shore, the otherness. Krishnamurti wanted to completely negate this. And to do this he had to negate it in totality, completely. If he made an exception, negation would not work. This is my way of understanding his position on methods.

Apparently we human beings are caught in a terrible tragedy of habit, tradition, of an activity of a brain that has become atrophic because we are functioning mechanically. We hold onto beliefs, to faith, to constant repetition of endless meaningless rituals in all the churches of the western world, and the rituals in the eastern world. All these rituals are put together by thought. Thought is a material process.

But if you examine thought, and the origin of thought, what is thinking, you will find that it is born out of memory, knowledge, experience, and from that experience, thought, thought in action, and so on. This is the chain in which the brain works at present. Experience, knowledge, memory stored in the brain, from that memory comes action, skilful or not skilful, and from that action you learn more knowledge. So you keep this chain going, which is gradually making the brain atrophied. When you repeat over and over and over the same thing, as they do in rituals, in having strong beliefs, convictions, conclusions, the brain must inevitably become not only atrophied but lack nourishment. And one of the factors of this atrophy is that man puts up with every kind of illusion—religious illusions, psychological non-facts, and so on.

Now we are asking if sorrow can ever end. Not only personal sorrow, but also the sorrow of all mankind. Sorrow is sorrow; it is not yours or mine. The sorrow that has been created through these five thousand years of war. The sorrow that human beings are preparing for wars. The sorrow of endless division between people, as the Catholics, the Protestants, the Hindus, the Buddhists, the Muslims, the Arab and the Jew, the American and the Russian, the Hindu and the Muslim, and so on.

J. Krishnamurti, Ojai, California, 6th Public Talk, 17 May 1981

Dharamsala, India, 2014, Day Two

Ritual Conditioning

M: *Being respectful, yet with this in mind, I got up with the sun and came to the main temple here in Dharamsala and the monks were chanting. They had their books, beads, their prayers; people were walking around a circle. They seemed deeply conditioned, not unlike people in the West addicted to their technology. Both seem completely occupied. How can we do these things and not become hypnotized by the doing?*

S: That is exactly what I am trying to say. Chanting becomes a repeated ritual. Counting the beads becomes a repeated ritual. All this makes no difference to the mind of the person, so there is no real progress, only conditioning, and we need to reject this conditioning. Even Buddhists would say these things do nothing. I have a very clear example from Atisha's biography. Atisha was visiting the central temple of Lhasa. Walking around the temple, he met a person sitting cross-legged reading a book, who invited Atisha's blessing. To the man he said, "Reading the book is good but why don't you practice the Dharma?"

M: *The book was on the Dharma, I assume.*

S: Yes. "Why don't you practice the Dharma?" The man was shocked and put down the book. But Atisha was not happy. "Oh," thought the man, "I think I should do some prostrations." The next time Atisha was at the temple, the man was prostrating and Atisha said, "Oh good, you are doing some exercise. Why don't you practice the Dharma?" The next time Atisha visited the temple, the man was repeating a mantra, using beads and with his eyes closed, and Atisha said, "Yes, reciting a mantra is also not bad. But why don't you practice the Dharma?" The man was completely confused and asked Atisha, "What should I do?" Atisha said, "Change your mind." This is not quoted from Krishnamurti but is completely consistent within orthodox Buddhist tradition and fits perfectly with Krishnamurti's teachings of *no methods*. This illustration helps us understand why Krishnamurti negates all this, why he insists that our repeated practices and rituals do not contribute to the liberation of the mind.

You want to find out what method the speaker will offer to reveal this extraordinary state. You want to learn how to approach this state step by step through the practice of certain forms of meditation, through the cultivation of virtue, self-discipline, and so on. But I do not think that any method will bring about clear perception; on the contrary.

When you practice a method you must have time to bridge the gap between what is and what should be. Time is necessary to travel the distance created by the mind between the fact and the dissolution of the fact, which is the end to be achieved. Our whole ideology is based on this sense of achievement through time, so we begin to acquire, to learn, and therefore we rely on the master, the guru, the teacher, because he is going to help us to get there.

Is perception or direct experience of that reality a matter of time? Is there a gap that must be bridged over by the process of knowledge? If there is, then knowledge becomes extraordinarily important. Then the more you know, the more you practice, the more you discipline yourself, and so on, the greater your capacity to build this bridge to reach reality.

We have accepted this idea and it may be an illusion; it may be totally false. Perception may be immediate, not in time. I think it is not a matter of time at all. If I may use the phrase "I think," not to convey an opinion, but an actual fact. Either one perceives, or one does not perceive. There is no gradual process of learning to perceive. It is the absence of experience, which is based on knowledge, that gives perception.

If we see that the method is false, an illusion, the product of time, and that time cannot lead to direct experience, then that very perception is the liberation from time. Our relationship is then entirely different.

The Collected Works of J. Krishnamurti. Benaras, India,
1st Public Talk, 11 December 1955 *(Abridged)*

The Method Is Not the End

M: *In your tradition, cultivating a clean intellect, being able to follow the logic of something deeply, takes experience, mentoring. One doesn't get up in the morning and run the marathon. You need to train for it, you need to practice. This is the point I was making about the state-specific nature of the brain, the false belief in psychological progress. When Krishnamurti says there's no psychological becoming, he's talking about the state of the mind. He's not talking about our capacity to do mathematics or follow logical sequences. Methods are like going to the gymnasium and developing intellectual capacities and using those brain muscles to see the mess that needs negating. There seems to be a value to methods but methods are not enough.*

S: A method is not the end. That is the Buddhist viewpoint and also Krishnamurti's viewpoint. The problem is that many people are not able to understand how to apply a method in their lives and not become even more conditioned by it, unless Krishnamurti shakes them by forcefully rejecting methods. Once this kind of challenge is given, you may adopt a different relationship with methods. The Buddhist training of the intellect involves repeated analysis until you find emptiness, *shunyata*. The analytical search has no end until you negate everything, including the intellect. Krishnamurti used to ask, "Can you live with the question, not finding a conclusion?" Buddhist training implies this question. Most Buddhists are trained to live with a question, with logic, until seeing the negation of everything, including the intellect that is questioning. So this is a very similar viewpoint.

Removing Misconceptions

M: *In the introduction to Nagarjuna's* Seventy Stanzas, *the author wrote: "Reality, according to the Buddhists, is kinetic, moving, not static, but logic, on the other hand, images reality stabilized as concepts and names. The ultimate aim of Buddhist logic is to distinguish between a moving reality and the static constructions of thought." We don't think of thought being fixed because one thought follows another so quickly it appears to be fluid, always moving, changing, but actually, each thought is like a little brick. It's a moment, an impression, frozen as concept in memory.*

S: The *shunyata* is basically to remove misconceptions about the inherent existence of an independent self. There is no inherent, independent

If you were listening to Krishnaji, he was not a guru. If you were accepting what he was saying, he was a guru. So the fact of whether he was a guru or not did not lie with Krishnaji; it lay in the audience who listened, in the person who felt that every word he said was biblical, to be followed without questioning. The listening is, in essence, the questioning and when listening is truly flowering, the guru is not.

Pupul Jayakar, Interview with Evelyne Blau and Michael Mendizza

J. Krishnamurti with Pupul Jayakar

A mystic is a man who perceives directly. St. John of the Cross, one of the great exemplars of this tradition, had a beautifully clear image. He said, "If I have my hand in front of my eyes, I cannot see the sun. If I have an image of God, I cannot see God." And it's as simple as that. So, in this sense, Krishnamurti was a mystic.

When I was living here on this property in 1944 and 1945, perhaps my most vivid perception of Krishnamurti was that he never talked shop, except by appointment. He was never that awesome person on the stage, nor was he given to impromptu analyses of the events of daily life. It almost amounted to a dual personality. The person with whom I related in daily life reminded me of an extraordinarily alert, intelligent, responsive, ingenuous, open-hearted child, and who used the simplest language, who never used abstractions.

So I have the impression that his mind was like a tool, like a hammer that he used very, very well indeed when he used it. And when he wasn't using it he put it aside, not dominating his consciousness, not in the forefront. And this is part of what I mean by his relationship of eternity and time and the art of living.

William "Bill" Quinn, Interview with Evelyne Blau and Michael Mendizza

existence of the *shunyata* (self as an entity), unchanging and so on, nor in any phenomena. Negation of an inherent independent existence of everything negates the existence of *shunyata*. When you remove all inherent independent existence, how can there be an independent self? Everything that exists is interdependently constructed. Apart from interdependent originations, nothing exists. So when we talk in Buddhist philosophy about absolute reality, the ultimate truth, using any word is inadequate. Words can only represent an image, not what lies beyond the image. Many people say, "Truth is one." One is always in relationship to some other number. If there is no *two*, no *three*, what does *one* mean? Thought always represents things as small fragments, not what lies beyond fragmentation. So when we go beyond fragmentation, then these words—*moving, changing, one*—only bring us back to fragmentation, back to the realm of relative truth, not absolute truth. In the realm of absolute truth, and in the way Krishnamurti uses the word *truth*, of course there is no path. If there is a path, then truth must be a destination. If you make truth a destination, then it must be very small, another fragmentation. What thought represents is not that which is beyond the word.

Truth and the Absolute

M: *Let's explore Krishnamurti's use of the word* truth *and the Buddhist use of the word* absolute. *Are they similar?*

S: As I mentioned before, when Krishnamurti uses the word *truth*, he is always referring to *absolute truth*, *choicelessness*. *Choicelessness* means *absolute*. He never regards relative truth, which he completely denies. Krishnamurti insists that unless you totally deny relative truth, you will never go beyond relative truth. That is the way he communicates.

M: *If the relative ceases, the absolute is?*

S: Yes.

M: *It seems so simple.*

S: It may be simple but we cannot experience this simplicity because of our thought, because of our language. Human beings are experts at making things complicated.

M: *You mentioned fragmentation.*

S: Yes.

We were talking over together the nature of consciousness. And in talking about it, we went into the question of attention, what is attention. And we said, this quality of attention is a state of mind in which all energy is there, highly concentrated, and in that attention there is no observer, there is not a center as the "me" who is aware, attentive. We went into that.

What we are going to do this morning is to find out for ourselves…what happens to the mind when there is this extraordinary attention, when there is no center as this observer or as the censor.

We must begin with seeing "what is."…

To understand "what is." you need energy. Now, these fragmentations of which we are are the division of these energies. "I" and the not "I", anger and the not anger, violence and the not violence—they are all fragmentations of energy. And when one fragment assumes the authority over the other fragments, it is an energy that functions in fragments.

So the mind sees that all fragmentations—as nation, not nation, my god, your god, my belief and your belief—are fragmentations of energy. There is only energy and fragmentation. This energy is fragmented by thought. And thought is the way of conditioning.

So consciousness is the totality of these fragmentations of energy. And we said, this fragmentation of energy, one of those fragmentations is the observer, is the "me", is the monkey, that is incessantly active.

Now to see that, which is "what is," can you see without the fragment as the observer? Can the mind see these many fragmentations which make up the whole of consciousness, and these fragmentations are the fragmentations of energy—energy—can the mind see this without an observer who is part of the many fragments?

We are asking, what is the quality of the mind that is highly attentive, in which there is no fragmentation.… What is the quality of the mind?

J. Krishnamurti, *The Impossible Question*. Saanen, Switzerland, 8th Public Dialogue, 9 August 1970 *(Abridged)*

Fragmentation Leads to Conflict

M: *In 1971 Krishnamurti noted that fragmentation in consciousness always implies conflict. Once this conflict begins, it sustains fragmentation by creating more conflict, including what we think of as the self, which is another fragment. Krishnamurti is saying that relative reality, and implicitly the self as we know it, is based on and sustained by conflict. Conflict is the source of our relative reality. Conflict keeps the relative reality going. He used India and Pakistan as a metaphor. As soon as the conflict between the images we have about India and Pakistan ends, India and Pakistan cease to exist.*

S: I have heard Krishnamurti say that fragmentation leads to conflict. Buddhists will not dispute this, but our way of looking at conflict takes a different form. Buddhists talk about cooperation and conflict. Either we cooperate or we are in conflict. Conflict leads to violence and destruction. Cooperation leads to creativity, in relationship with the environment, society, with all aspects of life. Think of a tree. Cooperation is the positive relationship between all the elements or forces necessary for a tree to grow.

M: *The Dalai Lama talks about happiness. One could say that the negation of unhappiness, the ending of unhappiness, results in happiness.*

S: Yes.

M: *This is similar to our saying earlier that the ending of the relative, which is conflict (using Krishnamurti's language), results in the absolute. The absolute is there, hidden by the relative conflict. Krishnamurti is saying that conflict is inherent in the relative, one image fighting another endlessly. The ending of conflict naturally results in cooperation. You don't have to do anything, make an effort to be cooperative. Negate, end conflict, and cooperation is there.*

S: Yes, that's right.

Two Types of Virtues

M: *In Alexandra David-Néel's* The Secret Oral Teachings, *there was a chart that listed two types of virtues. One column listed normal virtue, and the other was what was called* golden virtues *or* supreme virtues. *The difference between the two columns was the ego. The same virtue took on a different quality if the ego was active or not.*

The bhavacakra is a symbolic representation of samsara (or cyclic existence) found on the outside walls of Tibetan Buddhist temples and monasteries in order to help ordinary people understand Buddhist teachings. The bhavacakra is popularly referred to as the wheel of life, the wheel of cyclic existence, or the wheel of becoming.

S: Virtue with ego is different from virtue without the ego, yes.

M: *Eliminate the self-centered ego, which implies conflict, and cooperation is there, without effort. Krishnamurti is talking about cooperation that unfolds naturally, without effort. Effort implies conflict.*

S: Unless the ego is eliminated, virtue will not express the Buddha Nature.

M: *Walk out the door and there are beggars on the street. In the United States we have philanthropists, people who give away money and are supposed to be good. In the egoless state there is no good guy; there is no place for that badge to rest. This is the choiceless state Krishnamurti is referring to.*

S: Exactly.

Samsara Is the Result of Ignorance

M: *Ignorance and conflict go together. You have a word* samsara, *which I believe is ignorance, and with ignorance comes suffering, two sides of the same coin.*

S: Samsara is not ignorance. Samsara is the result of ignorance. Samsara is the cycle between death, birth, decay and death. This cycle involves unending misery and suffering that we call *dukha*, which is the result of ignorance. Because we are ignorant of the ultimate, the absolute truth, people have egos. The western word *ego* or the concept of the ego is a good generalization. Because of the ego, we accumulate karma. With karma comes rebirth and decay and again death with its *dukha*, suffering. Death is not the end of *dukha*. The reborn individual is bound and pushed around by the forces of karma and ignorance. This is samsara.

This is also sometimes called *bhavacakra*. You might have seen *bhavacakra* in the Buddhist temples. There is a picture with four circles. The innermost shows a pig that represents ignorance, a snake for anger, and a rooster for desire. The next circle shows individuals who have performed virtuous actions creating good karma moving upwards, and those who have performed bad actions, and so on. This is the classic image showing samsara.

Are we craving self-expansion, the constant nourishment of the ego, the me and the mine, or are we seeking to understand and so transcend the process of the self? Will self-expansion bring about understanding, enlightenment; or is there illumination, liberation, only when the process of self-expansion has ceased?

If you are aware you will realize that your mind is constantly engaged in the activities of the ego and its identification; if you pursue this activity further, you will find the deep-seated self-interest. These thoughts of self-interest arise from the needs of daily life, things you do from moment to moment, your role in society, and so on, all of which build up the structure of the ego.

We know how the self is built up and strengthened through the pleasure and pain principle, through memory, through identification, and so on. This process is the cause of conflict and sorrow.

The Collected Works of J. Krishnamurti.
Ojai, California, 1st Public Talk, 1946 *(Abridged)*

Ignorance Is the Ego: The Ego Is Ignorance

M: *The cycle is driven by ignorance.*

S: Yes. In Krishnamurti's language, ignorance is the ego. Krishnamurti always used the ego to represent ignorance. Buddhists say ignorance is the true nature of phenomena we call *the self*.

M: *We began with my inquiry into identity, the image we have about ourselves. The ego is this image. Understanding the truth and falseness about this image is fundamental to Krishnamurti's so-called teachings. He and David Bohm explored the nature of this image for many years, questioning why we treat it as an independent reality, when clearly it is just an image, why we are blind to the trick the mind is playing on itself.*

All beings are searching for this happiness. Though thy sons build impenetrable walls around their country, shutting out the happiness they seek, though thy learned priests fight for the Gods they shall worship, though the contentment of the wealthy be stagnating, though the oppressed and the exploited be suffering, though the man of thought has not found the eternal solution, though the sannyasi who renounces the world has not gained enlightenment, though the beggar who wanders from house to house for kindness has not found shelter, though thy people prefer the darkness of the night to the light of day, though thy people turn night into day—all are searching for that lasting happiness.

They buy and they sell, they build magnificent palaces, surrounding themselves with all the beauty that money can buy, they plant gardens, the exquisite delight of the refined, they cover themselves with jewels, they quarrel and they are charming, they drink without restraint, they eat without restraint, they are virulent and pacific, they worship and curse, they love and hate, they die and are born again, they are cruel to man and beast, they destroy and create, they produce and annihilate—yet they are all seeking happiness, happiness in transient things.

They bribe, they corrupt, they make unholy the earth, the seas and mountains. Their graven images do not answer their call. As the mountain stream sweeps all things before it, so is their structure of happiness destroyed in an instant; they destroy each other in their jealous love.... And, in an instant, sorrow is the outcome of their fleeting joy.

J. Krishnamurti, *From Darkness to Light*: "The Search"

Dharamsala, India, 2014, Day Three

Happiness

M: *Even Buddha said that the ultimate wisdom is happiness. Happiness is the natural order. A healthy body is a happy body. A clear unconditioned mind is a happy mind. That is the base, the natural state. If I recall, you have several terms for this optimum state: Buddha consciousness, Buddha mind. How do you frame or describe this natural state of happiness?*

S: This is a complex question. I cannot define what a happy state is. You ask about Buddhahood. Is Buddhahood a happy state? I would say yes; at the Buddha level, there's no unhappiness. Unhappiness is completely eradicated. So we may define it as a happy state. But all unenlightened sentient beings, all living beings, have one basic thing in common. They like happiness and don't like unhappiness. From a small insect to the elephant to the human being, they desire happiness and do not want unhappiness. The Buddhists say, in this way we are all equal. But what is happiness and what is unhappiness? In worldly life we have well-defined notions of what happiness is. In the Buddha's mind, worldly happiness is not happiness. What we consider happiness, the Buddha considered as unhappiness. In the ordinary world, I am unhappy because I feel hungry. I get delicious food. I eat with interest, enjoy it, and my stomach is filled, so I feel happiness. The Buddha says no, that is not happiness. What we call *happiness* is shifting from one unhappiness to another unhappiness. The Buddha categorized three forms of suffering: the suffering of suffering, the suffering of changing, and the suffering at the base of suffering.

The suffering of suffering is the intense feeling of hunger. Everyone knows it is happening. The suffering of changing is the feeling of being satisfied by taking food. Ah, I am full, as if that happiness can sustain itself, and eating more would increase your happiness. But if you go on eating, after some time, at some point that happiness will become unhappiness. So the suffering of suffering and the suffering of changing happen to an individual because of his or her bondage with the biological body. And the biological body is the vessel or container of all misery, in change, decay, and death. If you don't have a biological body, you can't feel hurts and all these things. So these three categories of suffering are

J. Krishnamurti, Bombay

The flashing river was now the light of the sky, enchanted, dreaming, and lost in its beauty and love. In this light, all things cease to exist, the heart that was crying and the brain that was cunning; pleasure and pain went away leaving only light, transparent, gentle and caressing. It was light; thought and feeling had no part in it, they could never give light; they were not there, only this light when the sun is well beyond the walls of the city and not a cloud in the sky. You cannot see this light unless you know the timeless movement of meditation; the ending of thought is this movement. The brain was completely still but very alive and watching, without a center. The otherness was there, deep within at a depth that was lost; wiping away everything without leaving a mark of what has been or what is. It was simply a fact, like a sunset, like death and the curving river.

Krishnamurti's Notebook

not happiness. When you leave these three, there is freedom from the bondage of karmic forces that bind your mind with your body. When karmic forces and their source are completely eradicated, you don't need to take a rebirth in a physical body. Or you take a birth by choice, not as a continuation of karmic forces. Then you will have the freedom of choosing when you are born and when to die, and in this case, birth and death is like changing a shirt. There is no pain. The freedom, the liberation from karmic forces, that is real happiness. That is the Buddhist view.

M: *Very clear.*

Conditioning or Freedom

S: Krishnamurti also describes unconditioning as freedom. On occasion he used the word *liberation.*

M: *One of the distinguishing qualities between the two perspectives is that Krishnamurti does not go so far as to separate the mind from the body. He may imply it, yet he doesn't make it explicit.*

S: He does not use these categories. He says conditioning/unconditioning. Simple.

M: *Very simple. The question arises: Is this subtle consciousness embodied, incarnate or not? Krishnamurti, on occasions, certainly in his* Notebook, *said there is something vast, immeasurable, something that the brain cannot grasp or understand. We are so material. We assume that consciousness, awareness, mind, emerge out of the body and brain instead of the other way around. Rather than using happiness or unhappiness, might it be more accurate to describe this optimum state as being free from conflict, as empty of unhappiness. That's more accurate. Both Krishnamurti and Nagarjuna used negation rather than trying to define the other, the positive, where we get lost.*

S: Yes.

Two Realities: Absolute and Relative

M: *We are left with two realities, something we touched on when we first met in Sarnath over thirty-five years ago: the absolute and the relative. The absolute seems to be the natural order we're talking about, uncontaminated, clear and direct. The other, the relative,* samsara, *may be true within its realm but mistaken*

When you understand the structure of your daily living—with its competition, greed, ambition and the search for power—then you will see not only the absurdity of theories, saviors and gurus, but you may find an ending to sorrow, an ending to the whole structure which thought has put together.

The penetration into and the understanding of this structure is meditation. Then you will see that the world is not an illusion but a terrible reality which man, in his relationship with his fellow man, has constructed.

But beyond all this, and not related to this struggle, this vanity and despair, there is—and this is not a theory—a stream that has no beginning and no end; a measureless movement that the mind can never capture.

J. Krishnamurti, *The Only Revolution*

or false when viewed from the absolute. Once set into motion, samsara *or relative reality seems to go round and round recreating itself. What you call* freedom, liberation *and* real happiness *breaks this cycle.*

S: These two realities, many scholars say, are two sides of one coin, inseparable. Other scholars argue that this metaphor is not very good. Two sides of one coin are separable. The truth is, in nature they are not separate. In appearance only, they appear opposite.

M: *In nature, you're saying there is one reality.*

S: I don't say *one*. In nature, what appears to be separate is inseparable. If I say *one*, then where is *two*? They are separable, opposite, only in appearance. In their nature the absolute and relative realities are inseparable because absolute truth is *truth*. All things exist within it. And relative truth is truth in the eyes of ignorance. When ignorance is eradicated, relative truth is also negated. What remains is absolute. When you remove ignorance, you need not make a second effort to remove relative truth. It is gone. When ignorance goes, there is no relative truth, no *samsara*, no suffering. But as long as ignorance remains, all these things continue. When Buddha removed ignorance, there was no relative truth. But for all sentient beings, there is the relative truth you and I have created, and Buddha sees that.

M: *Krishnamurti has a point of reference.*

S: A perspective, yes.

Look at What We Are Doing

M: *He would look and listen to those around him and see the confusion, the ignorance, and he would say, "Look at what you are doing." I don't think he had an opinion. This sounds similar to what you just described. He said, "We don't know ourselves and because of this, we are the enemy. We have created the society that we blame for our unhappiness." At the root, both Krishnamurti and Buddhism are pointing to the same dynamic.*

S: Yes, exactly.

M: *The next step seems so basic. We need to get rid of ignorance. That's it.*

S: Yes, that is the whole thing.

M: *Krishnamurti follows by pointing out that the content of our consciousness is created by ignorance, and that content, which is ignorance, is not capable of self-*

Although it is true that in some cases instantaneous spiritual experiences may be possible, they are rather unreliable and somewhat short lived. The problem is that when sudden experiences occur, like bolts of lightning, the individual may feel profoundly moved and inspired, but if the experience is not grounded in discipline and sustained effort, the impact will be rather limited.

We can now further our understanding of enlightenment by considering the presentation made by Maitreya in his Sublime Continuum (Ratnagotravibhaga). He states that all the pollutants of our mind are adventitious, meaning that they can be separated from the essential nature of mind. This indicates the possibility of being able to eliminate the affections of mind and heart, that is, affective emotions and thoughts. Maitreya then makes the point that as far as the enlightened qualities of the Buddha are concerned, we all possess within us the potential or seed for their perfection. This means that the potential for perfection, the potential for full enlightenment, actually lies within each one of us. In fact, this potential is nothing other than the essential nature of the mind itself, which is said to be the mere nature of luminosity and knowing.

The teachings of many other ancient spiritual traditions of India also contain notions of nirvana, moksa or spiritual freedom. It also seems that some traditions identify these states with a physical realm of existence. However, as far as the Buddhist understanding of nirvana is concerned, it is a state of mind and not an external reality.

According to Chandrakiriti, a famous Indian teacher of the Middle Way school, liberation or true cessation is the ultimate truth. His point is the true cessation can only come about on the basis of understanding the ultimate nature of reality, that is emptiness.

It is our ignorance of this ultimate nature of reality that lies at the root of all our obscurations, confusions and delusions.

Finally, it is the emptiness of the mind in its perfected state that is true liberation. So the basis of true liberation is emptiness, the knowledge by which we eliminate our obstructions is that of emptiness, and the final perfected stage in which we attain liberation is the emptiness of mind.

His Holiness the Dalai Lama, *Transforming the Mind*

correcting. We keep looking to ignorance to free ourselves from ignorance and this generates more ignorance.

S: We keep looking in the wrong place.

M: *Krishnamurti's and Buddhist teachings have the same ultimate goal, which is to eliminate ignorance.*

S: True.

M: *Simple.*

S: Yes.

M: *Krishnamurti uses the word* silence *to describe a mind that is free of ignorance. Buddhists refer to the state as* empty.

S: The Buddhist literature also, not very often, uses the word *silence*; in particular in Tantra practices, *silence* and *peace* are used equally.

M: *We can see how peaceful the ending of confusion would be.*

S: Yes.

M: *Krishnamurti describes how the ending of ignorance, beliefs, identifications, and endless conflicts release tremendous energy. Huge amounts of energy are released when we eliminate confusion. All that energy is then available to act with true intelligence. Our energy and attention are no longer wasted.*

Compassion Combined with Energy

S: Yes. Not only energy, limitless compassion will be there. Compassion combines with energy. In Buddhism, we have three different words: *Gyan*, meaning wisdom; *Karuna*, meaning compassion; and *Shakti*, energy. When these three come together, immeasurable things can be done.

M: *Tantra is a practice that unifies these three: wisdom, compassion, and energy.*

S: The other disciplines approach these one by one. In tantra, all three are unified. Ultimately you have to develop all three: wisdom, compassion, and energy.

M: *I understand the natural order and I understand the role of ignorance, at least as a concept. The question is, "What do I do?" You described the first step, gathering attention. The second is using reason to dispel the false images and emotions we have accumulated. Stop wasting energy and attention grasping after these. This frees tremendous energy for wisdom and compassion to act for the benefit of all life.*

Traveling in Europe with His Holiness the Dalai Lama, ca. 2008–2009

Tibetan Buddhism can be described as the most comprehensive system of Buddhism in the sense that it contains elements of all the aspects of the Buddha's teachings, including Vajrayana. The teachings of the Four Noble Truths form the core of the non-Mahayana teachings, and are really the foundation of the Buddhist path. Together with the training in morality, the Four Noble Truths also serve as the basis for the practice of bodhichitta.

Once the development of bodhichitta has taken place, the practitioner endeavors to apply the altruistic principle throughout his or her life. This leads to what are known as the "bodhisattva ideals," including the "six perfections"—the perfections of generosity, morality, patience, enthusiasm, meditation or concentration, and wisdom. Of these six, the last two are perhaps the most important because it is in the context of the perfection of concentration and insight that the Vajrayana methods are introduced. We can consider the Vajrayana teachings as more refined methods for realizing the perfection of concentration and wisdom. The highest practice for perfecting these, from the Tibetan Buddhist point of view, is said to be the Highest Yoga Tantra (anuttarayoga tantra) where a detailed explanation of the subtle levels of consciousness can be found.

His Holiness the Dalai Lama, *Transforming the Mind*

S: Yes.

M: *Tantra is a form of practice along with the other disciplines. In* The Secret Oral Teachings *by Alexandra David-Néel, she described how the level of difficulty of the practice is ideally tailored to the unique capacity of the listener or student. The secret oral teachings were of the highest level.*

S: Yes, the highest intelligence.

M: *The highest level of teaching is saved for those who have the capacity to understand the most complicated teachings.*

S: That is the Buddhist way. Buddha never tried to be consistent. If you read the whole of the Buddhist teachings, there are so many contradictions, variations. *You should do this. You should not do this.* Somewhere he says, yes. Somewhere he says, no. All this must be understood in terms of the listener. To a particular listener he said, no, and to another he said, yes. Yes is for listener A, his capacity, and no is for listener B, his capacity. Both of them will have to go beyond yes and no. Only then can the real intention of Buddha be understood. But this is not the way of Krishnamurti. He always remains at his level. He never comes down to the level of the listener.

It Is So Damn Simple

M: *Krishnamurti speaks from his level and not at the level of the listener. At lunch one day he leaned over and said, "I have only said one thing my entire life but I have said it a thousand ways." He then said, "It is all so damn simple, so obvious, as concrete as this table."*

S: Simple for him but not for everybody.

M: *Krishnamurti insisted his teachings were not exclusive, only for a few. Anyone who listens carefully, simply, to what he is saying can understand. Many traditions reserve their more difficult teachings or concepts for those deemed capable of grasping them.*

S: Ultimately you have to understand Buddha's highest teaching. In order to understand the Buddhist highest teaching, we have to increase our capacity to that level. When we function at the level of our conditioning, we cannot understand. To increase our capacity for understanding, we need to go step by step. There is a path. There is a method. You do this first, this second, and get a little bit better. This involves *becoming*. There

Has truth an abiding place? Has truth a fixed point? Has truth an abode, or is truth a dynamic living thing, and therefore without a resting place? Truth is in constant movement; but if you say it is a fixed point, then you will have to find a guru who will lead you to it, and the guru becomes necessary as a pointer. That means that both you and the guru must know that truth is there, in a fixed place, like the station. Then you can ask the way.

Also, if you want truth and you go to a guru, you must know what truth is. When you go to a guru you do not say, "I want to discover reality"; on the contrary, you say, "Help me to realize truth." Therefore you already have an idea of what it is; you already know its content, its beauty, its loveliness, its fragrance. Do you know what it is? How can a confused man know clarity?

If you "think" about truth, surely it is the product of thought, and therefore it is not true; and if the guru can tell you what it is, then he is still within the field of thought, therefore what he tells you is not true. So when you go to the guru, obviously you are going for gratification.... In other words, when you go to the guru, you are not seeking the truth, you are seeking security at a different level, permanency at a different point. But is truth permanency?

Your speculations, your thoughts about truth, have no validity. Truth is not in the distance; truth is near, in what you are thinking and feeling, in your relationship with your family....

There is no path to truth. You cannot discover the path, because there is no path. Truth is a thing that is living, and to a living thing there is no path—it is only to dead things that there can be a path.

So you can make me into a guru if you wish, but it will be your misery, because there is no guru to truth, there is no leader to reality. That reality is an eternal being in the present, not in the future; it is in the immediate now, not in the ultimate tomorrow.

You cannot enforce stillness, you cannot make the mind still, you cannot force thought to stop. You must understand the process of thought and go beyond all thought; only then will truth liberate thought from its own process.

The Collected Works of J. Krishnamurti. Poona, India,
6th Public Talk, 3 October 1948 *(Abridged)*

is the danger that you may get caught in the method. In spite of this, in spite of all the challenges, you keep on trying to reach that highest level. That is the Buddhist way.

Ultimately There Is No Path

M: *There are two schools: the one you just described with paths, steps, gradually increasing capacity; and the other, called the direct path, the high road, that has none of this. Your teachings have both.*

S: Yes. They also say, why are you wasting your time with this gradual process? There is the possibility of an explosion. Bam! Finished.

M: *Krishnamurti seems to be of that tradition. He said, "Do it now, sir."*

S: Yes.

M: *He said that psychological transformation is only possible now. Gradual change, he said, is no change. As the saying goes, "It is now, this moment, or never." Alan W. Anderson, PhD, who shared eighteen hours of rare dialogue with Krishnamurti in the '70s, began the series with a quote: "It's the responsibility of each human being to bring about their own transformation that is not dependent on knowledge or time." Without knowledge or without time means without relative reality.*

S: Of course, ultimately there is no path.

M: *Buddhists have their Dharma.* Dharma *seems to mean "the teachings, the path, living in accordance with universal cosmic laws." Krishnamurti used the phrase "to live the teachings." Living something is quite different from reading and studying.*

S: Dharma has two categories. The first is *agama*, which means literally *the teacher*, the Buddha's words that have been recorded. And the second is *adhigama*, which is experiential. The real Dharma is experience. Whatever you experience of the Buddha's teachings is the real antidote for ignorance. Experience is the real medicine, the real Dharma. So Dharma is the combination of these two. The experiential category includes your mental activity, hearing, contemplation, meditation. Then finally comes realization. Realization, the experience, is the real Dharma.

M: *We discussed how few people move from idea to experience. They study the map their whole life and never take the journey.*

K: K's teachings are a living thing, and the books, I am afraid, are not; no book is. When K dies, what is going to happen to the teachings? Are there people who have, if I may use the phrase, drunk at the fountain, and can carry on from there? Not merely quoting K but getting the spirit of it, the vitality of it, the energy of it?

Because for the last fifty-two years, one has talked a great deal about all these things, and I find—I hope you will forgive me for saying this—there is not one person who has seen that thing for himself and goes on with it…

EL: People for all these years have been looking to this one man, and the teaching of the one man.

K: Which is so fatal… People will say to you, "You've known him more than anyone else." They will ask you, "Are you living it; have you imbibed it?" If I were an outsider I'd say, "Well, you've known him for fifteen, twenty, thirty years, what the heck, have you gotten something, or are you just passing the buck?" If you have not, what shall we do?

Say I haven't been able to hear the Buddha, but I have heard about him, people have talked about him, and I am extraordinarily interested in what he has to say. And you have known him for years, so I will travel any distance because I am really interested to see what you have felt about him, what he said, how much you have imbibed, how much you have learnt. I come to you and you say, "Sorry, we're not of one mind, we don't want to represent him…"

DB: You are asking us here to be responsible for communicating this spirit that has come from the fountain. In other words, not merely to communicate the words. But I think I see a certain reluctance, a hesitation, from all of us here to say that we have actually got something from this fountain…

K: Have you got something of it? You as a group, or you as an individual, tell me. I'm tremendously concerned, interested. I might catch something from you. But if you say, "Sorry, we've spent our life in organizations, buildings," I'll say, "For God's sake…"

DB: It seems to me that a new purpose is required now, considering what will happen when Krishnaji is no longer here. The Foundations must assume a new purpose beyond what they have been doing.

K: I feel passionately responsible for this; what am I to do to prevent a circus happening from other people, stronger people? So that the thing doesn't wither, is not corrupted by some crook in the name of God, in the name of truth, in the name of peace, in the name of love of K, and so on? What am I to do? Now, not eventually in ten years' time when I am dead?

J. Krishnamurti, *The Perfume of the Teachings, A Dialogue with Trustees*, 1997 *(Abridged)*

S: Yes. Most study the map, talking about the roads, which is easier, which more difficult, but never start walking. That is the problem.

M: *And it seems universal.*

S: Not only for Buddhists, this applies to all other spiritual traditions. Of course there are many exceptions but as a whole this is true. And not only talking about the map, there is possessiveness, division, conflict. My Dharma is the best. My Dharma is in danger. I should die for it. As far as Buddhists are concerned, there can never be a danger to Dharma because Dharma resides in your mind, not in your property. Your books may be destroyed, burned, but your insight can never be taken away or destroyed unless you yourself destroy it. No outside enemy can destroy your insight, your wisdom. It is like a jewel that cannot be stolen. The huge monasteries can be destroyed. The symbols and statues can be destroyed, but that is not the destruction of Dharma.

Identity, Name, and Fame

M: *Similar observations have been made by Krishnamurti in his so-called teachings. To him, the teachings meant life. They are not in the books or videos. The teachings, he said, are living. In* The Opening of the Wisdom-Eye, *His Holiness noted, "One will not suffer in one's heart as long as one is not attached to name and fame."*

S: That's right.

M: *This touches again on our identity, name and fame being false. In order to not be affected by name and fame, one has to go beyond or not believe in a false identity. There's no transformation without a transformation of identity. That is my proposal.*

S: In the Tibetan tradition there are three things to which people are attached: food, clothes, and a name. Detaching from food and wealth, material things, clothes, is not so difficult compared to a name. People may completely renounce all their worldly possessions and still remain worried about their name and fame. Therefore they are unable to transcend attachment to their identity. I would say, from a Buddhist viewpoint, identity is the ego. Identity is ignorance. You cannot transform identity. To transform identity would mean that you are looking for a different kind of identity. You have to eliminate, destroy, the identity.

To me, the ego, that limited consciousness, is the result of conflict. Inherently it has no value; it is an illusion. It comes into being through lack of understanding, which in turn creates conflict, and out of this conflict grows self-consciousness or limited consciousness. You cannot perfect that self-consciousness through time; time does not free the mind from that consciousness. Please make no mistake; time will not free you from this self-consciousness, because time is merely postponement of understanding. The further you postpone an action, the less you understand it.

Whether you believe in reincarnation or not seems to me a very trivial matter; that belief is like a toy, it is pleasant; it does not solve a thing, because it is merely a postponement. It is merely an explanation, and explanations are as dust to the man who is seeking. But unfortunately you are choked with dust, you have explanations for everything. For every suffering you have a logical, suitable explanation. If a man is blind, you account for his hard lot in this life by means of reincarnation. Inequalities in life you explain away by reincarnation, by the idea of evolution. So with explanations, you have settled the many questions concerning man, and you have ceased to live.

The Collected Works of J. Krishnamurti.
Adyar, India, 6th Public Talk, 3 January 1934

The ego cannot be transformed. It has to be eradicated. Consciousness is transformed from seeking identity to not seeking identity, from being attached to an identity to not being attached. That is transformation of the person, not transformation of the identity.

Brain-Mind, Reincarnation, Past Lives

M: *Let's touch again on the notion that the mind is not in the brain. Reincarnation makes no sense if the mind is emergent from the brain. His Holiness, in his early writings, describes that the existence of past lives has been confirmed by those practicing* samadhi, *deep meditation. Some meditators of wide experience have recalled, even in great detail, many previous lives. This is a personal question. You must have meditated. You have been through some of these experiences or you know other people who have. Can you describe any personal experiences that you have had or people that you know have had that confirmed past lives?*

S: I recently received a scientific paper stating that consciousness is much bigger than the brain and the body. Personally, no, I have not remembered a past life. I had no time to meditate to look into my past lives. But I was told by my parents and my childhood teacher that I did have some remembrance of my past life. My teacher scolded me several times for forgetting scripture, the teachings of the Dharma, but I remember my horses and my dogs. I know many people who have remembered past lives and have been recognized as a reincarnation, but of course they do not share it with everybody. And apart from that, this happens not only in the Buddhist field. A girl somewhere in Agra remembered her past life. She insisted on going to a street where she named everybody. Today scientists study remote memory and easily go to past lives. They are able to find out where a trauma started. The basic argument of having a past life or not in Buddhist terms is to understand the beginningless and endless continuum of consciousness.

M: *Reincarnation and past lives brings up the relative nature of time. Interdependent origination, creation, is always happening. It never stops.*

S: Yes, it's always flowing.

M: *Krishnamurti used the phrase, "Reincarnate now."*

S: Yes.

Nechung: The State Oracle of Tibet

Like many ancient civilizations of the world, the phenomenon of oracles remains an important part of the Tibetan way of life. Tibetans rely on oracles for various reasons. The purpose of the oracles is not just to foretell the future. They are called upon as protectors and sometimes used as healers. However, their primary function is to protect the Buddha Dharma and its practitioners.

In the Tibetan tradition, the word oracle is used for a spirit which enters those men and women who act as mediums between the natural and the spiritual realms. The mediums are, therefore, known as kuten, which literally means "the physical basis."

In early times it is believed that there were hundreds of oracles throughout Tibet. Today, only a few survive, including those consulted by the Tibetan government. Of these, the principal one is the Nechung Oracle. Through him manifests Dorje Drak-den (Nechung), the principal protector divinity of the Tibetan government and the Dalai Lama. It is because of this that Nechung Kuten is given the rank of a deputy minister in the exiled Tibetan government hierarchy.

In his autobiography, *Freedom in Exile*, His Holiness the Dalai Lama writes:

"For hundreds of years now, it has been traditional for the Dalai Lama, and the Government, to consult Nechung during the New Year festivals. In addition, he might well be called upon at other times if either have specific queries. I myself have dealings with him several times a year. This may sound far-fetched to twentieth-century western readers. Even some Tibetans, mostly those who consider themselves 'progressive,' have misgivings about my continued use of this ancient method of intelligence gathering.

"But I do so for the simple reason that as I look back over the many occasions when I have asked questions of the oracle, on each one of them time has proved that his answer was correct. This is not to say that I rely solely on the oracle's advice. I do not. I seek his opinion in the same way as I seek the opinion of my Cabinet and just as I seek the opinion of my own conscience. I consider the gods to be my 'upper house,' The Kashag constitutes my lower house. Like any other leader, I consult both before making a decision on affairs of state. And sometimes, in addition to Nechung's counsel, I also take into consideration certain prophecies.

"Dealing with Nechung is by no means easy. It takes time and patience during each encounter before he will open up. He is very reserved and austere, just as you would imagine a grand old man of ancient times to be. Nor does he bother with minor matters: his interest is only in the larger issues, so it pays to frame questions accordingly. He also has definite likes and dislikes, but he does not show them very readily."

From the Government of Tibet in Exile Website

M: *Are we not all reincarnating now? Every second there is a birth and death. Isn't it possible to reframe or redefine the concept of past lives because the last second was a past life?*

S: Buddhist logic is so subtle. The language used to describe spiritual matters must be very precise. Care must be taken to use the correct word, the meaning of which everyone agrees on. If asked in a real sense, being very precise, a Buddhist would say no one is reincarnated. An incarnation cannot be reincarnated. Once it is born, it is already past and cannot be reborn. So the expression *reborn* is not the correct expression. The past life, the present life, the future life — the future life is not the rebirth of the past life. The future life is freshly born, so it is not repeating. It is always fresh. In that way, each moment, the very smallest, subtle moment is passing away, creating anew, passing away. The principle of impermanence is always there. Consciousness is not static. It is always moving. So this morning, talking with you is dead and this moment is fresh. The next moment is fresh. Consciousness is a moment-by-moment transition in continuum. You can remember a hundred years past because there is continuity. In our usual language however, there is rebirth and reincarnation. This is the Buddhist way to look at it.

M: *Krishnamurti talked about life, death, and love being one simultaneous movement, not even two sides of the same coin. You can't have one without the other. Our consciousness is reincarnating moment to moment. This always-changing creation is implicit in Krishnamurti's teachings, and most clearly in his statement, "There is no psychological becoming."*

S: Each moment we are dying, each moment we are born. This is it, yes.

Mediums, Oracles, and Celestial Realms

M: *I was reading the Dalai Lama's biography where he described his childhood before the Chinese invasion. Things were grim. He consulted the High Lamas and the Oracles. I've never heard of Tibetan Oracles. There were Greek Oracles. I am somewhat familiar with Shamanic traditions, but not Oracles in this context. Later, reading the Dalai Lama's first western publication,* The Opening of the Wisdom-Eye, *he described honoring transcendent Masters and made reference to celestial realms. All of this seems mixed together in a harmonious way in your culture. I presume Tibet's isolation allowed remnants of the oracle tradition, pre-Buddhist traditions, and Buddhism to co-exist. Do they co-exist today?*

Top left and right: KahYah Elias; Above: Courtesy of Tibet Group Tour

S: We have to be careful. Similar words are used by many different traditions. We have to understand a word as it is used by one particular tradition. That is important. The pre-Buddhist religion in Tibet was Bon. In the past, the Bon religion was not well studied by Western scholars, so it was generally classified in the Shamanic tradition, but I do not think this is accurate. The present Bon religion is in name only. The entire content is Buddhist. Bon is only the bottle; the wine inside the bottle is Buddhist. They have borrowed Buddhist metaphysics, Buddhist philosophy, and Buddhist tantra. And at the same time, whatever was suitable, they maintained, and whatever was not, they gave up. Now nobody knows exactly what Bon was before Buddhism. The Bon tradition is oral. Before Buddhism reached Tibet, Tibet did not have a script or written language. We do not have recorded teachings of the pre-Buddhist religion. The so-called pre-Buddhist religions were recorded post-Buddhism. Therefore it is very difficult to say what they were.

M: *It was said there was great skepticism about putting sacred meanings into writing, that the truth being shared orally would be lost if written.*

S: It was a fact. There was a great deal of resistance from the Bon tradition to the spread of Buddhism. A number of kings were assassinated by the Bon to stop the spread of Buddhism. Many people were killed and tortured. But they did not succeed. At the same time, Buddhists, being nonviolent, never tried to wipe out or completely do away with pre-Buddhist traditions. That is why the Bon co-exist in parallel with Buddhism today.

Coming to the Oracle, which is maintained by both the Bon tradition and Buddhism, it is the same only in name. Actually, they are quite different. During the Bon period, a dead person is called back and inhabits a medium. For example, one month after my father died I went to a Bon priest and explained that I had lost my father and wanted to know where he had hidden our property, jewelry, and money. I asked the priest to contact the soul or the spirit of my dead father to tell me where the treasure was hidden. At that time, the Bon priests used a medium to call back the dead person.

What Buddhists mean by *the Oracle* is quite different. In Buddhism there are so many protectors of Dharma. Dharma protectors are not beyond the world. They are in a kind of spirit realm within the worldly status.

ALWAYS AWAKENING

Scattered throughout the sutras are references to as many as thirty-one distinct "planes" or "realms" of existence into which beings can be reborn during their long wandering through samsara, the cycle or wheel of birth, death and rebirth, and these are most often represented by six.

1. Realm of Devas (Gods) and Heavenly Beings: godlike beings who enjoy great power, wealth and long life
2. Realm of Asura (Titans) governed by hate and jealousy
3. Realm of Hungry Ghosts: insatiable hunger and craving, addiction, obsession and compulsion
4. The Hell Realm: unchecked anger and aggression
5. The Animal Realm: marked by stupidity, prejudice and complacency
6. The Human Realm: the only realm in which beings may escape samsara

They are in the realm of goddesses. They have some clairvoyance and can look back and look ahead thousands of years, and they know many things. Their responsibility is to protect the monasteries and the teachings of Dharma, and therefore they are called *Dharma protectors*. They can be called into the body of a medium, who then becomes unconscious. All the sensory organs of the medium's body are temporally hired by that spirit, because the spirit cannot contact the worldly realm directly, so through the medium, we can ask for answers to our problems.

M: *Do the High Lamas and the State Oracle still exist?*

S: Yes, it is still here. I think the State Oracle did a good job, otherwise His Holiness may not have escaped. The uprising was the tenth of March. From the tenth to the seventeenth of March, each day the State Oracle would go into a trance. All the advisors knew that we could not protect His Holiness unless he escaped, but the State Oracle continued to say, no. His Holiness will not go. He will stay. And many people lost faith in the Oracle because it was very insistent. This secret information leaked to the Chinese spies and they thought he would never leave because the Oracle said so. On the morning of the seventeenth, the Oracle said His Holiness must go, this is the way, around the people, this night. And that is how the Dalai Lama escaped.

M: *This blending of traditions rest upon the concept that there are aspects of mind that are not in the brain. The brain translates fields of meaning that are not in the brain, in a way similar to a television converting a broadcast signal into a physical image on the screen. What is being imaged is not in the tubes or transistors. Without that concept, none of these things would happen.*

S: Yes, that's right.

M: *All cultures had this blending, honoring, listening to the ancestors. Then it got wiped away by the Western material clockwork mentality. Another thing that caught my attention was His Holiness's reference to* celestial realms.

S: *Celestial* is translated in many different ways. Some English translations say *higher status*. In Sanskrit it is *abhyudaya*, which is translated literally in the Tibetan language as *abhi* is *ngon*, *udaya* is *tho*. One refers to the realm of human beings and the other, the realm of goddesses. Buddhists believe there are six realms in which people are reborn. Hell, the realm of hungry ghosts and animals, is the lower status or bad realm. The three higher realms are called *celestial*; there you find human beings.

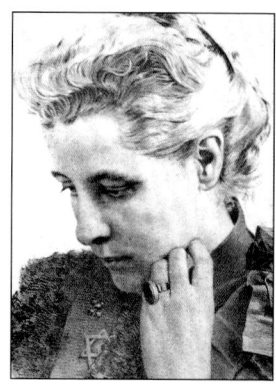

Annie Besant

The first great Aryan people, there they had as the World-Teacher the great One known under the name of Vyasa, and He taught the one truth by the figure and the symbol of the Sun.

Then when He came to the second sub-race, and taught in Egypt under a different name, the name of Thoth whom the Greeks called Hermes, there He took the Light as symbol.

Then He came to the third sub-race, to the Iranians, and He came then under the name of Zarathustra, better known as Zoroaster, and there the Fire was the symbol by which the same great truth was taught.

Then a fourth time He came to the fourth sub-race, the Greeks, now as Orpheus; but He no longer spoke in Light but in Music, and by the mysteries of Sound he taught the unfolding of the Spirit in man.

Then that Mighty One returned to earth but once more, to become the Lord Buddha, and to found the religion that still outnumbers any other faith on earth. And then He passed away, never again to take a mortal form, and handed on the duty of the world-teaching to His Brother, who had come side by side with Him through many ages, to Him who is the World-Teacher of today, the great Lord Maitreya, whom Christendom calls the Christ.

If, during five sub-races, ever the Teacher has appeared to teach and help, shall the one that is now being born be alone left without a Teacher? Shall the World-Teacher refuse to come, as He has come in every similar case before?

Oh, would you and I recognize such a teacher, if He came in the London of today instead of in the Jerusalem of 2,000 years ago?... If it be so amongst some of us, enough of us to influence the public opinion of our time, then when the Lord of Love comes again, it shall not be a Cross that will meet Him....

> Annie Besant, "The Immediate Future, The Coming of a World Teacher," Queen's Hall, London, 1911 *(Abridged)*

The second are with gods and goddesses. And the third are called *demigods*, beings that have achieved certain meditative concentration and then have taken a birth in which they maintain the state of meditation throughout that life. They are not visible to human beings, but can, by their own will, become visible if needed.

M: *The Oracles exist in one of these celestial realms. Normal human consciousness is in another realm. The medium is a doorway or window between these different realms.*

S: Yes, in this case between the Dharma protector and human beings.

M: *Where transmissions occur.*

The Theosophists' Idea of a Vehicle

S: That's right. This concept is similar to the Theosophists' idea of a *vehicle*. Krishnamurti said there was a tremendous energy using his body, a tremendous intelligence passing through his brain. These are parallel.

M: *Your tradition has a structure for understanding what was taking place in Krishnamurti.*

S: For us it's not difficult to understand. For us it is not a belief. We have the direct perception of how energy comes into the medium and how difficult it is for them. Sometimes they are not able to communicate. There is a lot of pain and suffering. To use a medium requires a great deal of preparation. But these mediums are very ordinary. An Oracle uses their body only for an hour or a half-hour to make a few communications and then it goes away. But what Krishnamurti did was permanent, lifelong. He represented a much higher quality window.

M: *The period from 1922 until 1926 was a very important window when something similar began to happen in Krishnamurti's life, now called* the process.

S: Yes, that's right.

M: *Drawing from your tradition, the leaders of the Theosophical Society, dating back to the late 1800s, used the idea of a medium, something they called* a vehicle, *to describe what was about to happen, that the Maitreya, the future Buddha, would take a human body and teach. After* the process *began, Krishnamurti insisted that he was not a medium. "There is a blending," he said. This refers to the much higher quality window you just described. With a medium, the blending of consciousness is transient. With Krishnamurti it was permanent, lifelong.*

This has been really a question that's been asked over and over again all over the world, in India, in the West, here and so on. Has suffering changed man?

I am not being personal, sir, but you have heard all this. You, as a human being, have been through a great deal of anxieties, suffering insecurity and confusion. Why don't you change? What prevents you? If each one of us asked that question, not verbally or merely intellectually as an entertainment, but asked that question most seriously and deeply, what is your answer? What's your answer to this problem that human beings have lived this way for millennia upon millennia—why haven't they changed?

Why haven't you who are listening now, why haven't you changed? You know if you don't change, what the consequences are. You will be national, nationalistic, you will be tribal, insular, isolated and therefore having no relationship globally—fighting, fighting, fighting, building up more and more armaments to destroy each other.

Why don't you ask yourself that question? Why am I, a human being, who have been through all this, why haven't I changed? What would be your answer? Either you're not serious—you want to live a very superficial life, and that superficiality temporarily satisfies you—or you really don't care. As long as you have immediate pleasures, immediate satisfactions, you really don't care. You don't care for your children if they're murdered. You really have no deep love, affection for them. If you had, you would prevent all wars. So apparently, none of these things mean anything to you. Or probably you're so deeply conditioned psychologically and one is not aware of it. Unless there is freedom from that conditioning, you will go on this way. Now, why don't you change?

J. Krishnamurti, Interview with Michael Mendizza

J. Krishnamurti in Indian dress, Castle Eerde

This caused a great challenge to the beliefs held by the Theosophists. They thought it was presumptuous for Krishnamurti to say he was not a medium but something much more.

S: A different perception, because the members of the Theosophical Society could not understand exactly the intentions of the Masters.

M: *I'm glad you mentioned the intentions of the Masters. Masters are beings in this celestial realm.*

S: Yes.

M: *They exist in this other dimension.*

S: They're not non-existent but they don't exist for ordinary people.

M: *That's a great way of describing this. I was reading about* Shambhala. *Shambhala is a hidden kingdom whose reality is visionary or spiritual as much as physical or geographic. Shambhala is not visible to ordinary people. Shambhala's existence isn't dependent on itself; it is dependent on who is looking. It is the same with the Masters. What good is it for one who perceives the absolute directly to communicate to somebody who has not? They can't hear it. It can't be done. We discussed that when Buddha became realized, he said the same thing. Why bother?*

S: Yes, he would keep quiet.

M: *And yet Krishnamurti and Buddha, along with others, try. What could they do differently than what they have done? Krishnamurti was as clear as anybody could be about what he was saying. He was very precise.*

S: Sometimes he became impatient. "Why can't you see it?"

M: *He asked this question of Bohm: "What else can I do?" What is it that prevents us from being able to hear? That is one question. The other is, what else could they have done to bridge this gap?*

S: As we discussed earlier, use symbols, metaphors, and negation. I will tell you a story. In the Lalitvistara Sutra, Siddhartha Gautama became Buddha. He saw the ultimate truth. He ended his ignorance and became liberated, and he wanted to communicate it but he saw he would not be able to verbalize it. No one would understand. Then he thought, "I will remain in silence." One week passed. Two weeks passed. The third week passed. Brahma and Indra in the celestial world became worried. "Siddhartha is enlightened, but he is not teaching. We must go and ask him to preach." Both of them went to Buddha. Brahma offered him the

With His Holiness the Dalai Lama and Sikyong Dr. Lobsang Sangye, Theckchen Choeling, 2011

Threefold Training (Trisiksa)

By the practice of collectedness taught in the Buddhadharma, one may experience the supermundane bliss of Nirvana. For this reason, the collectedness taught by Lord Buddha cannot be labeled "ordinary" but is said to be "special" or "supreme." The samadhi taught by outsiders only has the effect of calming the mind, preventing its disturbance by sense-objects, hence leading to happiness here and at most to arising as a god (deva) in the celestial realms of form or formlessness (rupapabhumi), which is one of the six divisions of the wandering-on. As it does not destroy the stains of the mind and its evil imaginings (since only calm [Samatha] is developed without vipaSyana or insight), so these samadhi of outsiders cannot be called "supreme."

Thus, worldly collectedness is that which has worldly objects and produces a worldly result, that of calm and happiness in this life and for the next, gives rise to a celestial birth (the experience of "heaven," "paradise," etc). Unworldly or transcendental means that this sort of samadhi is aimed at freedom, its objects being essence-lessness and not-self-soulness (nihsvabhavata, anatmata). In order to achieve worldly and transcendental absorptions, one should first develop calm and insight (samatha-vipaSyana). Although at first one may seem to develop these aspects of samadhi separately, finally one must develop the collectedness in which they are yoked together.

His Holiness the Dalai Lama, The Opening of the Wisdom-Eye

golden chakra and Indra gave him a conch shell, and they asked the Buddha to preach. Buddha told Brahma, "What I have perceived is beyond words, beyond thought. How shall I communicate because our instrument is only the word and the word is the product of thought? This will not be adequate to communicate." Brahma said, "Yes, my Lord, I understand. But you can use metaphors, similarities. This is one way. And you can use symbols. And you can use negation—'this is not the truth, that is not the truth.' You cannot describe the truth directly, but using these three ways you can accomplish a great deal."

The Most Effective Is Negation

M: *This is exactly what Krishnamurti did too.*

S: Symbols and metaphors are used many times but the most effective is negation. If you can negate what you are grasping, that means opening the window. Krishnamurti used metaphor, he used symbols, but the most effective weapon was negation. "Jealousy is not love. Lust is not love. Attachment is not love." When you negate everything that is not love, love is there.

M: *Let's return to the Dalai Lama and* The Opening of the Wisdom-Eye. *He describes* three-fold training.

S: Yes.

M: *The quality of training used in your tradition he calls* supreme, superior. *He said the methods used by others are limited. Yours are not. "Samadhi taught by outsiders only effects the calming of the mind, preventing its disturbances by sense objects, hence leading to happiness and the celestial realms and so on." What is the difference between outsider practices and the special or supreme practices found in your tradition?*

S: There is an ancient Indian technical word that describes this: *Adhisheel-adhisamadhi-adhipragya*. The *adhi* is special or superior. Why is Buddhist meditation superior? Why is Buddhist moral conduct superior? Why is Buddhist insight superior? Because it negates the ego. Whatever practice is done by the ego implies a practitioner; there is a practice and there is a goal. These three things are all good, but will not take you beyond. You remain in the same realm. If you do a moral act without the ego, without the doer, then it becomes real morality. Otherwise, whatever practice

To see clearly what is at any time needs the attention of all energy; and in this there is no contradiction or duality. This total energy does not come about through abstinence, through the vows of chastity and poverty, for all determination and action of will is a waste of energy because thought is involved in it, and thought is wasted energy: perception never is. The seeing is not a determined effort. There is no "I will see," but only seeing. Observation puts aside the observer, and in this there is no waste of energy. The thinker who attempts to observe, spoils energy. Love is not wasted energy, but when thought makes it into pleasure, then pain dissipates energy. The summation of energy, of meditation, is ever expanding, and action in daily life becomes part of it.

J. Krishnamurti, *The Only Revolution*

you do adds to your conditioning. You are conditioned by immorality and you are conditioned to be moral. Both are conditioning because the ego, the "me", the image, is there.

M: *Yes, completely.*

S: And similarly, if you've achieved a concentrative or analytical mind and you still have the ego and your ego uses this, then you will convert *samadhi*, the concentrative mind, into conditioning, not into freedom. The wisdom adds to your conditioning. Negating the ego changes this. That is why His Holiness describes our practices as *superior*.

M: *Most of Krishnamurti's discourse in his early years, what he called self-preparation, negated the ego. This began in 1922 with the beginning of the process.*

S: That's right.

M: *This focus on negating the ego continued for the rest of his life but it was very intense through the years 1924 to 1927.*

S: Yes.

M: *The essence of self-preparation was to get rid of the ego. If we don't get rid of the ego, there may be a great deal of activity but nothing really changes. Ending the ego is the beginning of something real. This is similar to what you just described. Virtue with an ego is one thing. Virtue without an ego is completely different.*

S: Your act of killing is done with the ego, and the act of refraining from killing, not killing, is done with the aid of the ego. One is negative. One is positive. But the positive is not the supreme positive. It is still contaminated by the presence of the ego.

Wisdom Cannot Be Achieved by a Partial Mind

M: *You described various forms of meditation, practices, and methods. Krishnamurti said many times that repeating methods dulls the mind. Methods used to awaken the mind instead dull the mind. He also said that thought is dead, is the past. Books are dead. They are not living, moving. Truth is moving, living. He said that one needs to be extremely sensitive, have tremendous energy. Do the meditations in your tradition bring about this energy and clarity, this lack of dullness?*

I am not all the time measuring myself or others. This freedom from measurement comes about when you are really living with what is—neither wishing to change it nor judging it in terms of good and bad. Living with something is not the acceptance of it: it is there whether you accept it or not. Living with something is not identifying yourself with it either.

Total negation is that freedom. To negate everything we consider to be positive, to negate the total social morality, to negate all inward acceptance of authority, to negate everything one has said or concluded about reality, to negate all tradition, all teaching, all knowledge except technological knowledge, to negate all experience, to negate all the drives which stem from remembered or forgotten pleasures, to negate all fulfilment, to negate all commitments to act in a particular way, to negate all ideas, all principles, all theories—such negation is the most positive action, therefore it is freedom.

It is only when there is emptiness in oneself, not the emptiness of a shallow mind but the emptiness that comes with the total negation of everything one has been and should be and will be—it is only in this emptiness that there is creation; it is only in this emptiness that something new can take place. Fear is the thought of the unknown, so you are really frightened of leaving the known, the attachments, the satisfactions, the pleasurable memories, the continuity and security which give comfort. Thought is comparing this with what it thinks is emptiness. This imagination of emptiness is fear, so fear is thought. Can the mind negate everything it has known, the total content of its own conscious and unconscious self, which is the very essence of yourself? Can you negate yourself completely? If not, there is no freedom. Freedom is not freedom from something—that is only a reaction. Freedom comes in total denial.

J. Krishnamurti, *The Urgency of Change:* "Conditioning" *(Abridged)*

S: Since you have read *The Opening of the Wisdom-Eye*, you are familiar with the three-fold training, which encompasses the entire process of the Buddhist tradition, how to attain enlightenment, how to be liberated. Liberation is freedom from ignorance, which can be achieved if you have wisdom, superior wisdom, *adhipragya*. Superior wisdom cannot be achieved by a partial, fragmented, or distracted mind. Therefore, in order to gain wisdom you need *samadhi*, the concentrative and analytical mind, one-pointed concentration with attention. Krishnamurti distinguished between concentration and attention. We also differentiate between them.

Concentration with attention is the highest level or quality. When mixed, they bring out the entire capacity of the mind. Normally we only use a very small segment of the mind. Even modern scientists say we do not use the complete capacity of the human brain. This is similar. There are two kinds of meditation: one is *shamatha* and the other is *vipashyana*. *Shamatha* means the capacity to give attention without distraction, complete fully concentrated attention on one object for a period of one-fourth of a day (about four hours). Then you are at the beginning of achieving concentrative meditation, which has two obstacles: sinking and scattering. *Scattering* means your thought processes come and go. And *sinking* means you are concentrating but without clarity and energy. There is no force. You become drowsy.

M: *One can be concentrating but without attention, without energy.*

S: Yes, without energy. You are scattering.

M: *There may be focus but you're dull.*

S: Yes, basically dull. In India and Tibet, many people thought sinking was concentration and they became duller and duller and sometimes less intelligent. So that is the greatest obstacle, the wrong way. Meditators spend a lifetime cultivating dullness and waste their lives. When you achieve steady, clear concentration, you use it for analyzing without scattering, without losing concentration and attention. We do contemplative meditation within that state of concentration. By this practice you achieve two things: a quality of mind and a quality of body. First you feel a pleasurable sensation in the body. It is not in the category of good hearing or good seeing but the body is in soothing, deep peace, no stress from conflict. That soothing feeling in the body disappears and soothing

Is it possible to remove this conflict between the censor and the thing that is censored? That is really a very important question if you ask yourself, because that removes all conflict, all contradiction. A mind in contradiction, in conflict, is a wasting mind, is a deteriorating mind; every problem which is given time, deteriorates the mind unless the problem is solved immediately, instantly. And the problem which we are talking about is very important, because that is the center from which all problems arise.

Is it possible to think, to feel, to act, to do everything that we do, without the center? The things that we do, and the misery, the chaos, the confusion, the sorrow, the extraordinary despair that we have—will they exist if there is no center, if there is no entity that is committing itself and acting from a thing that has become merely a bundle of memory and which has assumed such importance? Surely, there is only thinking, and not a center which thinks. But thought has created the center.

This may sound extravagant and absurd. But if you have gone into the question of thought, into the question of idea, and as you cannot live without action, you ask, "Is it possible to live without an idea, without a word, but only with action?' It is only when the mechanism of thought is understood, that there is action which is not an approximation. Surely, if you think about this yourself, you will see what an extraordinary thing it is.

Thought creates all the divisions that exist in life—godly love, human love, and all the rest of it. Is not the quality of the mind that has complete leisure that has come into being through understanding, through observing, quietness, a sense of silence? For me, this whole process of investigation into oneself is meditation. Meditation is not the repetition of words and formulas, mesmerizing oneself into all kinds of fanciful states.

Meditation is actually this process of investigation into oneself. If you go into it deeply yourself, you are bound to come across all this, when it is possible to think without the center, to see without the center, to act so completely without idea and approximation, to love without the center.

The Collected Works of J. Krishnamurti. Varanasi, India,
6th Public Talk, 12 January 1962 *(Abridged)*

comes to the mind. In the third stage, awareness of the body and mind disappear, leaving only concentration. Then you can use the mind as a precise tool. You can concentrate on one point for weeks without sinking or scattering. The mind is at your will. If you want to meditate for ten hours, there will be no disturbance, no feeling of aches, thirst or hunger. The body and mind will do exactly what you want. That mind/body is able to achieve wisdom. This is how three-fold training is interdependent. If your meditative practice is not in the right direction, your meditation becomes yet another form of bondage and conditioning.

Complete Attention Without a Center

M: *Krishnamurti make a distinction between concentration and attention.*

S: Yes.

M: *Concentration is like drilling a hole is the metaphor he used. Choiceless awareness is not concentration. It has intensity, complete attention, but not on an object.*

S: Yes.

M: *No object. There's no boundary. What's the different between the practice you just described and choiceless awareness?*

S: The last step is without the object. In the beginning when we practice concentration and attention, we need an object. Then we go beyond the object, and it gets real. If you put your mind on an object and concentrate, it can stay like a mountain without shaking. And if you use the mind all pervasively, it is like the sky, no boundary, nothing, no images, limitless, but full energy is there. The mind is not dull.

M: *In the beginning you use the object like a tool.*

S: That's right.

M: *When you take away the object, the energy, intensity, remains, vast like the sky.*

S: Yes, empty like the sky.

M: *In 1968, the first time Krishnamurti allowed his talks to be filmed in California, he said, "Because you're serious, because you are intent, then you are aware of the whole process of the observer, which means that you're totally attentive, completely attentive. In that attention, there is no border created by a center. When there is complete attention, there is no observer." That last line I*

If the whole of life is a movement, a flux, then how can it be watched unless there is a watcher? Now we are conditioned to believe, and we feel we know, that there is a watcher as well as a movement, a process, so we think we are separate from the process. To most of us there is the thinker and the thought, the experiencer and the experience. For us that is so; we accept it as a matter of fact. But is it so? Is there a thinker, an observer, a watcher, apart from thought, apart from thinking, apart from experience? Is there a thinker, a center, without thought? If you remove thought, is there a center? If you have no thought at all, no struggle, no urge to acquire, no effort to become something, is there a center? Or is the center created by thought, which feels itself to be insecure, impermanent, in a state of flux? If you observe, you will find that it is the thought process that has created the center, which is still within the field of thinking. And is it possible— this is the point—to watch, to be aware of this process, without the watcher?

Can the mind be aware of itself in action, in movement, without a center? I think it can. It is possible when there is only an awareness of thinking, and not the thinker who is thinking. You know, it is quite an experience to realize that there is only thinking. And it is very difficult to experience that, because the thinker is habitually there, evaluating, judging, condemning, comparing, identifying. If the thinker ceases to identify, evaluate, judge, then there is only thinking without the center.

What is the center? The center is the "me"—the "me" that wants to be a great person, that has so many conclusions, fears, motives. From that center we think, but that center has been created by the reaction of thinking. So can the mind be aware of thinking without the center—just observe it? You will find how extraordinarily difficult it is just to look at a flower without naming it, without comparing it with other flowers, without evaluating it out of like or dislike. Experiment with this and you will see how really difficult it is to observe something without bringing in all your prejudices, all your emotions and evaluations. But however difficult, you will find that the mind can be aware of itself without the center watching the movement of the mind.

The Collected Works of J. Krishnamurti.
Stockholm, Sweden, 3rd Public Talk, 21 May 1956

have always loved. It's such a simple key to understanding everything he says. "The observer comes into being only when in that looking there is inattention, which is a distraction." He goes on, "We have put away the observer. Therefore, there is complete attention, which may last a second. That's good enough. Don't be greedy to have more. In that greed to have more you have already created the center and then you are trapped." Is there a parallel in your tradition to that statement? With complete attention, there's no observer?

S: Yes, of course there are references, but our language is entirely different. We are talking about meditation with duality and meditation without duality. As long as the meditator, the meditation, and the object of meditation are all there, the mind is caught in fragmentation. That meditation is in duality. When all three disappear, there is no center, no meditation, no object without distractions, no drowsiness, without the hindrances of thought, then the observer and the observed are transcended. They become equal. There is no separation, no division or fragmentation. That is non-duality.

M: *Krishnamurti does not call meditation with duality meditation. In his world, meditation is only when the observer is the observed.*

S: In order to eliminate ignorance, you must reach the state of non-dual meditation. This is quite similar to Krishnamurti's *choiceless awareness*.

M: *The observer is the ignorance.*

S: Yes.

M: *Of course.*

S: We do not say, "This is not meditation." We simply say this will not eliminate ignorance. This is not the antidote to ignorance. We say you are trying to reach the antidote to ignorance.

M: *To see that the observer is ignorance is like the light switch we described. It is on, with a center, the observer, and the duality of ignorance is there or it's not, moment by moment.*

S: Very simple.

M: *Again, His Holiness in* The Opening of the Wisdom-Eye *talked about the four formless accomplishments. I assume this is non-duality. He says, "All Dharmas are like infinite space.... Consciousness is like the infinity of space."*

S: The four forms and the four formless accomplishments exist in very deep meditative states but all of them remain in duality. They are not

> Perceptions can emanate from the body, the brain, and those the brain cannot reach. The source may be anywhere.
>
> Samdhong Rinpoche

During World War II the British employed two mathematical savants who served essentially as computers. They were, so far as is known, infallible. One mathematical savant was shown a checkerboard with a grain of rice on the first of its sixty-four squares and asked how many grains there would be on the final square were they doubled at each one. The answer took the savant forty-five seconds to deliver, since that answer is a number greater than our estimate of the atoms in the sun. My mathematical friends tell me the answer is 1.8447×1019, or 18,447,000,000,000,000,000. (The zeroes here represent place figures only in this quintillion number, since my friends did not have computers powerful enough to run the complete sequence.) Ask these savants how they get their answer and they will smile, pleased that we are impressed but unable to grasp the implications of such a question.

The issue with these savants is that in most cases, so far as can be observed, the savant has not acquired, could not have acquired, and is quite incapable of acquiring, the information that he so liberally dispenses. If we furnish the savant with the proper stimulus, a question about his specialty, he gives the appropriate response, but he can't furnish himself with that stimulus, can't develop the capacity as an intelligence, and can't move beyond his narrow limits.

Quantum physicists use the term non-locality for those organizing forces that are not "temporal-spatial," not in time-space, and this term offers a way to explain this aspect of the frequency-realm. We can't locate the potential, only our lived translation of it. Since the neural fields of our brain and the non-localized potential operate as a dynamic of resonant frequencies, our brain's neural-fields are obviously "quasi-temporal-spatial," both in and not in the time-space they give rise to. No research has been able to determine where in the brain perception actually takes place, because perception isn't localizable, yet every response we make to the stimulus of awareness changes the field from which our awareness springs. Our lived experience is a dynamic between a non-localized potential and our particular localizing of that potential as our perceived time-space world.

Joseph Chilton Pearce, *Evolution's End (Abridged)*

transcendent. They are all worldly. When people finish the power of the meditation, they are still in bondage. This is a temporary relief.

M: *Temporary relief. It's like taking an aspirin for half an hour to get rid of your ignorance but it comes back.*

S: Yes, it comes back.

M: *About this formless state, which I equate to Krishnamurti's choiceless awareness, His Holiness says there's no gross perception but there's no absence of subtle perception.*

S: Yes.

M: *What does "no absence of subtle perception" mean?*

S: That is the detail of *Abhidharma*, how the four formless states are differentiated. First those meditating will eliminate unpleasant physical feelings. Then they eliminate pleasant feelings. They do away with all kinds of feeling. But this is for a certain period of time. When the force of the meditation ends, they return to where they began. Temporary relief.

M: *But there's no absence of subtle perceptions. His Holiness seems to be saying that after we've eliminated these forms that we normally consider to be realities, something else, subtle perceptions are there. Do subtle perceptions emanate from the brain or do they emanate from the mind that is not in the brain?*

S: They can emanate from anywhere. Perceptions can emanate from the body, the brain, and those the brain cannot reach; the source may be anywhere. There are many sources.

M: *You described how each sense has its own consciousness: eye consciousness, touch consciousness, all the senses plus mind consciousness. All these are active, percolating in what we call* conscious awareness.

S: Yes.

M: *In addition to the impressions the brain produces, there are other realms or frequencies emanating from beyond the brain. These too are available, present. A great deal of our effort seems to be negating the gross so we can perceive the subtle, what Krishnamurti called* intelligence. *Intelligence may express in the body and it can express as insight.*

S: It is not always when we negate the gross that subtle perception necessarily comes. The formless states negate the gross temporarily. They do not negate the seed or the source of the gross.

After having attained the fourth absorption, one turns away completely from touch, sight and physical dharmas, even subtle ones, while developing the thought: "All dharmas are like infinite space." One should fix the mind on this and develop it. Upon development, one has achieved the Sphere of Infinite Space. Having accomplished this, one should go on to develop the thought: "Consciousness is like the infinity of space." After some time one will achieve the Sphere of Infinite Consciousness. These two accomplishments having been won, and perceiving that they have objects and are established upon objects, one should develop the thought: "No thing is to be grasped," thus coming to accomplish the Sphere of No-thingness. Finally, having come to see that these three spheres have objects even though they are subtle, one should develop further by thinking thus: "While there is no gross perception, there is no absence of subtle perception," in this way accomplishing the sphere of neither-perception nor-non-perception. This last accomplishment is called the Summit of Becoming.

The superknowledges (abhijna) are various worldly powers which arise in one who has practiced the four form-absorptions. These knowledges are five, as follows:

1. DivyacakSu, the divine-eye by which one is able to see forms, even subtle ones, both far and near.

2. DivyaSrota, the divine-ear whereby sounds though very faint can be heard from far away.

3. Paracittajanna, knowledge of others' minds, possessing which one is able to know what is passing in the minds of others.

4. Purvanivasanusmrti, "past-dwellings-recollection," that is, the knowing of past lives both of one's own continuity and in the continuities of others, remembering such details as place of birth, name and status of one's family, and many other matters.

5. Cyutyupapattijnana, knowledge of the death-moment and the rebirth-moment of beings who arise in their several bourns according to their karma.

His Holiness the Dalai Lama, The Opening of the Wisdom-Eye

So long as there is an observer, space is the narrow yard of the prison in which there is no freedom at all.

J. Krishnamurti, The Only Revolution

Permanent Relief from Ignorance

M: *Temporary relief. Liberation, realization, is permanent relief from ignorance, from the source that produces the ego.*

S: Yes.

M: *The Dalai Lama goes on, "The super knowledges are various worldly powers which arise in one who has practiced the four form absorptions. These knowledges are five, as follows: the divine eye by which one is able to see forms, even subtle ones, both near and far; the divine ear whereby sounds though very faint can be heard from far away; knowledge of other's minds, possessing which one is able to know what is passing in the minds of others; knowing of past lives both of one's own continuity and in the continuities of others, remembering such details as place of birth, name and status of one's family and many other matters; knowledge of the death-moment and the rebirth-moment of beings who arise in their several bourns according to their karma."*

S: Yes. Past, future, both.

M: *"Knowledge of death and rebirth."*

S: Yes.

M: *"These knowledges are peculiar to the realm of form and cannot arise in the formless realm." What does that mean?*

S: In the realm of form, they enjoy a border status as in the realm of man. They can go into deep meditation. They can come out of the meditation. We call it *samadhi* and *after samadhi*. When they awaken from samadhi, then they can see everything and can talk, eat, can do whatever we normally do. With the help of their concentrated mind, their samadhi, they can practice to develop these five knowledges and use them after samadhi for the purpose of serving others or one's self.

In the four formless states, there is no *after samadhi* privilege. They are born. They go into samadhi and when samadhi is finished, they die. They cannot acquire or use any knowledge after samadhi. That is the limitation of the formless. They have no body. They are nothing.

J. Krishnamurti, Pergine, ca. 1924

Meditation is the total inaction which comes out of a mind that sees what is, without the entanglement of the past. This action is not a response to any challenge but is the action of the challenge itself, in which there is no duality. Meditation is the emptying of experience and is going on all the time, consciously or unconsciously, so it is not an action limited to a certain period during the day. It's a continuous action from morning till night—the watching without the watcher. Therefore there is no division between the daily life and meditation, the religious life and the secular life. The division comes only when the watcher is tied to time. In this division there is disarray, misery and confusion, which is the state of society.

So meditation is not individualistic, nor is it social; it transcends both and so includes both. This is love: the flowering of love is meditation.

J. Krishnamurti, The Only Revolution

The Western Concept of Soul

M: *This seems similar to our Western concept of the soul? You described* soul *as subtle consciousness. It doesn't begin. It doesn't end. I asked, "Is there one soul or are there many?" You replied that this is a very old question. I still struggle with what holds a soul together? The soul doesn't have a material form but apparently has some kind of energetic form that holds together. Something keeps it individualized so that it doesn't merge back to the sea. A raindrop disappears in the ocean. That's one metaphor. When I die, my subtle consciousness merges back into the ocean. How do I maintain my individual soulness if I'm the ocean? What holds the soul together?*

S: The ocean and the drop metaphor is used mostly with the non-Buddhist tradition in India. Buddhists use it very seldom. It arises from the belief in a creator. The Indian tradition can be classified into two groups: *Ishwarvaadin* and *Unishwarvaadin*. *Ishwarvaadin* means, using Christian language, you believe in God, Ishwar, who created the universe. And the universe cannot move, not even a single leaf, without the intention of Ishwar. This kind of believer is considered an *Ishwarvaadin*. The other, *Unishwarvaadin*, consists of three living traditions. One is the old Sankhya, and the next is the Jain who practice silence, and then Buddhism. Only a portion of the old Sankhya, Jain, and Buddhists do not believe in a creator. To them there is not a common soul or creator into which you can merge and disappear. Each soul is individual and has no beginning or end. Even if you go back to the ocean, it is not the end of the individual.

The Buddhists say the Buddha Nature has three qualities: the truth body, *Dharmakaya*, which embodies the principle of enlightenment and knows no limits or boundaries, meaning nature and the body; the body of mutual enjoyment, *Sambhogakaya*, which is a body of bliss or clear light manifestation, meaning the apparent body; and the created body, *Nirmanakaya*, which manifests in time and space. So the *Dharmakaya* is nature in the body of the Buddha Nature. Your *Dharmakaya*, my *Dharmakaya*, all *Dharmakayas* become a single consciousness. No one can differentiate. They are all inseparable. But the Buddhas can trace back which drop in the *Dharmakaya* is Michael's *Dharmakaya*, which drop in the *Dharmakaya* is Rinpoche's *Dharmakaya*. So each individual identity is still there but not separable and differential. All *Jatakas* of each Buddha are different because each Buddha was individual in past lives and

There was the human being, Krishnamurti, who functioned as a teacher to the world. Supporting that, there was an etheric, great energy without identity that, when called upon or when the atmosphere was right, came to the human being of Krishnamurti. In his books, talks, conversations, and some few recordings, Krishnamurti referred to "the other," "otherness," the "benediction," "presence of the Mighty Beings," "it," and "immensity" to acknowledge the presence of the great energy. Sometimes, sensitive people could perceive that energy. Such phenomena, and the way Krishnamurti dealt with and described them, must be considered part of the larger Teaching. It seems to me those energies were not personal to Krishnamurti but are universal phenomena, as evidenced in the writing and myths of most cultures in the world. Krishnamurti was himself a phenocopy of humankind—a changed organism that mutated without dependence on heredity or circumstances. Therefore, the phenomena are part of, or may even originate in, that mutated state. The usual tendency in humankind is to move from the gross, the phenomenal world, to the subtle, less obvious. This striving has resulted in religions and cults with associated conflicts and frustrations. But in the spiritual world, the opposite direction from the subtle to the gross is the only way for transcending energy to manifest.

Being able to read the thoughts of others; being able to physically transmogrify (to change completely or transform physically); being able to heal corporeal bodies; being able to speak profoundly without or in spite of normal brain function; to be seated in and exist concurrently in several different consciousness; to contain disembodied voices; to see non-physical phenomena like fairies and angels; to be able to magnetize objects; and, strangely, to deny all phenomena as cheap tricks—all these Krishnamurti could do, and did, in the presence of a few people. He made nothing of any of it for himself nor gave it any importance. We heard from others that he was quick to play it down or dismiss phenomena as unimportant, a trap to be wary of.

There are enough statements like this by Krishnamurti to lend credence to a hypothesis that his early experiences of the metaphysical were not imaginary. Nor did he try and hide them; he just didn't talk publicly about them. In modernizing his perennial Teachings to make ancient wisdom contemporary, and to avoid all the pitfalls of spiritual hypnosis, cultism, blind following of leaders, faith and belief, and spiritual snobbery, Krishnamurti built into his Teachings absolutist denials of the importance of the esoteric and the arcane. He did not deny or renounce the Theosophical Masters, reincarnation, or karma; he just refused to make them a part of his Teachings or give them any credence that would add strength of belief or faith in them as part of a religion. The Teachings are austere, missing the esoteric that would confuse or lead to misunderstanding, as belief generally does. Religion, then, stripped of all the traditional elements that trapped centuries of followers, is reduced to its essential truths—to quality of life fundamentals, practically and actually attainable.

R. E. Mark Lee, *Knocking at the Open Door: My Years with J. Krishnamurti*

remains identifiable in the Buddhahood also. It will remain identifiable, who is who. This is the Buddhist way.

All Buddhas See the Same Truth

M: *To return to Krishnamurti, he made the observation that when two individuals are looking at the same thing, with the same energy, with the same passion, with the same clarity, they will see the same thing. This is an important concept. From one perspective, the relative, we all see a different reality. We're all actually seeing our own relative reality and there is no real commonness within the relative. My question has to do with the assertion that you made that Krishnamurti always spoke from the absolute. Buddha spoke from the absolute, whichever Buddha it was. According to Krishnamurti's statement, what they saw would be common. They would see the same thing. How they might express what they saw could be quite different because of culture, time, and language. This concept is critical. There is one root, the Buddha mind or the Buddha Nature, but there can be many Buddhas who have arrived at that common absolute reality.*

S: That's what I am trying to say. When Buddha's mind is within the absolute truth, you cannot say this is this Buddha's mind or that Buddha's mind. All Buddhas see the same truth and their way of seeing is not different. The capacity, the intensity, the force, in everything there is no differentiation. It just merges into the ocean of the absolute mind. Each drop has no individuality but that does not end the individual Buddhas. Two men see the same reality and their way of seeing is not different but you still have two men.

M: *His Holiness goes on: "By persistent practice of the Noble Eight-Fold Path, one enters the Path of Development where the stains to be destroyed by mind-development are in fact destroyed. In the process of discarding them there are two methods: the 'gradual' and the 'single-stroke.'" We discussed this before, the gradual and the instant.*

S: The gradual path and the instant path are not at the level of the Buddha Nature. It is for those who are not completely free from all conditioning. They still have to attend the Eight-Fold Path to attain the Buddha Nature. In the Buddha Nature there is no differentiation between the gradual and the instant. The transition from no Buddha Nature to Buddha Nature is always spontaneous.

K: Why has mankind created this "I," which must inevitably cause conflict? "I" and you, and "me" better, and so on and so on and so on.

DB: I think that was a mistake made a long time ago, or as you call it, a wrong turn, that again having introduced separation between various things outwardly we then, not knowing better, kept on doing… Not seeing what they are doing.

K: I am inclined to observe that the origin is that, the ego, the "me," the "I"… If there is no ego there is no problem, there is no conflict, there is no time—time in the sense of becoming, not becoming, being or not being.

DB: But it might be that we would still slip into whatever it was that made us make the ego in the first place.

K: Wait a minute. Is it energy being so vast, limitless, has been condensed or narrowed down in the mind, and the brain itself has become narrowed down because it couldn't contain all this enormous energy—you are following what I am saying? …And therefore gradually narrowed down to me, to the "I."

DB: I understand that that is what happened, but I don't quite see all the steps.

K: It couldn't handle it.

DB: But if it can't handle it, it seems as if there is no way out then?

K: Why has the brain, with all thought and so on, created this sense of "me," "I"? Why? Outwardly, the family, you follow, outwardly it had to be that way.

DB: We needed a certain sense of identity to function, to know where you belong.

K: Yes, and so on. And is that the movement that has brought that in? The movement of the outer, where I had to identify—the family, the house, and so on gradually became the "me"?

DB: Yes.

K: To me that is the enemy… the origin of man's misery… Inwardly, that is what I am talking about… Is that the cause of this—man's confusion—introducing time as a means of becoming, and becoming more and more perfect, more and more evolved, more and more loving? You follow?

DB: Certainly if we didn't do that, the whole [ego] structure would collapse.

K: Collapse, that's it… I am not talking theoretically, personally. To me the idea of tomorrow doesn't exist psychologically… If psychological time doesn't exist, then there is no conflict, there is no "me," there is no "I," which is the origin of conflict … Now, if there is no inward movement as time, moving, becoming more and more, then what takes place?

DB: If we say this whole movement of time ceases—whatever that means—the word "ceases" is wrong because that is time.

K: Time ends.

> J. Krishnamurti, *The Ending of Time*. Conversation with Professor David Bohm, "The Roots of Psychological Conflict," 1 April 1980 *(Abridged)*

M: *Is the ending of ignorance, the ego state, enlightenment?*

S: No.

M: *No?*

S: You just stop the dependency on karma, being born back in Samsara, and you get a state of permanent peace. That's all. The elimination of your ignorance is not accompanied by a combination of vast merit. You have not practiced the *Bodhisattvacharya*. The *Bodhisattva* path to the Buddha Nature and the path to *Arhathood* are entirely different. *Arhathood* is for the individual. To obtain the Buddha Nature means that you become omniscient, omnipresent, and universally present, and you have to eliminate all hindrances. *Arhathood* has only eliminated the hindrance of *kleshavarana*, meaning identifying with mental concepts. The Buddha Nature demands that you awaken the entirety of your mind and eliminate all hindrances to see the whole, the vastness. Buddha and *Arhat* are very different states. Many people not familiar with Buddhism are unable to see the difference between liberation from bondage and liberation from the hindrances that prevent seeing everything. These are very different.

M: *Krishnamurti made none of these distinctions.*

S: No, he speaks only at the highest level. You cannot draw a parallel between Krishnamurti and the Buddhist concept.

M: *Krishnamurti said simply, stop being ignorant.*

S: Yes.

M: *And wait and see.*

J. Krishnamurti, Valley School, Bangalore

Who is there to tell you what to do? When we are children the parents tell us what to do. That same mentality is cultivated right through life. In school we are told what to do. In college you are told what to do. In the university, right through life, somebody tells you this is right, this is wrong, this should be done, that should not be done. Which means what? There is no self-investigation. There is no saying, I am really the rest of mankind, which you are, because every human being goes through a great deal of suffering, a great deal of pain, a great deal of anxiety, uncertain, confused, insecure, like you, like the rest of the world. We don't accept that. We think that our suffering is totally separate from other people's suffering. And so we have this mentality that I must have somebody to tell me what to do—right from the Pope down to the poor parish priest.

Why should I accept what somebody else says, when I realize that I'm the rest of mankind?

Mankind is me and me is the history of mankind, the book of mankind. If I know how to read it, I don't depend on anybody. Can I, without distortion, without prejudice, without choice, be aware of the content of this book, which is me? To read it very carefully, never distorting it, requires a great deal of attention, a great deal of energy, intensity, immediacy. We are not willing to do all that because we think that it's too tiresome. Tell me quickly what to do and I will do it or I will not do it. We generally may not do it.

I personally think that the psychological guidance by another, whether it is the religious guidance or the guidance of the psychologist, is totally wrong. Because you're making humanity into children who have to be guided, told, encouraged. We are all grown-up human beings after five or ten million years.

J. Krishnamurti, Interview with Michael Mendizza

Dharamsala, India, 2014, Day Four

Krishnamurti Was Able to Stand on His Own

M: *The Theosophical Society based many of its ideas and systems on your culture.*

S: That is true. Nobody can deny that.

M: *There is both truth in the inspirations and information an Oracle can transmit or express, and there is untruth.*

S: Yes, both.

M: *They are not infallible. After Krishnamurti began to stand on his own in the mid-1920s, he grew more and more dissatisfied with many of the leaders of the Theosophical Society. They assumed the role of the Oracle, bringing through or communicating with the other side. Krishnamurti grew increasingly skeptical. What is your understanding of this history, not wanting to toss out the baby with the bath water?*

S: This is very difficult to discuss these days. And I appreciate Krishnamurti's position, saying this is all rubbish. Don't discuss it, forget it. Yet I trust the wisdom of the early founders of the society, Madame Blavatsky, Colonel Olcott, and in particular Annie Besant. All of them were authentic. I don't mean that they did not make mistakes but the mistakes they made were innocent, without any bad intention. They were good people. But the society became too large and there were many who became over-zealous and wanted to have an important role when the New World Teacher and the New World Religion appeared. "I will be so important," and that sort of thing. These are all too common, worldly, and have nothing to do with the teachings or spirituality. This corrupted and spoiled the Theosophical leadership. Fortunately Krishnamurti was able to step out of that system and stand on his own, which allowed the fulfillment of the original intent that the Masters desired and planned. That original intent has not been distorted, and for this we have to give one hundred percent responsibility to one person, Krishnamurti himself.

M: *We discussed virtue with an ego and virtue without an ego. This applies.*

S: Absolutely.

M: *Imagine having an ego and being placed in a position of authority, representing the New World Teacher, Maitreya, the future Buddha. This is very powerful. If you have an ego, and just about everyone does, that ego will be affected by*

In 1900, nine years before J. Krishnamurti was "discovered," a certain Mr. B. K. Mantri of India wrote a letter to Dr. Besant, then in England. When Dr. Besant opened the letter she found on its back a message from Master K.H., in His well-known handwriting.

Last K.H.-letter to Annie Besant

A psychic and a pranayamist [referring to Annie Besant] who has got confused by the vagaries of the members. The T.S. and its members are slowly manufacturing a creed. Says a Tibetan proverb, "credulity breeds credulity and ends in hypocrisy." How few are they who can know anything about us. Are we to be propitiated and made idols of'? Is the worship of a new trinity made up of the blessed M., Upasika [referring to HPB] and yourself to take the place of exploded creeds? We ask not for the worship of ourselves. The disciple should in no way be fettered. Beware of an esoteric popery....

The T. S. must safely be ushered into the new century. You have for some time been under deluding influences. Shun pride, vanity and love of power. Be not guided by emotion but learn to stand alone. Be accurate and critical rather than credulous. The mistakes of the past in the old religions must not be glossed over with imaginary explanations....

No one has a right to claim authority over a pupil or his conscience. Ask him not what he believes. All who are sincere and pure minded must have admittance. The crest wave of intellectual advancement must be taken hold of and guided into spirituality. It cannot be forced into beliefs and emotional worship.... At favorable times we let loose elevating influences which strike various persons in various ways. It is the collective aspect of many such thoughts that can give the correct note of action. We show no favors. The best corrective of error is an honest and open-minded examination of all facts subjective and objective. Misleading secrecy has given the death blow to numerous organizations.

The cant about the "Masters" must be silently but firmly put down. Let the devotion and service be to that Supreme Spirit alone of which one is a part. Namelessly and silently we work, and the continual references to ourselves and the repetition of our names raises up a confused aura that hinders our work.... The T.S. was meant to be the cornerstone of the future religions of humanity. To accomplish this object, those who lead must leave aside their weak predilections for the forms and ceremonies of any particular creed and show themselves to be true Theosophists, both in inner thought and outward observance. The greatest of your trials is yet to come. We watch over you but you must put forth all your strength.

K.H.

all this. The Masters understood this. In 1900, ten years before the boy Krishnamurti was discovered, Annie Besant received a letter from a businessman in India. When she opened the letter, she found written in the customary blue pencil a note from Master KH. It said, "Be careful, you're under delusion, get rid of the ceremonies, don't talk about the Masters, all this popery, walking around like a pope. We do our work quietly. Don't talk about us. Don't use us." When you examine Krishnamurti's mature teachings, all the core points are in this letter.*

S: But all these things happened.

M: *Yes, in spite of being warned.*

S: In spite of being authentic, the leaders were unable to prevent these things from happening.

M: *Ignorance again, that darn ego.*

S: Yes, ignorance. They were not able to realize what was going on. But it is very sensitive to talk about them now. After people pass away, talking about their mistakes is not appropriate. They can't come back and defend themselves.

M: *I'm simply giving voice to Krishnamurti's concerns. He was suspicious. He turned away.*

S: I did not meet any of that generation except Rukmini Devi Arundale, but I can sense what they felt from her.

Krishnamurti Is Talking About the Human Mind

M: *This is from an address Krishnamurti gave in 1927 to a small group of the most devoted. "When Krishnamurti dies, which is inevitable, you will make a religion. You will set about wanting rules in your minds because 'K', the individual, has represented to you the truth. So you will build a temple. You will then begin to have ceremonies. You'll invent phrases, build systems, beliefs, creeds, and create philosophies. If you build great foundations on me, the individual, you'll be caught in that house, in that temple, and so you will have to have another teacher come and extricate you from that, to pull you out of that narrowness. But the human mind is such that you will build another temple around him. And so, it will go on and on." You have been around the Krishnamurti Foundations for a long time. Is this what they are doing?*

S: Krishnamurti is talking about the human mind. We are all unenlightened human beings. So we will have to admit that is what we do. I think

K: I'm going to answer all these questions.... I know you would all like my answers to be based on authority, but I'm afraid you will be disappointed. I'm not urging you to accept what I hold to be the absolute Truth, but I am leaving it to your own judgement, which alone is valuable.... Please have patience and listen diligently... if you do not understand wisely, you will ask these same questions next year.

Q: In 1925 you selected seven Apostles... Now you say you have no disciples.

K: I say again, I have no disciples. Every one of you is a disciple of the Truth, if you understand the Truth and do not follow individuals. I have no followers.... If you understand the Truth which I put forward, in all its simplicity... for its own beauty, then you become a disciple of that Truth. To be a disciple of another is to betray the Truth. The only manner of attaining Truth is to become disciples of the Truth itself without a mediator.

Q: You tell us that ritual and ceremony step down the Truth.

K: No organization, however seasoned in tradition, however well-established, contains the Truth. If you would seek the Truth you must go out, far away from the limitations of the human mind and heart, and there discover it—and that Truth is within yourself. Is it not much simpler to make Life itself the goal—Life itself the guide, the Master and the God—than to have mediators, gurus, who inevitably step down the Truth and hence betray it?

Q: You tell us that stages on the path are unessential.

K: You are no longer children and yet you are worshiping a toy.... Finding and establishing the Truth depends on you and on no one else. If I destroy for you all your present crutches, you will invent others to satisfy your craving for support; you will invent other fantastic ideas.... I neither believe nor disbelieve. To me belief has very little value compared to the most precious jewel in the world, which is Life.... I refuse to be your crutch. I'm not going to be brought into a cage for your worship. When you bring the fresh air of the mountain and hold it in a small room, the freshness of that air disappears and there is stagnation and no man who is wise will allow himself to be caught in things that pervert and bring about stagnation of his mind and heart. I am free. I have found this Truth which is limitless, without beginning or end. I will not be conditioned by you.

J. Krishnamurti, *Let Understanding Be the Law*.
Castle Eerde, The Netherlands, 2 August 1928 *(Abridged)*

this is inevitable. The people in the foundations do some of these things but with some degree of hesitation and doubt. But hesitation and doubt do not prevent us from doing them. Perhaps we might say we are a little bit better than some other groups.

M: *We have a vague notion that we are doing it, but we do it anyway.*

S: That's right.

M: *Those representing Krishnamurti should be constantly reminding themselves that this is taking place. We all need to be very careful.*

S: Yes.

M: *This was an interesting quote from 1928 to a similar group, a year later. "No organization, however seasoned in tradition, however well-established, contains the truth. If you would seek truth you must go out far away from the limitations of the human mind and heart and discover it. That truth is within yourself." Krishnamurti is saying we have to go far beyond the human mind and heart but then he says we will find it in our self. Doesn't this imply a vast contradiction?*

S: It is quite simple in the sense that the truth is within you, with you, and the truth is everywhere, which prevents our seeing it. What prevents our seeing it is the ego, as Krishnamurti used the word ego. And unless you go far away from the ego, you can't see it. When you go far away from the ego, it is not a discovery of truth. It is only removing the ego.

The Entire Process Becomes Distorted

M: *He cautioned that we negate the ego not to discover truth, but simply to negate the ego.*

S: Yes, and then the truth is there. As long as we live with the ego, we push truth far away. We make it a destination and then want to go there and see it with that big ego. The ego is blinding. You are not trying to remove it *here*, you are trying to get *over there*. Then the entire process becomes distorted. Nothing works. Whatever you do strengthens the ego.

M: *Your description is different but what you are saying is in perfect alignment with Krishnamurti's core message.*

S: Yes. A Tibetan scholar, the second Panchen Lama, wrote Dharma poetry. He put the ego on one side and himself on the other and had them argue. The ego says, "You are so weak. You are so difficult to internalize by anyone because of my power. Whatever you do to find liberation, I will dilute it."

We could say that knowledge has become self-centered by building up contradictory commitments of absolute necessity, especially of the self. Knowledge of the self then assumes supreme necessity, which dominates, distorts and leads knowledge into self-deception and destruction. This trap is very subtle because the unconscious presupposition of absolute necessity operates before one can think reflectively. By the time you begin to think in this way, it's often too late. The mind has already begun to defend itself through various forms of self-deception.

This activity generates a kind of darkness. I suggest that what is needed to penetrate this darkness is insight. Not just particular insights, such as those of Newton and Einstein. These are valuable, but there's something much greater, as Krishnamurti brought out in all his work. This is, an insight into the whole activity of knowledge, where the mind can actually see what it's doing.

David Bohm, An Informal Talk, "Knowledge and Insight," 1981

The Ego Says, "I Have Done This"

M: *And everything you do will make the ego stronger.*

S: Yes, it strengthens the ego's defense. Panchen Lama expressed this very dramatically, relating it to our day-to-day life. About all our speeches and religious activities, our organizations and activities in the name of religion, the ego says, "I have done this. Look how very well I have done. No one has been able to touch wisdom. No, everything is under the ego's command. All your spiritual efforts strengthen me and you can't get rid of me."

M: *A great deal of what we think of as religion, the cathedrals in Europe, were displays of family vanity. Medieval churches were built by rich families as displays of wealth and social power. They built these massive structures to puff up and make the family name and image even bigger.*

S: Yes, and they talk to the people and say, "Look what I have done, how nice it is." *Me, me, me.*

M: *Regarding this image, the ego, David Bohm noted in one of our interviews: "First, there is an assumption that ego or self-image is more than an image, that it is real and therefore it feels absolutely necessary to meet its needs. The image becomes a reality and takes priority over everything. And because the image is actually false, everything becomes distorted." This is a dramatic illustration of the power of ignorance.*

S: The Buddhist's general use of the term *ignorance* and Krishnamurti's term of *ego*, they are the same.

M: *David went on to describe how once this assumed reality has taken hold, anything that challenges it is defended against. There is a built-in defensiveness to anything that challenges the authenticity or integrity of that assumed reality, the ego, and the first line of defense is concealment. When someone like Krishnamurti challenges the image, the image changes the subject or rejects the messenger.*

S: Right, yes.

M: *Are there parallels in your teachings, how the ego defends itself and just gets stronger and stronger even when we're trying to get rid of it?*

I have suggested that today's challenges cannot be met by existing knowledge. Attempting to solve the environmental, social, cultural, and ultimately political problems with the crude and fragmented structure of thought which is now common will never work. The point is, knowledge is limited. And proper application of knowledge requires that knowledge know its limitations.

For example, suppose you have a computer with a "virus" that is doing all sorts of crazy things. A number of computers could soon become so completely occupied that they no longer respond to the programmer, and necessary programs may even be destroyed. This is a good analogy of what has happened to the mind. This "virus" has communicated itself throughout society, and the brain is thoroughly occupied, as well as being disrupted in its function.

As a result, intelligence, which can be compared to the programmer, is no longer able to properly affect the brain. We are overwhelmed by all sorts of meaningless misinformation, and the more television and newspapers we have, the more rapidly the virus spreads. I am saying that we need a perception or insight which is not dependent on memory and therefore is able to see the limitations of thought and knowledge.

I have to emphasize strongly that knowledge without insight will ultimately lead to self-deception because of the pressures implicit in that knowledge. There is little realization of the ultimate inability of science to avoid the self-deception implicit in the active functioning of knowledge which is not penetrated by insight.

Insight is universal, and its origin or essence is not restricted to great scientific discoveries or to artistic creations, but rather is of crucial significance to everything we do. The negative operation of insight removes blocks and barriers, while the positive is the new perception that this removal makes possible.

David Bohm, An Informal Talk, "Knowledge and Insight," 1981

Ignorance Cannot Be Removed by Ignorance

S: In the Buddhist teaching the final act of negating ignorance is the clear seeing of the manner in which ignorance grasps the image we have of "I". The perfect way to see this grasping, clinging, and holding onto this nonexistent "I" is not being able to find it as something real, independent of thought. Then logic and all the arguments that reveal that the "I" is an image created by thought come into play. Without seeing this, everything we do strengthens the image. This is very clearly defined.

M: *This requires an insight, stepping out of the structure that created the image, which is thought, and from another position seeing what is taking place.*

S: Because ignorance cannot be removed with the help of ignorance. But most people do not have any instrument other than ignorance. That is our paradox.

M: *There seems to be a leap of faith. Ignorance is all we know. It is what we consider to be reality. It is our words, our language, our concepts, our beliefs, the whole semantics-generated realm, and the self as image is inseparable from that. They're all one. When we say, "I must negate this," I have no concept of anything else.*

S: Yes.

M: *David Bohm was drawn to Krishnamurti by his statement that "the observer and the observed are one." Krishnamurti meant by this that the thinker and the thought are the same thing. The thought process is real. It is actually going on, and out of that movement emerges an image of self that is assumed to be an independent reality.*

S: You will find in Buddhism almost everything Krishnamurti is saying, using different words and descriptions. Buddhists generally will say, as long as thought exists, thought will make a separate thinker. It is thought's production or thought's image that makes a solid thinker exist out there. We can see this in two ways. If you are awakened and you remove the thinker's independently inherent existence, thought will come to end. Or if you remove the thought, the independent thinker will automatically disappear. In this way, it becomes clear that thought is the thinker and the thinker is thought. This is how Buddhists see this.

Without interfering with the necessary and useful function of memory, insight dissolves the mind's attachment to all kinds of absurdities that hold us prisoner to the past. This affects all functions of the mind, physical, emotional, and intellectual, as one undivided act which does not involve time in any basic way. It not only takes place in a flash with no sensible duration, but its essence cannot be captured in thought. There's no meaning in choosing to have an insight and then trying to find some means of producing this result. Rather, the action of insight is immediate, total, and not analyzable.

The key point is that everyone must be able to question with great energy and passion whatever is not clear. It is necessary to sustain this questioning in spite of whatever difficulties may arise. This questioning is not an end in itself and its purpose is not mainly to give rise to answers. Rather, it's essential in the whole movement of life, which can only be harmonious when this ceaseless questioning frees the mind of the tendency to hold indefinitely to contradictory and confused knowledge. If you question in this way there may be the energy of insight, which is crucial for opening up the mind to new directions. To do this is a tremendous challenge, not only because of our habit of wanting important ideas to be secure, but because of very deep and subtle questions involving how the mind operates.

At present, insight is not generally given great value in society nor in education. Rather, there's a very strong bias in favor of accumulating knowledge, and doing this far beyond the point where it actually makes sense, while the spirit of questioning, necessary for insight, is ignored and, in fact, is discouraged if this questioning disturbs strong beliefs.

We have to see that insight itself has very high value. Then we'll have a different attitude to knowledge, values and education. The whole of life will be a field in which there is no end to the possibility of fresh and original perceptions.

David Bohm, An Informal Talk, "Knowledge and Insight," 1981

With or Without the Ego

M: *This brings up a fundamental question that is rarely explored. Bohm and Krishnamurti went into this quite deeply. As we said, virtue with an ego is one thing. Virtue without the ego is another. The same thing is true of the thought process itself. Thought without the ego operates one way. Thought in the service of the ego or self-image operates completely differently.*

S: But this is a little difficult. Virtue without an ego is there, but I question if thought without the ego is there.

M: *David raised the question, "Is there a form of thought without an image, non-verbal thought?" He used the example of insight, insight being a non-verbal image in the mind. Words cause the brain to create mental images. Flashes of insight, non-verbal imagination, are images but not images produced by words. There seems to be some bridge between insight, which is intelligence or wisdom, and imagination, translating that flash into meaning that the brain can understand. Krishnamurti responded, no, there is a direct action from insight. It doesn't need imagination to act. Is there action born out of insight independent of action born out of imagination and thought?*

Buddhists Believe That Thought and the Ego Are Always Combined

S: Professor Bohm's viewpoint has some logic behind it but the Buddhist position would be a little different. Freedom from thought, according to Buddhism, is achieved only at the Buddha's level. A person in deep meditation, who is not able to engage in other kinds of activity, is on a human level. When that person is engaged in worldly activities, he is not able to remain in deep meditation. When that limitation is removed, he or she becomes the Buddha. Then the person is in the deepest meditation all the time, yet his mind is able to engage in all kinds of other activities. And there is no thought. Everything is a perception and then action is effortless. There is no need to think, to plan, create the intention, "I will do that." Action flows immediately, automatically. At the Buddha's level, all Buddhas are free from the ego, free from ignorance. Up to the Buddha's level, thought comes automatically and whatever they do, thought contaminates it, at least a little bit. That is why I say, as long as thought is there, it is not free of ego. Thought and ego are always combined.

> You need a very, very sane mind to see, and to be free.
> These two, seeing and freedom, are absolutely necessary.
> Freedom from the urge to see, freedom from the
> hope that man always gives to science, to technology, and to
> religious discoveries. This hope breeds illusion. To see this is
> freedom, and when there is freedom, you do not invite.
> Then the mind itself has become the measureless.
>
> J. Krishnamurti, *The Only Revolution*

During offering of long life prayers, Gyuto Tantrik Monastery, Dharamsala, 2014

M: *Krishnamurti said, "Thought is conditioned."*

S: Yes.

M: *Call it what you will, thought, the ego, is conditioned and it can never not be conditioned or limited.*

S: Buddhists also say that.

M: *There is an action that's free from thought, not dependent on thought, unconditioned, and this can express itself in the world daily, moment by moment.*

S: Yes, that's right.

Bringing the Action of Enlightenment into the Relative World

M: *How do we bring the action of enlightenment into the relative world? Isn't that what Krishnamurti was talking about? He asked the question, "What is truth and what is reality? Have they any relationship or are they eternally separate?" He said, "Truth is not a thing." How do we live in this relative world once the ego is negated? Do we just sit and stare?*

S: "Truth is not a thing" is a different question. The Buddhists also say, "Emptiness is not a thing, it is no thing." The Buddha sees relative truth as it is seen by unenlightened people, because relative truth is true for unenlightened people. This is the bridge between unenlightened people and the Buddha, so they can communicate and live together.

I can share a story. Long ago in India there used to be great magicians who made magic by hypnotizing people. For example, they used a small piece of wood and the hypnotized people saw the wood block as an elephant moving around. Now we have three different onlookers. One is the hypnotized person. The second is a person who is not hypnotized. The third is the magician himself. All three have a different view. The hypnotized person sees the elephant and believes that it is an elephant. The person who is not hypnotized sees only a wooden block, not an elephant. And the magician sees the wooden block but knows it's not an elephant. Buddha sees the elephant but Buddha knows it's not an elephant. That is the difference.

M: *What a great story.*

S: Yes.

K: To worship another is to worship oneself; the image, the symbol, is a projection of oneself. After all, your idol, your book, your prayer, is the reflection of your background; it is your creation, though it be made by another. You choose according to your gratification; your choice is your prejudice. Your image is your intoxicant, and it is carved out of your own memory; you are worshipping yourself through the image created by your own thought. Your devotion is the love of yourself covered over by the chant of your mind. The picture is yourself, it is the reflection of your mind. Such devotion is a form of self-deception that only leads to sorrow and to isolation, which is death.

Q: Is search devotion?

K: To search after something is not to search; to seek truth is not to find it. We escape from ourselves through search, which is illusion; we try in every way to take flight from what we are. In ourselves we are so petty, so essentially nothing, and the worship of something greater than ourselves is as petty and stupid as we are. Identification with the great is still a projection of the small. The more is an extension of the less. The small in search of the large will find only what it is capable of finding. The escapes are many and various but the mind in escape is still fearful, narrow and ignorant.

The understanding of escape is the freedom from "what is." The "what is" can be understood only when the mind is no longer in search of an answer. The search for an answer is an escape from "what is." This search is called by various names, one of which is devotion; but to understand "what is," the mind must be silent.

The "what is" is that which is from moment to moment. To understand the whole process of your worship, of your devotion to that which you call God, is the awareness of "what is."… It is only when the mind is silent that the truth of "what is" unfolds.

J. Krishnamurti, *Commentaries on Living, Series II (Abridged)*

M: The Buddha insisted on the necessity of examining the propositions put forward by Him, and of understanding them personally before accepting them as true. There is a classic quote: "Do not believe on the strength of traditions even if they have been held in honor for many generations and in many places; do not believe anything because many people speak of it; do not believe on the strength of sages of old times; do not believe that which you have yourselves imagined, thinking that a god has inspired you. Believe nothing which depends only on the authority of your masters or of priests. After investigation, believe that which you have yourselves tested and found reasonable, and which is for your good and that of others."

This brings up devotion. Teachers are like ladders. We stand upon their insights to see further. But we don't then turn around and worship the ladder. What is the right relationship with teachers such as His Holiness and Krishnamurti? Respect is one thing. Devotion, placing another in a position of psychological or spiritual authority, is quite another. I'm reminded of the Zen saying, "When you meet the Buddha on the road, kill him."

Devotion and Belief or Wisdom

S: Good question. Nagarjuna talked about devotion and belief on one side and wisdom on the other. Nagarjuna said that wisdom is supreme. Devotion is just part of the journey to wisdom, sometimes a prerequisite so people could debate how important belief and devotion really are. With devotion or belief that is not substantiated by wisdom, all the dangers are there. When devotion comes out of wisdom or when devotion has been substantiated by wisdom, the dangers are not there. This is similar to the golden virtue and good virtue.

In Buddhism we talk about the Three Refuges: Buddha, Dharma, and Sangha. *Sangha* refers to a spiritual or monastic community. We take refuge in all three, not just one. But in reality, what saves or gives refuge is only Dharma. Not Buddha and not Sangha. In spite of that, we consider there are three refuges. How do you take refuge in the Buddha? You must have tremendous respect and total faith. How is this done? You internalize the Dharma. When the Dharma is internalized in you, you see the truth. When you see the truth, you verify the truth by your own wisdom. This is true. I have seen it. This truth is talked about by

A: May I read a sentence out of your book?... "Through negation, that thing which alone is the positive comes into being."

K: May I put it this way? I must negate—I mean negate not intellectually or verbally—actually negate the society in which I live. The implication of immorality which exists in society, on which society is built, I must negate totally that immorality. That means that I live morally. In negating that, the positive is the moral.... I negate totally the idea of success.... Not only in the mundane world, not only in the sense of achievement in a world of money, position, authority, I negate that completely, and I also negate success in the so-called spiritual world.

A: Oh, yes. Quite the temptation.

K: Both are the same. Only I call that spiritual, and I call that physical, moral, mundane. So in negating success, achievement, there comes an energy. Through negation there is a tremendous energy to act totally differently, which is not in the field of success, in the field of imitation, conformity, and all that. So through negation—I mean actual negation, not just ideal negation—through actual negation of that which is immoral, morality comes into being.

A: Which is altogether different from trying to be moral.

K: Yes, yes. Of course, trying to be moral is immoral... When we use the word "negation," as it is generally understood, it is an act of violence.

A: Yes.

K: I brush it aside. And we are using the word "negate" not in the violence sense, but the understanding of what success implies. The "me", who is separate from you, wanting or desiring success, which will put me in a position of authority, power, prestige. So I am, in negating success, I am negating my desire to be powerful, which I negate only when I have understood the whole process which is involved in achieving success. In achieving success is implied ruthlessness, lack of love, lack of immense consideration for others, lack of a sense of conformity, imitation, acceptance of the social structure—all that is involved, and the understanding of all that when I negate success. It is not an act of violence. On the contrary, it is an act of tremendous attention.

A: I've negated something in my person.

K: I've negated myself... The "me" which is separate from you.

A: Exactly.

K: And therefore I am negating violence which comes about when there is separation.

> J. Krishnamurti, *A Wholly Different Way of Living*.
> San Diego, California, 3rd Conversation with Allan W. Anderson, 1972

Buddha, and he is not lying. I see myself what he is pointing to. Faith that comes out of understanding or wisdom is real devotion. Then it is free of all the dangers of blind faith.

M: *When you see for yourself, from wisdom, faith ends.*

S: Yes. But before that, before seeing from wisdom, you have to have a little faith in the Buddha. If you think Buddha's talk is not true, you will drop it and not examine for yourself what is being said. You begin to examine because of an unsubstantiated faith in the Buddha, which encourages you to discover wisdom for yourself. And you are able to remain in this process because you are helped by Sangha, the community. This is why we consider there are three refugees; otherwise there's only one refuge, the Dharma.

We use a metaphor. You are seriously ill. You need a doctor. You need medicine. And you need a nurse. The cure of the disease comes from the medicine, not from the doctor and not from the nurse, if the person takes it. If you put medicine there and say it is very good but don't take it, the medicine will do nothing. And unless it is prescribed by an authentic doctor who recognizes what the cause of your disease is, there is no cure. An ignorant doctor cannot prescribe the right medicine. So you need Buddha, Dharma, and Sangha. That is why we conceive of these three refuges, although the freeing of misery comes from the medicine, the Dharma. Faith created by wisdom is positive faith. Faith created because many people say so, faith because it was written long ago, faith because you feel God inspired you, without examination, without direct experience—this is dangerous blind faith.

Negating the Basis of Our Inaction

M: *Krishnamurti is quite forceful in saying, forget the doctor, forget the nurse, forget them. They will only confuse you. Take the medicine.*

S: Yes. That's right.

M: *Krishnamurti is saying that inwardly, psychologically or so-called spiritually, we spend all our time chasing after the doctor and never take the medicine. How do you feel about this position, which is so radical for most? He says, no spiritual authority, no guru, be a light unto yourself. Everyone else is standing in line at the doctor's office.*

The serious man, surely, is he who is capable of dropping all his conclusions because he sees that only then is he in a position to inquire.

If my mind is tethered to the peg of belief, experience, or knowledge, it cannot go very far; and inquiry implies freedom from that peg, does it not? If I am really seeking, then this state of being tethered to a peg must end, there must be a breaking away, I must cut the rope. There is then never a question of how to cut the rope. When there is perception of the fact that inquiry is possible only when there is freedom from obstinacy, or from attachment to a belief, then that very perception liberates the mind.

If you would really inquire into this whole problem of seeking and what it is to be serious, then the mind must find out how to inquire, and what inquiry is. Any assumption, any conclusion, any attachment to knowledge or experience, is an impediment to inquiry. As long as the mind is tethered to some conclusion, inquiry is an immense struggle, a process of effort, striving, breaking through; but if the mind sees the truth that there can be inquiry only when there is freedom, then inquiry has quite a different meaning altogether.

If one realizes this, one is never a slave to any guru, to any formula, to any belief. Then you and I can pool our inquiry, and out of that we can cooperate, act, live. But not as long as one's mind is tethered, there is "your way" and "my way," "your opinion" and "my opinion," "your path" and "my path," and all the many divisions and subdivisions which come between man and man.

The Collected Works of J. Krishnamurti. Benaras, India,
2nd Public Talk, 18 December 1955 *(Abridged)*

S: Krishnamurti is speaking in the twentieth century, a century in which people forgot about the medicine. They start and stop with the doctor and the nurse and only talk about the medicine.

M: *Yes.*

S: My medicine is much better than your medicine. My doctor is much better than your doctor. They're not consuming the medicine.

M: *This is so common.*

S: Yes, very common, absolutely common. Human conditioning, if we analyze it deeply, has been created by the gurus, the Masters, the authorities, and we tend to glorify them and stop there. In such a world, denying the doctor becomes necessary. That is why Krishnamurti negated this basis of our inaction.

M: *Our not taking the medicine.*

S: Not taking responsibility.

M: *This man Krishnamurti was so forceful, black and white. People, even back in the '20s, were shocked at how absolute and clear-cut his message was. He gave one no room to wiggle back and stand in line with the doctor. This was both wise and necessary. This forcefulness was part of his uniqueness.*

S: That's right.

M: *His ability to shake us out of our habits.*

S: Yes. That's part of it. Having said this, Krishnamurti does not deny your capacity to see the truth. And Krishnamurti does not deny the necessity of seeing the truth. He did not deny taking medicine.

M: *He called it, "living the teachings."*

S: By denying the doctor and the nurse, he empowered you to take the medicine voluntarily. "Do it now, sir. It will be OK," he said. Without shaking us from our habits, we might not do it. We would say, "The medicine is there, but my nurse will come sometime and put it into my mouth. Until then, I will stay right where I am."

M: *Yes, I will get to it tomorrow.*

S: That's right.

A: Mr. Krishnamurti, I was very taken with a recent statement of yours in which you said that it's the responsibility of each human being to bring about his own transformation, which is not dependent on knowledge or time.

K: Are we asking this question, sir? What place has knowledge in the regeneration of man, in the transformation of man?

A: Yes, yes.

K: So, when we talk about change, we mean not the mere bloody revolution, physical revolution, but rather the revolution in the makeup of the mind.

A: Of each...

K: Of human beings.

A: Right.

K: The way he thinks, the way he behaves, the way he conducts himself, the way he operates, he functions—the whole of that. What place has knowledge in that?... After all, human beings have created this society. By their greed, by their anger, by their violence, by their brutality, by their pettiness, they have created this society.

A: Precisely... If he changes, everything changes. If he doesn't change, nothing changes.

K: If we accept that, if we see that not intellectually but feel it in your heart, in your mind, in your blood that you are that, then the question is, is it possible for a human being to transform himself inwardly and therefore outwardly?

A: Yes.

K: So we come back to the point... man has collected such enormous information, knowledge, and has that knowledge changed him into goodness? You follow, sir—into a culture that will make him flower in this beauty of goodness. It has not.

A: No, it has not.

K: So saying all that, what place has knowledge in the regeneration of man?

J. Krishnamurti, A Wholly Different Way of Living.
1st Dialogue with Allan W. Anderson (Abridged)

The First Step Is the Last Step

M: *Let's look at another phrase that is at the very core of Krishnamurti's approach. On the one hand his message is absolutely clear, but on the other, he's somewhat hard to grasp. For example, "The first step is the last step." One of the most insightful statements was used by Allan W. Anderson to begin their eighteen dialogues together: "It's the responsibility of each person to bring about their own transformation, which is not dependent on knowledge or time." This statement is as radical, as challenging, as "the first step is the last step."*

S: Krishnamurti observed very carefully, in great detail and in minute clarity, the present state of human conditioning, which comes from many sources. It comes from so-called spiritual teaching, education, society, social systems and customs, rituals. Everything that takes place around us is the cause of our conditioning. All the sources of liberation we have made into causes of bondage. And in this, an important aspect of conditioning is the desire to become, to achieve something. Therefore psychological time, within which the rest of our conditioning is related, has become more and more important. Unless and until that is smashed, you will not be able to step out of conditioning. The first step, the second step, last step, if you accept that, the first step will itself condition you and you will never be able to take the second step. This I think is very clear.

M: *One either ends conditioning on the spot, which is knowledge and time, or you don't and all the steps deepen your conditioning.*

S: Therefore, based on Krishnamurti's insight, there is only one step. Otherwise all the steps are the same, leading nowhere.

The Individual Mind Is Part of a Universal Mind

M: *(Referring to* The Secret Oral Teachings*) Krishnamurti challenged the feeling that my mind is uniquely mine. Rather, all humanity shares the same sense perceptions, is influenced by the same basic conditioning. Krishnamurti used the statement, "You are the world."*

S: Yes.

M: *You are society. I believe that in the Buddhist approach there is a realization that what I call* my mind *is not mine. Is what I call* my mind *part of something must vaster?*

The psychological content of consciousness of man is almost universal. In that consciousness man suffers, goes through a great deal of agony, conflict and depression and elation. He has enumerable beliefs, great many images about himself and about others. There is fear and the pursuit of pleasure. And there are the various types of religious divisions with their superstitions, illusions, saviors, and all that. That is the content of one's consciousness, which is really the content of humanity.

So, one must question deeply whether you are an individual at all. You are the result of your parents psychologically and genetically. You have inherited certain conditions as an American, as a Russian, as an Englishman, and so on. And according to religion, you are a separate soul. But is that so?

God will save you, or Jesus; somebody will save you. That pattern has been established after 2,000 years in the Western world, and probably 3,000 to 5,000 years in the Eastern world—that you are a separate human being because you have a separate body, separate name, and so on. From the physical they move into the psychological, which becomes the individual, the soul. Personally I question all of that because your consciousness is similar to the rest of mankind. So we are not an individual.

J. Krishnamurti, Interview with Michael Mendizza

S: Buddhists may not say there's no individual mind. They would also not say the individual mind is part of a universal mind. These expressions are not in Buddhism. The Buddhist believes that your mind, my mind, and all the other minds, are individual minds. This remains up to the Buddha Nature. Until then, individuals will remain individual. Buddhists would say there is nothing inherently *mine*. However, as long as your ego, your ignorance is there, the division—*my* and *others*, *my* and *his*, *my* and *hers*—cannot be removed until you remove the ego. When you remove the ego, then nothing will be mine or the other's. *Mine* is a result of the "I". Once the "I" is removed, then you can't say, *it is mine*. There's no need.

Above: Group photo, Benares, September 1910
Left: J. Krishnamurti, Adyar, 1910

Many of the world's religions speak of a hero or savior who appears in a time of crisis to help mankind. In *The Secret Doctrine*, Blavatsky described how such a teacher would define truth in terms suitable for a new civilization. Over the years this theme had been developing in Besant's mind. By 1900 she was convinced that time had come for the reappearance of a great spiritual leader. Even now she was lecturing in India, Europe, and the United States on the coming of a World Teacher. Expectations were spreading throughout the Society and thousands thronged to hear her lectures.

The year was 1909. C. W. Leadbeater had moved to India and was now living at Adyar, the Theosophical headquarters near Madras. Each day, he would stroll with a group of friends along the beach on the Bay of Bengal. It was there that the young Jiddu Krishnamurti was discovered.

In spite of the child's thin, uncared-for appearance, Leadbeater saw a quality so remarkable that he announced that this Brahmin boy would fulfill the long-awaited prophecy. Krishnamurti was to be prepared as the vehicle for the World Teacher. This discovery was not an isolated revelation, for it was believed by some that humanity was entering a new age, an age that would bring with it a new Messiah.

J. Krishnamurti, *The Challenge of Change*

Dharamsala, India, 2014, Day Five

The Maitreya Prophecy

M: *I find Krishnamurti's story one of the most unusual, amazing, and thought-provoking in modern history, if not most of history. It's a very strange story. There was a prophecy in the mid-1800s. The Maitreya, the future Buddha, would take a physical body, teach, and bring about a New World Religion, completely unlike anything that had existed before. This was to take place in 1975, at the end of the dark* Kaliyuga, *which began at midnight (00:00) on 18 February 3102 BCE or 14 January 3102 BC in the Gregorian calendar. Later, two leaders of the Theosophical Society charged with preparing humanity to accept the New World Teacher, Annie Besant and C.W. Leadbeater, pushed it forward to 1910.*

Leadbeater was told through clairvoyant communion with his Tibetan Master that there would be a special boy that day on the beach. Krishnamurti's discovery was not by chance or random. Leadbeater was instructed. By all accounts, confirmed by Krishnamurti's own account and by his talking with people who were there at the time, the boy was thought to be moronic, retarded. Krishnamurti had a sister who was mentally retarded, and his behavior was similar to hers. He would stand and stare, mouth open, for hours. His outward capacity was not inspiring. After his so-called discovery, the boy and his younger brother were trained by Besant and Leadbeater in the Theosophical system, its beliefs, dogma, magic, rituals, and ceremonies. Krishnamurti claims that none of this stuck. He may have been told all sorts of things that went in one ear and out the other. This is a very strange prophecy, given this unusual boy. At the end of his life, if we ask if he fulfilled the prophecy I would have to say, yes. I'm curious what you think about this story.

S: I don't have anything to contribute because I don't attach any importance to the story or to the history or to the sequence of events. They happened or they did not happen or they happened in another way. All this is possible. One thing that no one can deny is that Krishnamurti appeared in this world. He talked for sixty to seventeen years and no one will be able to contradict his statements through logic or in any other way anything that he has said. We may understand. We may not understand. But no one can prove them wrong. This is a fact that is undeniable. This is the history. He was with us as an ordinary human being. He walked around. He had happiness and sorrow. He had relation-

*Right: J. Krishnamurti with Star medal, 1911;
Below left: Group photo, Taormina, 1912; Below right:
C.W. Leadbeater and Annie Besant; Bottom: Group
photo, Villa Cevasco with J. Krishnamurti in shawl*

ships, some good, sometimes strained. All the things that happen to ordinary human beings happened to him. His reactions may have been different, but everything that happens to ordinary human beings happened to him. No one can change what he said. Not only said, his words were recorded. A thousand years in the future, people will witness the publications and the videos. This is for the entire world. That is most important. No other teacher in human history has been so accurately documented.

Was the prophecy correct or incorrect? Is this really relevant? As I mentioned before, the organization of the Theosophical Society, its coming into being, was not completely a human idea. It was a divine design. That has to be accepted. But in that divine design we cannot say that the human beings involved never made mistakes. The human actors had their own egoistic ways of doing things. But the mistakes that may have been made did not prevent or block the message that Krishnamurti wanted to give. This is how I look at this story.

M: *Well done.*

So Many Mysteries

S: If we indulge in the re-digging of history, there is no end. You will find hundreds of things that are false and hundreds of things that are true. Both are of little use. I remember one of the authors of Buddhist logic. He said, "Yes, Buddha had clairvoyance and all the attributes of the enlightened person. But what value has any of this for me? Does he know how many insects live in the ocean? He may not know or he may know. This knowledge is of no concern to me. I am concerned only with his teaching of how to get out of the ego. That is my concern."

M: *Mark Lee, who was with Krishnamurti from the mid-1960s, produced a publication called* Under the Pepper Tree *that dealt with the strange process that occurred in Krishnamurti's life, beginning in 1922. Mark wrote, "Theosophy opened the door to the unknown. Krishnamurti walked through the door and never looked back." There are so many mysteries, unanswered questions, speculations.*

S: It is our responsibility to preserve the documents. I do not think there's anything we should be hiding, keeping secret. There is also little use in publicizing them. Documents are documents. The history is there.

July 9th: As one sat in the aeroplane amidst all the noise, smoking and loud talking, most unexpectedly, the sense of immensity and that extraordinary benediction which was felt in Italy, that imminent feeling of sacredness, began to take place. The body was nervously tense because of the crowd, noise, etc., but in spite of all this, it was there. The pressure and the strain were intense and there was acute pain at the back of the head. There was only this state and there was no observer. The whole body was wholly in it and the feeling of sacredness was so intense that a groan escaped from the body and passengers were sitting in the next seats. It went on for several hours, late into the night. It was as though one was looking, not with eyes only but with a thousand centuries; it was altogether a strange occurrence. The brain was completely empty, all reaction had stopped; during all those hours, one was not aware of this emptiness but only in writing it is the thing known, but this knowledge is only descriptive and not real. That the brain could empty itself is an odd phenomenon. As the eyes were closed, the body, the brain, seemed to plunge into unfathomable depths, into states of incredible sensitivity and beauty. The passenger in the next seat began to ask something and having replied, this intensity was there; there was no continuity but only being. And dawn was coming leisurely and the clear sky was filling with light. As this is being written late in the day, with sleepless fatigue, that sacredness is there. The pressure and the strain too.

Krishnamurti's Notebook

If someone is interested, let them see for themselves. Why should we hide anything? Some foundation people think this or that should not be shared. I do not subscribe to that idea. They should be open. They should be available. They need not to be advertised, publicized, and talked about to make a sensation out of this. The past is the past. What is important is here and now. Why should we hold on to the past?

M: *I mentioned Krishnamurti's pepper tree experience and the strange process. As you know, it went on most of his life.*

S: It was consistent.

M: *It wasn't just a day, it was weeks. Many times when Krishnamurti was involved with the process, he would talk to entities no one else could see or hear. From Krishnamurti's letters and those of his brother, what was taking place in Krishnamurti's body was described as an experiment. No one, not even the so-called Masters, knew if it was going to work or not. When you say Theosophy was divinely inspired, this implies some other dimension influencing what was taking place. Is there anything like this in your culture, your history, or is this just another mystery?*

No One Can Understand What Was Going On with Krishnamurti

S: I don't think there's any way to know these things. *The process* was experiential for Krishnamurti only. No one can understand what was going on with him. Sometimes people can witness pain or physical discomfort, otherwise we cannot know what is going on internally. The evidence of the combination of *the process* is the work of Krishnamurti, his work being his teachings, and *the process* is evidence that he went through an amazing experience. What Krishnamurti has said, his teachings, is not a compilation of past references. It is fresh, authentic, and substantial. He spoke for sixty years or more. No one can say this came without preparation. What preparation? It is not study. It is not learning. It is not research. It is not memorization. All these are not the preparation. It was not something transplanted in his brain by an operation. But he gave it to us for over sixty years, consistently. And each one of his words is, as I mentioned before, irrefutable, undeniable. This is the greatest evidence of his preparation. Therefore, we should be satisfied

July 20th: The room became full with that benediction. Now what followed is almost impossible to put down in words; words are such dead things, with definite set meaning, and what took place was beyond all words and description. It was the center of all creation; it was a purifying seriousness that cleansed the brain of every thought and feeling; its seriousness was as lightning which destroys and burns up; the profundity of it was not measurable, it was there immovable, impenetrable, a solidity that was as light as the heavens....

July 23rd: Why should all this happen to us? No explanation is good enough, though one can invent a dozen. But certain things are fairly clear. 1. One must be wholly "indifferent" to it coming and going. 2. There must be no desire to continue the experience or to store it away in memory. 3. There must be a certain physical sensitivity, a certain indifference to comfort. 4. There must be a self-critical humorous approach. But even if one had all these, by chance, not through deliberate cultivation and humility, even then, they are not enough. Something totally different is necessary or nothing is necessary. It must come and you can never go after it, do what you will. You can also add love to the list but it is beyond love. One thing is certain; the brain can never comprehend it nor can it contain it. Blessed is he to whom it is given. And you can add also a still quiet brain.

Krishnamurti's Notebook

with the truth he has shared with us and very passionately asked us to understand deeply; to do it here and now, to live it. So what was *the process?* Was it easy? Was it difficult? What did it do to him? We have no instrument to look into that. He passed through a door and did not look back. And no one has the responsibility or the privilege to look back, whether that door is open, closed, damaged, whatever. That is long passed. Krishnamurti himself never looked back to reconstruct or remember the past.

M: *Something would happen and he would begin to ask, and stop, knowing that whatever thought made of it would not be able to hold the truth.*

S: Yes. So we have to agree with his statement. Even if we were able to reconstruct the whole of his preparation process, we cannot prepare a second person at this moment through that method.

M: *He didn't deny that extraordinary things went on.*

S: No, he never denied it.

M: *Krishnamurti raised the question many times with David Bohm; "Is Krishnamurti a freak?" Was this process some form of epileptic or mental disorder? Krishnamurti said, "No. I'm not a freak, I'm a human being." He also said that other people didn't have to go through what he went through in order to benefit from what he's saying. This implies that the jump or leap he made could be understood without preparation. "You don't have to be Edison to switch on the lights," he said. That is my question. It seems that at least some form of preparation may be required in order to understand, to perceive or experience, not the process but to live the teachings. Can one live the teachings without some form of preparation?*

Can You Live with the Question?

S: As I have mentioned before, Krishnamurti denies preparation. He also does not deny whatever preparation he went through. These two different aspects are clear. He may not consider preparation necessary. He may not accept it. But he did not deny that his preparation was very intense and it went on for years. Our focus must be to understand why he denies preparation for us. Why he insists that we do the thing, experience and live what he was describing, here and now, that our transformation is not dependent on a path, graduation, preparation, time, becoming. We have to understand that all these things that he has emphasized throughout his

We rarely listen to anybody. We are so full of our own conclusions, our own experiences, our own problems, our own judgements, so we have no space in which to listen.... And to listen is only possible when you put aside your particular opinion, your particular knowledge or problem, your conclusions, then you're free to listen, not interpreting, not judging, not evaluating, but actually the art of listening, to listen with great care, attention, with affection. And if we have such an art, if we have learnt such, rather, if you are capable of such listening, then communication becomes very, very simple. There'll be no misunderstanding.

In the art of listening one learns immediately, one sees the fact instantly.... And if you, if one listens rightly, as we pointed out the meaning of that word correctly, accurately, not what you think is right, or wrong, but in the art of listening there is freedom and in that freedom every word, every nuance of word has significance and there is immediate comprehension, which is immediate insight, and therefore immediate freedom to observe.

Also there is the art of seeing, to see things as they are, not as you wish to see them. To see things without any illusion, without any preconceived judgement or opinion, to see actually "what is," not your conclusions about "what is."

So the art of learning implies freedom to observe, to listen without prejudice, without argumentation, without any emotional, romantic responses. If we have these three arts, not merely as a verbal conclusion or an intellectual comprehension, but actually, in our daily life, to put everything in its right place, where they belong, so that one can live a really very quiet, harmonious life.

And with that attention of listening, which is an art, when the speaker says, "Thought is time, thought is measure, thought is a movement in time, which creates fear," if you see that, if you actually listen to it, to that statement, and not make a conclusion of that statement, but actually listen with your heart, with your mind, with all your capacity, attention and care, then you will see that fear has no place at all. The art of listening is the miracle.

The Krishnamurti Reader. Ojai, California, 4th Public Talk, 10 April 1977 *(Abridged)*

life have a specific objective. He used very few ways to convey his message—his talks in public or in groups, followed by dialogue, discussion, questions and answers. Dialogue was, I think, a major way of his sharing the truth with us. During this process of dialogue he always said that conclusions have no meaning. Conclusions are still in the realm of thought. And sometimes he said not to be in a hurry to reach a conclusion. Many times he asked, "Can you live with the question?"

Questioning means searching in a state of wonder and inquiry. Living with a question is preparation, a consistent dialogue with oneself, a constant dialogue with others. It means constantly challenging the ideas, thoughts, and conclusions that we have accumulated, all of which have been heavily contaminated by one's ego and the ego of others. *Living the teachings* means always challenging and trying to destroy those impediments. If the ego takes hold of our preparation, we will be stuck in it throughout our life. The ego will manage to make it so beautiful, consistent, convincing, that we will be taken in by that, thereby avoiding living the teachings. On the contrary, we may prepare ourselves to always be preparing, and thereby remain separate from the teachings, which means we are not disassociating from the ego. It means, on the contrary, living in the world of the ego.

This is the danger and Krishnamurti always warned us of this. Because of this, it is better not to say *preparation*. Just say, *live the teachings*, knowing that is to remain with the question, to continually inquire, to question, like a child who is full of innocent curiosity and wonder. This state of ongoing searching, questioning, without words and with words if necessary, is the only instrument to challenge the ego and our habits of thought, ignorance, and conditioning. That, in my view, is living the teachings.

M: *Each thought is actually discrete, fixed, frozen in time. Thought is similar to persistence of vision. Our fluid sight is made up of discrete images, one following the other in rapid succession. As one fades, it is replaced by another. This gives the impression that sight is moving. But it is not. Thought is similar. Every thought is a separate brick, fixed. Inquiry, wonder, and curiosity are not fixed.*

S: Until it becomes an idea.

M: *Yes, until it becomes a conclusion. Wonder is a state. Curiosity becomes frozen in time as a thought. As long as complete attention as curiosity is active, the ego isn't. As Krishnamurti said, with complete attention there is no center. The center*

It is one of the characteristics of our human species that we can entertain these remarks cerebrally and even dilate upon them intellectually, yet without meeting them viscerally or being touched by them emotionally. Such a bloodless relation to the obvious has through technology given us great material power over our physical environment. Unhappily, it has done nothing to generate or to advance self-inquiry. Without self-inquiry, human nature cannot reach its essential promise, which is to become free of self-misunderstanding.

Allan W. Anderson, *Practical Wisdom:*
Reflections on the Teaching of J. Krishnamurti

It's hard work to put away all illusions—the political, the religious, the illusion of the future. We never discover anything for ourselves. We think we do, and that is one of the greatest illusions, which is thought. It is hard work to see clearly into this mess, into the insanity which man has woven around himself. You need a very, very sane mind to see, and to be free. These two, seeing and freedom, are absolutely necessary. Freedom from the urge to see, freedom from the hope that man always gives to science, to technology, and to religious discoveries. This hope breeds illusion. To see this is freedom, and when there is freedom, you do not invite. Then the mind itself has become the measureless.

J. Krishnamurti, *The Only Revolution*

exists when curiosity, inquiry, attention become fixed as thought. The idea is to maintain the state of open wonder and curiosity, what Krishnamurti calls inquiry, and not get stuck grasping at conclusions. A conclusion may arise but we hold it lightly as an encouragement to deeper inquiry.

S: Yes, that's right.

Without Being Touched by Them Viscerally

M: *From Allan Anderson:"One of the characteristics of our human species is that we can entertain these remarks," referring to Krishnamurti's teachings, "cerebrally and even dilate on them intellectually without meeting them viscerally or being touched by them emotionally." This goes back to this core question of what prevents us from living the so-called teachings. Allan is describing how we spend all day appreciating intellectually but something different must happen to embody the insight, as Krishnamurti would say, in our blood, our guts, our entire being. How do we make that jump from intellectual entertainment to living something?*

S: You may recall when we discussed with him or engaged in dialogue, Krishnamurti would ask us over and over again, "Can you listen?" Here you have people listening very attentively to his words and yet he is asking, "Can you listen?" Their immediate reaction is, "I am listening." But the impression, "I am listening," means the listener is not destroyed. On the contrary, the listener is being substantiated, supported, and strengthened. This is happening. Anybody can experience it. What Krishnamurti demands is to listen to him without any pre-suppositions in your mind. To make your mind completely empty and remove the listener, and just receive the statements given by him, word by word, not adding your imagination to what is being said, your image, your previously supposed interpretations, free from all these with a completely empty mind to receive his insight.

M: *If any of these things is active, we are only listening partially.*

S: Yes.

M: *In the state of active listening there is no room for "me", no room for the ego.*

S: Yes, no room for "me". The ego does not exist. So we have to jump into that state. And you ask, how? Asking how is not the jumping. Nobody can ever tell you how. If someone tells you how, how will become the instrument of the ego.

Why does my mind, your mind, compare? Look at it, sir. Why? Is it from childhood we have been taught to compare? That's one factor. All our social structure is based on that too. Our religious environment is based on that—you are nothing, you must be like a saint; this whole business is based on comparison.... My life, my education, the culture in which I have been born, all bring about or shape the mind, the brain, everything, to compare myself with others, or compare myself with what I have been. Compare in the present, in the future, and in the past. And when I am aware of it, I find excuses for it: why should I compare, what's wrong with comparison, all the world compares.

And then I condemn it; how terrible to compare myself, why can't I be myself, I won't compare any more.... So you are constantly in battle between the past, the future, and what you have, what you think is right in comparing yourself. All that is based on comparison. And then you say, "I'll be myself, I don't give a pin for others, what others—I'll be myself, identify myself." What is yourself? Yourself is part of this momentum of comparison. Now, when you don't compare, what takes place?... I want to find out what happens to my mind when there is no comparison at all—and I don't say, "I will be myself"—all that's part of comparison. What takes place?

The mind is free of one burden, isn't it? It says, "The thing which I have about all my life, I've put it aside." So the mind, by examining, observing, being aware what the content of comparison implies, suddenly realizes the futility of it, the stupidity of it, the utter unintelligence of it. Therefore the mind has become intelligent.

Then the question arises, why does the mind identify; why do you identify yourself with your furniture, with your house, with your belief? Why do you identify?... I have identified myself with my books, with whatever it is, family and all the rest of it, country, belief, and so on.... Why do I do this?

When there is no identification, no attachment, what takes place in the mind? You've got rid of another burden, haven't you? The mind says, "All right, I've lived in a kind of fantasy, in a myth, which has given me tremendous pleasure; also it has given me a great deal of pain...." Then what takes place? Then you're dealing with facts, and that will give you tremendous vitality.

J. Krishnamurti, Saanen, Switzerland, 3rd Public Dialogue, 4 August 1972 *(Abridged)*

M: *The darn ego again.*

S: Yes, the ego again.

M: *The ego is very clever.*

S: Yes. He is a very clever guy.

M: *As you said, he will follow you wherever you go and take credit for everything you do.*

S: Yes, exactly.

What Will I Achieve?

M: *What is the significance of Krishnamurti's so-called teachings, the significance of his life?*

S: We must define what we mean by *significance* and *value*. With the conditioning of the human mind, particularly in the modern age, modern civilization, what we call significance and value are reduced to a very small channel. You can't go here, you can't go there. You must go this way and not that. This way of assessing, not that—perfect input, perfect output. Measuring things in this way, human love and compassion have become commodities, measurable. If you are not able to measure them, you think they have no value. So we try to evaluate Krishnamurti, the significance of his life and his teachings. If we do this, we are moving away from his teachings, making his teachings a new sect or one of the many hundreds or thousands of sects, a new tradition. I would stay away from talking or thinking in terms of significance, value or benefits.

Today the most important questions everybody asks are, "If I do this, what will I achieve? How will I benefit?" Professor Krishnanath used to ask, "What is the benefit of the benefits?" There is no end. Having a benefit implies that we are making our ego happy. But in this regard, if the ego is happy, there is no benefit. This is our way of measuring. So we cannot measure the significance, the benefits or utility of Krishnamurti's life or his teachings.

I simply look at Krishnamurti. He lived and spoke to the very end of his life. He did not remain silent. He shared something day in and day out with large numbers of people. And now the world has his message. It has touched, partially or fully, undistorted or distorted, millions of people, young and old. Students know the name *Krishnamurti*. They have a vague

J. Krishnamurti, Oak Grove School, Ojai

Dawn wouldn't come for a couple of hours, on waking, with eyes that have lost their sleep, one was aware of an unfathomable cheerfulness; there was no cause to it, no sentimentality or that emotional extravagance, enthusiasm, behind it; it was clear, simple cheer, uncontaminated and rich, untouched and pure. There was no thought or reason behind it and neither could one ever understand it, for there was no cause to it.

This cheerfulness was pouring out of one's whole being and the being was utterly empty. As a stream of water gushes out from the side of a mountain, naturally and under pressure, this cheer was pouring out in great abundance, coming from nowhere and going nowhere, but the heart and mind would never be the same again.

Krishnamurti's Notebook

idea that he talked frankly, and that he denied, negated, many things. They know he was not traditional. He was different. They have read his books or listened to his talks. They are being challenged to the core. Nobody is left unchallenged. They may have different theories, but no one who reads Krishnamurti can add to what he was saying, happily boosting their egos. It does not happen.

Constant Challenge Is Krishnamurti's Real Contribution, His True Legacy

S: Krishnamurti made it a bit uneasy, challenging. Not being able to easily disagree prevents us from reaching conclusions and casting Krishnamurti into another brick. That challenge stimulates curiosity, and stimulating curiosity and inquiry is a great thing. It is a great thing to stimulate the inner intelligence that we have set aside for such a long time. You might say this is the significance or value of his life. Constant challenge is his real contribution, his true legacy.

M: *Because our consciousness is embedded in the ego state, we feed and strengthen our own and others' egos by the mirroring of our relationships. If the mirror affirms the ego's self-image, we are pleased. If not, we are unhappy.*

S: Yes, right.

M: *Krishnamurti's mirror is different. When you look in Krishnamurti's mirror, be it a book or a video, the reflection we see is this challenge you're talking about.*

S: Yes.

M: *It doesn't matter which book, which page, which paragraph of thousands of pages one reads. You're going to get the same challenging reflection.*

S: His mirror is not the usual mirror. It reflects a very strange image, one we are not used to seeing. We look at this strange reflection he presents and we are challenged. Our ordinary mirrors, our traditions, religions, our cultures, reflect the images that boost the ego and we say, yes. Krishnamurti challenges all that.

M: *I appreciate the way we came to this, redefining the meaning of significance, seeing the essence of Krishnamurti's life and teachings as this pervasive challenge, and using the image of a mirror to see this challenge. In talking with Krishnamurti, Allan Anderson said, "There are two types of thinking; calculative, to calculate meaning measure, and meditative, to ponder." One measures and*

All human beings throughout the world, after so many millions of years, are conditioned. That's a fact. They are conditioned by their religions, by establishments of governments, by economic conditionings, climate, food, clothes, by their family, by their education, and so on. All human beings right through the world are conditioned. That's an obvious, acceptable, reasonable fact. And there are those philosophers and psychologists who say that you must accept this conditioning.... The human conditioning can never be transformed. There can never be a mutation from this conditioning, and so make the best of it.

If you accept that, which is very convenient and happy, you can trot along for the rest of your life, living in a small circle of conditioning and say that is inevitable. But if one goes into it much more deeply, if one wants to find out what the conditioning is and whether it is possible to really, very deeply, at the very root of it, this conditioning, be free of all that.

When the brain is conditioned, that conditioning brings various forms of conflict. Right? I am conditioned as a Hindu, suppose, or a Catholic, or a Protestant, or whatever it is. Naturally the brain being so conditioned becomes atrophied.

If you keep on repeating that you are a Christian, that you must behave this way, that you must be like that, that there is only one savior, and so on and so on, this very repetition, this constant acceptance of something unreal, which has no factual actuality, then the brain must inevitably become more and more atrophied... There are many other factors of this conditioning, which are separation, division; where there is division there must be conflict.

Is it possible to be free of all this? Is it possible to be aware without any prejudice, without any choice, just be aware of my conditioning? And then is it possible, not allowing time as a factor to dissolve this conditioning.... Time being, I will do it gradually. So is it possible to look at this conditioning without the time element at all?

The mind can never be free from conditioning if the mind allows time to interfere with the dissolution of conditioning.

J. Krishnamurti, Ojai, California,
1st Public Question & Answer Meeting, 5 May 1981 *(Abridged)*

asks is it possible? The other wonders and asks is it appropriate? One is purely mechanical, intellectual, and abstract. The other is based on relationship, empathy, and wisdom. Calculative thinking is necessary in our material world to survive. Yet, ironically in our time, the misuse and abuse of it and of technology is threatening the world, which may include our extinction.

In one of his publications, the Dalai Lama talked about how in years past the activity of ignorance was local, small, held in the village or neighborhood. Now, through technology, the consequences of ignorance have compounded dramatically. David Bohm and Krishnamurti discussed this at great length. We are talking about these two types of thinking, one that calculates and one that ponders. My question relates to the trend, how things are going. Professor Anderson is advocating that the calculative—and of course the ego loves to calculate, to predict and control—is dominating. I remember Krishnamurti and David Bohm being apprehensive about the misuse of calculative thinking. Buddhist teachings and Krishnamurti's insights have been available for a long time, yet calculative thinking is dominant. Your thoughts?

Exploitation of the Ego by the Ego Is the Root of All the Problems We Have Today

S: The collective conditioning of the mind of each individual in modern society is immense and is very difficult to decondition. It is a fact, particularly for the last two hundred and fifty years or so, that we have experienced what is called *calculative thinking*, and with it the systematic exploitation of human greed has been practiced consciously. Historically, in ancient societies, everyone produced something. Consumable goods or anything necessary for human beings were manufactured by hand and produced to meet real demand. In a village of two hundred people, there would be a cobbler who made shoes. He might make two hundred and fifty pairs of shoes in a year. He could live comfortably, honorably, and meet the demands of the entire village. His work did not overconsume natural resources, nor did it harm the environment. There was a harmonious balance between human beings and other living beings, and with nature. The natural order was not disturbed. We have four different seasons. During the rainy season the rain will come. The winter will bring snow. In summer it will be hot. And according to that, the food, fruits, flowers, and vegetables grow. There was no waste, no exploitation.

There is no savior. You are the only savior. Don't seek light at the feet or the knees of any person. You are responsible for all the things that you are doing. When you send your son to war, you are responsible for that, which means you don't love your son, which means you love yourself, your comfort, your position, your daily safety. So you sacrifice your son for your own personal comfort.

And it means also to be a light to one's self. That's really a marvelous sense of freedom without a single burden, because then, if you are a light to yourself, there is no shadow in that light.

J. Krishnamurti, Interview with Michael Mendizza

At the Old Kashag Office, Central Tibetan Administration, Dharamsala, ca. 2009–2010

The minds of beings are, in reality, always void, being really not-self-nature. This natural voidness of the mind is variously called "the lineage of the self-existent," "the lineage of the Buddhas," "the seed of the Buddhas," or "the womb of the Tathagatas," this last name being found in many Mayayana scriptures. This Buddha lineage exists in the minds of all beings, and it is for this reason that all beings are able (given suitable conditions) to attain to Buddhahood.

His Holiness the Dalai Lama, *The Opening of The Wisdom-Eye*

But science and technology have given human beings the ability to produce much more than is needed. Producers then had to think of how to sell all these things in the market and to make disproportionate, enormous profits. They could not increase the true nature of human need, so they had to find ways to escalate human greed; then the question of need would no longer be relevant. People would consume everything. All this is the intelligence of the ego comparing. And comparison leads to competition and will make the individual compete throughout his or her life, comparing with neighbors or with what is being promoted by advertising. This exploitation of the ego by the ego is the root cause of all the problems we have today. The widening gap between the very rich and the rest of humanity is itself a global form of violence.

In ancient times, violence was for revenge or for gain, such as for land or trade. Today violence is an industry. Violence is the only way to maintain the market of the weapons industry. Wars are not fought to win or lose. Wars are fought only to consume armaments. The over-consumption of natural resources and the transportation of over-produced material goods degrade the environment beyond its tolerance. As long as this pattern persists, this ignorance, there is no way to stop us from destroying the planet Earth. This is so obvious. It is not complicated, it is obvious. The challenges are clear.

This is the human predicament today. Now, you ask, why are the message of Buddha, the message of Krishnamurti, and the messages of many other people not effective? In my view, despite such deep conditioning, there are still many concerned people who are worried about these challenges. Each year more people are talking about the environment, about nonviolence, about equality and justice. Their voices are growing. At this moment they may not be effective but the power of their voices is growing. And behind these right-thinking people is the force and inspiration of these teachings. We cannot say these teachings will save the planet or save humanity or not save humanity. That is in the hands of humanity. But humanity cannot say, we were completely ignorant, we were not told. We have been informed about the challenges and the consequences. We have been given the alternatives. The great teachers have done everything they can. They have honored their responsibility, their duty. But they cannot transfer their wisdom to each individual person. They cannot

It has been said that Krishnamurti began where Buddha ended. Buddha is supposed to have brought rationality into spirituality. Krishnamurti goes beyond and he shows us the limitation of thought as a means of psychological mutation, and he shows that pure perception, which is not related to time or to thought, acts, and that perception which acts breaks away the pattern of the brain, in which the human being has been caught for over a million years, repeating the same thing over and over again.

Padma Madholkar, MD. Interview with Michael Mendizza

force humanity to see what they are doing and change, as Krishnamurti would say, change radically. The responsibility is ours.

Krishnamurti's Consciousness Touched Everything

M: *Krishnamurti said many times that what we call his teachings aren't in the books, are not in the words or videos. The teachings, he said, are living, alive. This brings us to a challenging point. If it is not in the books or in the words, it must be in the state he was in as he authored the books and the words, his way of seeing himself and his relationship to the world. His particular realization or enlightenment was a state, not an idea. He lived that. He was it. Some have suggested, and even he said, if one human being changes, because we all share the same human spirit and mind, that change will affect everything, not as an intellectual abstraction, but as a vibration, as a state or as a quality of energy, perception, way of living. This radiant, non-verbal presence, vibrating like a tuning fork with similar tuning forks, ordinary human beings, was his true purpose and value.*

S: I think that's true. It has radiated; it has touched everyone and everything and it is still radiating. And *radiating* means not only an invisible influence but even the books and the words that Krishnamurti used to share his insights. Of course the word, the symbol or metaphor is not the real thing. But the words, the books and videos carry Krishnamurti's challenge to people all over the world; the challenge, as we just described it, is the real meaning being transmitted. And that shakes the core, the foundation of ignorance, that is the ego.

M: *The words, the books and videos challenge humanity intellectually. This nonverbal radiance, this living quality being present and active, is also operating but in a different way. Both are challenging, not just one or the other. They are working together. The radiance, we might say the realization, is coming from the inside, and then the intellectual challenge is coming from the outside.*

S: Yes.

The first time I really met him was in Brockwood, my first year, in a student meeting, and it was a shock to see this ninety-year-old man just walking in, really frail; I mean, he was frail and it was strange to see him like that. He was very old. And he sat down, and he was very innocent, you know. He looked around and looked at us, smiled at us, but I didn't see intelligence here, as I knew it, you know, knowledge.

And when he started talking, we questioned him, first, a lot—you know, we're students we questioned him—and he got involved, quite involved, very involved, in what he was saying, and then you couldn't see the old man at all; he was so fresh, so young, so in charge of everything, aware of us, yeah, aware.

And in talking to him—I was fourteen and he was ninety—but I was older than him; he was so young and fresh, yeah? And the talk ended and there again the old man who forgot everything he had talked about.

Loic Lopez, Student, Interview with Evelyne Blau and Michael Mendizza

Thought Cannot Function Clearly When It Is Contaminated by the Ego

M: *We described how ignorance, the ego, and thought are one process. Realizing this tends to make thought and thinking less respected than we generally treat them. Professor Anderson suggested with Krishnamurti that thought might be corrupt. Krishnamurti and David Bohm also explored this idea that thought can be misused, and often is. However, they concluded that it is not necessarily the structure that is corrupt; rather that it is how it is used. Again, thought that is used in the service of the ego, self-centered thought, what we call ignorance, leads to self-deception and distortion. There is also the undistorted use of thought, as in proper science and the use of various arguments found, for example, in Nagarjuna's text and many of your intensely analytical meditations. Is thought inherently corrupt or distorted, and how is one to know?*

S: According to the Buddhist viewpoint, thought has limitations. Of course we do not deny that thought can be misused. Thought can be used in ways that cause tremendous violence, and thought can be used in positive ways that benefit others. Thought can do many good things but thought cannot do good when it is contaminated by the ego.

M: *Yes, thought can operate free from the influences of the ego; the expression of compassion may be an example. And thought can be filtered by the images we have of ourselves, our ego that tends to distort.*

S: Inherently we are not dealing with fact but with images produced by the ego. That's why we say that thought can operate at the level of the Buddha Nature. The old thoughts are not there.

M: *Krishnamurti was very clear that insight is expressed as direct action. For ordinary people, insight arises, is filtered by thought, and we act.*

S: As we discussed, Buddhists may not say that ordinary people can act without thought. For ordinary, unenlightened people, thought is indispensable because thought comes automatically. Without thought, we may be unable to act. This is the limitation of the unenlightened person, and thought has its own limitations. Humanity is influenced by both these limitations.

On the first of February I went to see him in his bedroom at Pine Cottage, because by that time he had been discharged from the hospital, and when I met him in the morning I was utterly shocked at his condition. He could hardly raise his hand to shake mine. He didn't recognize me. His attention span was less than two seconds because his eyes couldn't keep open. It wasn't only with me because my aunt and my cousin were there too, and the same thing happened with them. So we were in a state of great shock to see him like that, when a month earlier he had been the old Krishnamurti, talking to 6,000 people and going for walks and engaging in serious discussion.

When I went to see him the next day, an astonishing thing happened. He smiled and he held my hand and I felt a strong pulse beating and suddenly, in his old voice, a strong voice, he said, "Sir, where is your anchor?" So I said, "In you, sir." And he replied instantly, "I'm going." And then he said, "If you have touched that, you must be anchored in it, otherwise you will go to pieces." And then he smiled and he said, "You are a nice chap but you are wasting your life." And then he closed his eyes.

Asit Chandmal, Interview with Evelyne Blau and Michael Mendizza

J. Krishnamurti

To Understand the Real Teaching, You Need to Transform Yourself

M: *Speaking to the international trustees, Krishnamurti said that no one had understood him. No one is living the teachings. Allan Anderson noted that Krishnamurti's enigmatic or mysterious announcement that no one had understood him is not without precedent. Lao Tzu, of the* Tao Te Ching, *said, "My teachings are easy to understand and easy to practice but no one understands and no one practices." Lao Tzu described how his teachings are sourced in nature and his deeds are destined by the Tao. And because people don't understand this—nature, the Tao—they don't understand him. Confucius stated that no one knew him except Heaven. Jesus said to his disciples, "There are many things I would have told you, but you cannot bear them." Anderson described how Krishnamurti stood up, shrugged his shoulders and said, "I've been saying these things for fifty years," and then fell silent. This is a common theme. Can the teachings actually be understood? Or if they are understood, have we already taken and converted the absolute to the relative? Have we reduced something living, indescribable, back into something that can be measured?*

S: As Buddhists we say, all the teachings of any great person are understandable, knowable, but they are not easy. To understand, to know, the real teaching you need to transform yourself. Transformation is not common, not so easy. Apart from that, once a person is transformed, they will no longer fit in with the unenlightened crowd. He or she will have stepped out of that stream. Because I do not interpret the utterances of these great teachers, this does not mean that no one was transformed by their teachings. Many people may have understood and understand today. These statements address those who are not transformed, not enlightened, listening to these teachings. None of them had understood and therefore these statements are true.

Apart from that, I want to say something general about the old religious and spiritual traditions as they relate to Krishnamurti. Our general view of past teachers and their teachings is that they appeared in the world at different times, in different circumstances, and spoke to the majority of people with different attitudes than today. Buddha appeared. Buddha first summoned five disciples and all five were transformed. They understood. They lived the teachings. After that, the Buddha taught during his entire lifetime and each day many people were transformed, enlightened.

J. Krishnamurti, Ommen Camp, ca. 1929

I maintain that Truth is a pathless land and cannot be approached by any path whatsoever, by any religion, by any sect.... Truth being limitless, unconditioned, unapproachable by any path whatsoever, cannot be organized, nor should any organization be formed to lead or coerce people along any particular path.... If you do, it becomes a creed, a religion to be imposed on others.

No man from outside can make you free; nor can organized worship, nor the immolation of yourselves for a cause, make you free; nor can forming yourselves into an organization, nor throwing yourselves into works, make you free.

I have now decided to disband the Order, as I happen to be its Head. You can form other organizations and expect someone else. With that I am not concerned, nor with creating new cages, new decorations for those cages. My only concern is to set men absolutely, unconditionally free.

J. Krishnamurti, *Truth Is a Pathless Land*.
Ommen, The Netherlands, 3 August 1929 *(Abridged)*

Because Buddha appeared for them and they were prepared, the spark from both sides converged. When this happens it is easy to become enlightened. After Buddha's passing, when people had to depend on scripture, on interpretation, on commentary, or on the various traditions, this sparking power was no longer there. It gradually gets diluted. The same thing has happened to every spiritual tradition. During the founder's lifetime, many people benefit directly. Afterwards, the understanding goes down, down, down, but the tradition remains. In the twentieth century when the Theosophists appeared, almost every tradition had become dogma.

M: *All of the world's spiritual traditions had become dogma, lost their spark.*

S: Yes. And very few people are living it. Most simply repeat the words, believing they are achieving something else. In such a world, the need of the hour is to be challenged, to shake dogma. And for shaking dogma, a new vocabulary is needed; a completely new approach and new type of challenge is necessary. It was in that set of circumstances that Krishnamurti appeared. And his basic task was to challenge, to shake up, to make people think, to not take everything for granted. Taking everything for granted is the most dangerous form of conditioning at this moment in history. Krishnamurti worked in this way throughout his life. We may not understand his process or understand him completely but we are all challenged. And because we are challenged, our conditioning, our ignorance is shaken, which demands that we begin to inquire, begin to question. If you say this is the significance or value of Krishnamurti's life and teaching, I have no objection.

THE MYSTERY

Below are quotes describing a number of mysteries that surrounded Krishnamurti's life. From each in their own words, these selections are from Krishnamurti; his biographer, Mary Lutyens; Richard (Dick) Clark, Krishnamurti's first teacher; and Nityananda, Krishnamurti's younger brother.

It's interesting that when Krishnamurti first asked me to write his biography, he said to me, if he was writing the biography he would start with a vacant mind; and then he went on to enlarge how he'd always had, he said, a vacant mind. And he seemed to think that the vacant mind was so much a part of him, a part of his teaching. And he said it was because of the vacant mind that all he'd learnt and been taught, rather, about Theosophy and all the Theosophical jargon, had never taken root; it was all on the surface of his mind.

The Theosophical Society, which was founded by Madame Blavatsky and Colonel Alcott, was really an ecumenical movement to show that all religions were equal. That was the basis of it, which most people joined. There was also an esoteric side which Madame Blavatsky worked out, saying that a great hierarchical figure, called the Lord Maitreya, came to earth about every two thousand years and took the body of a human being, when they were most needed for the evolution of humanity.

Mrs. Annie Besant became the President of the Theosophical Society after Colonel Alcott's death and then she with her colleague, C. W. Leadbeater, started looking very seriously for a vehicle who they thought would be suitable for the World Teacher.

The boy who was eventually chosen to be the Messiah was an Indian boy from South India called Jiddu Krishnamurti. He and his brother and other boys used to play on the beach every afternoon, because Adyar is on the sea.

> *One day Leadbeater saw this boy on the beach and he was tremendously struck by his aura, which he said had not one trace of selfishness in it, and he immediately felt that this was the boy.*
>
> Mary Lutyens

> *I arrived in Adyar in 1909, in August, and within a few days I met C.W. Leadbeater. And almost immediately he introduced me to two Indian boys, J. Krishnamurti and his little brother, Nityananda.*
>
> *Krishnamurti was shy, reserved, mystically inclined, seeming outwardly to be rather dull and not quick on the uptake, whereas his little brother sparkled with intelligence. They were in poor condition, very poor condition. And Leadbeater said, "We have a task and when Annie Besant arrives in India, she will help."*
>
> Richard Clark

> *CWL and Dr. Besant were corresponding about the older boy, K. By then they had taken the boys to the Master and the Master apparently, according to them, said, "That is the boy." They had received, they said, instructions from their respective Masters that K was going to be the vehicle for the World Teacher. And so Leadbeater, CWL, took charge of training these two boys.*
>
> *Nobody was to touch anything that K touched. If they said they liked oranges, for the rest of the year they had oranges. If they said they liked porridge, they had porridge every morning for the rest of the year. If they said they wanted to go on a bicycle ride—right! You went on a bicycle ride for the rest of the year, every morning from seven to eight. So the boys never said after that that they liked anything.*
>
> *CWL had written to Dr. Besant in England that his Master had told him that K was to take his initiation. And Dr. Besant wrote to CWL saying: "Use my room. If necessary, close all the headquarters and do what you are instructed." So this boy was prepared, bathed properly and dressed, and all the rest of it, and taken to Dr. Besant's room and went to sleep or became unconscious, it is not clear all of this for me, for twenty-four hours or more.*
>
> J. Krishnamurti

> *Krishna was placed on Annie Besant's bed in her own room, and Leadbeater had a mattress on the floor. We, Nitya and I, used to supply hot milk. And Krishna would come back to his body and take some milk, because the whole period was three days. He was practically away from his body, more than not, for three days.*

After, he came back to his body, bathed and robed in silk, looking like a god; I will never forget it. In fact he looked so outstandingly remarkable that his little brother prostrated himself at his feet as he came out of the room, and I did the same.

He had taken a step up in physical appearance. He was no longer a skinny little, sorrowful-looking boy with a rather open mouth and a vacant look. He was a very alive, aware young boy ready to step into early manhood.

Richard Clark

There was a sense of tremendous feeling about all this, not just an intellectual concept, an intellectual invention, but a feeling that a great event, a great thing was around this boy.

People were talking around the boy, all the theosophical things, theosophical jargon about discipleship, and how the Master treated the disciples and so on and on. All that went around him all the time; not just for a few days or a few weeks, all the time. And apparently, nothing of that entered into the boy.

He said he saw the Masters then. He was highly probably sensitive, somewhat perceptive, clairvoyant and all that, because he used to see all kinds of things. All that in no way seemed to touch the boy, which is quite strange.

You see, my difficulty is now that I don't remember what he was like. I wish I could. I have thought a great deal about it, but I can't; I actually don't remember when I met CWL, Dr. Besant, about any of those things.

J. Krishnamurti

And Mrs. Besant's idea was that this boy should be trained and educated in England for this tremendous role. And the following year she founded a thing called "The Order of the Star of the East." And she was the protector, with Leadbeater; they were the two protectors of the Order, and Krishnamurti was made the head of it.

She thought that he must be educated in England so she took him, first of all, on a visit in 1911 to England with his brother. And the following year she took him to England to be educated.

Mary Lutyens

He was taken to Europe, lived with people who were so-called British aristocracy; butlers, yacht, clothes, servants, Rolls-Royces. Never smoked, never drank. Girls used to come around him and he didn't know what it was all about. And so there was this peculiar state of mind which could not be held in a pattern. And they had put him at the head of an organization, The Order of the Star of the East, where he was literally worshiped. And he used to shrink from all that.

He was vague. He would tell everybody: "I'll do whatever you want." That used to be his favorite phrase. "I'll do what you want." Even now sometimes it happens.

J. Krishnamurti

Of course, the object of the Order of the Star of the East was to spread the gospel, so to speak; to prepare people to prepare themselves to become disciples of the Lord when he came, and that might be in twenty years, thirty years, fifty years' time. So there was a tremendous surge of interest in this and people absolutely flocked, Theosophists and non-Theosophists, to join this Order, and the word was spread all around the Theosophical Lodges all around the world, because it was a worldwide movement. And it became a very, very great thing. And, as you can imagine, everybody was tremendously excited to think that when they came they might be chosen as a disciple, and all this. And my mother was very much into this because she met Krishna in 1911 and she befriended him all the time he was in England.

In 1921 Mrs. Besant, who was then in India, thought that Krishna had been educated enough and it was time that he started speaking and lecturing for the Society and for the Order of the Star. So she sent for him to come back to India and by that time he was thoroughly disillusioned with his role as Messiah. He didn't believe any of it and he was terribly unhappy.

Adding to his unhappiness was that his beloved brother, Nitya, had contracted tuberculosis, but he had been to Switzerland and he was pronounced cured.

On their way to Europe they stopped in San Francisco. They were lent a cottage in the Ojai Valley and were told it was a marvelous climate for tuberculars. And it was the first time in their lives that these two boys, these two brothers who were still very young, had been alone and quite suddenly they felt this tremendous youth and happiness.

And I think it was out of that happiness, for the first time, that in August of that year, Krishnamurti went through a completely unexpected transformation, one might almost call it; a terrific psychic or spiritual experience which changed him and changed him fundamentally and he found something which people, I suppose, always search for, one of these marvelous, transcendental experiences, and really he kept it for the rest of his life.

He was in fact, from that moment, a changed being. And my mother, who heard of this, she wrote to other people wonderful accounts of it, saying, "Isn't it wonderful that Krishna is happy and has found himself at last."

Mary Lutyens

I meditated regularly every morning. Then on the 17th of August I felt acute pain at the nape of my neck and I became almost unconscious. This went on for some time till eventually I wandered out and sat under the pepper tree which is near the house.

I felt myself going out of my body. I saw myself with the delicate tender leaves over me. In front of me was my body and over my head I saw the Star, bright and clear.

I could still see my body and I was hovering near it. There was such profound calmness, both in the air and within myself, the calmness of a deep unfathomable lake. Nothing, nothing could disturb the calmness of my soul. The Presence of the Mighty Beings was with me for some time and then they were gone.

J. Krishnamurti's letter to Annie Besant

The place seemed to be filled with a Great Presence and a great longing came upon me to go on my knees and adore, for I knew that the Great Lord of all our hearts had come Himself; and though we saw Him not, yet all felt the splendor of His Presence. Then the eyes of Rosalind were opened and she saw. Her face changed, as I have seen no face change, for she was blessed enough to see with physical eyes the glories of that night. Her face was transfigured, as she said to us, "Do you see Him, do you see Him?" for she saw the divine Bodhisattva Himself, and millions wait for incarnations to catch such a glimpse of our Lord, but she had eyes of innocence and had served our Lord faithfully. And we, who could not see, saw the Splendors of the night mirrored in her face, pale with rapture in the starlight.

Never shall I forget the look on her face, for presently, I who could not see, but who gloried in the presence of our Lord, felt that He turned towards us and spoke some words to Rosalind; her face shone with divine ecstasy as she answered, "I will, I will!" and she spoke the words as if they were a promise given with splendid joy. Never shall I forget her face when I looked at her; even I was almost blessed with vision. Her face showed the rapture of her heart, for the innermost part of her being was ablaze with His presence but her eyes saw.

Letter from Nitya, J. Krishnamurti's younger brother

After that amazing experience, Krishnamurti was perfectly happy to go on with his role of training himself, really, being trained as a vehicle for the Lord Maitreya. But then quite suddenly Nitya had a very bad relapse and was very, very ill again. And Mrs. Besant wanted Krishna to go to Adyar for the Jubilee Convention of 1925, because it was important that he should be there in his role.

And he didn't want to go because Nitya was so ill. But he was promised by all the leaders, including Leadbeater and Mrs. Besant, that Nitya was much too valuable to die and that Nitya would not die; he would recover.

And because of that promise, which he believed, Krishna agreed to go to India that year, leaving Nitya very ill, well looked after, very ill in Ojai. And on the voyage out, in fact, when he got as far as Port Said on the way to India, a telegram arrived saying that Nitya had died.

And this was an absolutely shattering blow to him. He never believed it could happen. And it destroyed his faith, very largely, in the Masters, who were part of the hierarchy of Theosophy who promised this through the clairvoyant people like Leadbeater, and he was absolutely distraught by this. And he said that he had now suffered, he now knew what death was, and he knew now that there was a love that transcended death, and death was no longer to be feared.

Mary Luytens

When the brother died, you know, I was here [in Ojai, California] and we left, and I didn't know he was going to die. When I got to England, they [the leaders of the Theosophical Society] said, "We are the disciples. If you accept us, your brother will live." And when he died I said, "What a joke this is." That is the phrase he used.

J. Krishnamurti

And after that, for another couple of years, he still believed in the Lord Maitreya and he said at that time, the Lord will come more and more often. It wasn't a question that he had taken possession, but the Lord would come more often to him, but it would still be the Lord speaking through him. But all this time something was going on in his own mind. He was searching for something himself.*

---

* Leading up to dissolving the Order of the Star, in a major break with the Theosophical ideal, Krishnamurti denied that he was a vehicle or a medium, that a separate entity was speaking through him. First, he insisted that there was a blending of consciousness, and later even that distinction completely disappeared.

But as late as 1927, Mrs. Besant declared in America to the press, the World Teacher is here, but it was after 1927 that he gradually began to feel that none of this was true or right, that he had to go his own way but he had to go very gently so as not to hurt Mrs. Besant, because he loved her dearly. There was a tremendously close relationship between them and so it was a very, very difficult time in his life, because he knew that all the leaders, everyone was against him.

In 1929 in Holland at one of these big annual camps he used to hold and had for several years, he announced at the meeting that he was the Head of the Order of the Star and he was going to dissolve it. He said that it was quite unnecessary to have such an order, such an organization. He said that it was ridiculous—I mean, the gist of what he said, I'm not quoting him at all—to be told how spiritual you were; only you knew whether you were corrupt or not corrupt inside.

Nobody could tell you, and that his only objective in life from then would be to set men absolutely free to discover truth for themselves and not to be told what truth was, or be led in any way; they had to find it, if they wanted to find it, for themselves, and he was going to help them to be free.

Mary Lutyens

I maintain that Truth is a pathless land, and you cannot approach it by any path whatsoever, by any religion, by any sect. That is my point of view, and I adhere to that absolutely and unconditionally. Truth, being limitless, unconditioned, unapproachable by any path whatsoever, cannot be organized; nor should any organization be formed to lead or to coerce people along any particular path. If you first understand that, then you will see how impossible it is to organize a belief. A belief is purely an individual matter, and you cannot and must not organize it. If you do, it becomes dead, crystallized; it becomes a creed, a sect, a religion, to be imposed on others. This is what everyone throughout the world is attempting to do. Truth is narrowed down and made a plaything for those who are weak, for those who are only momentarily discontented. Truth cannot be brought down, rather the individual must make the effort to ascend to it. . . .

So these are some of the reasons why, after careful consideration for two years, I have made this decision. It is not from a momentary impulse. I have not been persuaded to it by anyone. I am not persuaded in such things. For two years I have been thinking about this, slowly, carefully, patiently, and I have now decided to disband the Order, as I happen to be its Head. You can form other organizations and expect someone else. With that I am not concerned, nor with creating new cages, new decorations for those cages. My only concern is to set men absolutely, unconditionally free."

J. Krishnamurti, Ommen, The Netherlands, 1929

Perhaps the most significant thing he ever said was to Mary [Zimbalist] when she asked before he left Brockwood if she would ever see him again: "I won't die all of a sudden.... It is all decided by someone else. I can't talk about it. I'm not allowed to, do you understand? It is much more serious. There are things you don't know. Enormous, and I can't tell you." ("All decided by 'someone else'" not 'something else.'" ML addition.)

Mary Lutyens, *Krishnamurti: His Life and Death*

So you want to know now what K thinks of the World Teacher? You were brought up in the very center, in the thick of it all. What is your answer? I really don't know. He has never said, "Who am I?" He has never said, "Is the World Teacher true or not true?" Is this question relevant at all? What is relevant are the teachings. Who the teacher is is not relevant. But to investigate who the teacher is, we have to find out if you can grasp the mind of the teacher.

Personally I feel it's something so immense that the brain saying, I am going to find out, can't find out. But there is something extraordinary which happens, which shows, which occurs, which gives hints and opens the door. And after that, I don't want even to open the door to say what is all this. No, I don't think the brain can understand it.

J. Krishnamurti

Selections from: Krishnamurti with KFA Trustees, January 9, 1972; Biographer, Mary Lutyens interviewed by Evelyne Blau and Michael Mendizza, 1987, and a brief selection from *Krishnamurti: His Life and Death*, 1990; Krishnamurti's first teacher, Richard (Dick) Clark, interviewed by Evelyne Blau and Michael Mendizza, 1979; Letter from Nityananda, Krishnamurti's younger brother, to Annie Besant, August 1922

EPILOG

In physics it is understood that a small coherent force can bring a large chaotic field to order. The same is true of consciousness. Personally preparing and taking this journey with Samdhong Rinpoche was like pouring cloudy water through a fine filter. What appeared at first to be very complex distilled into clear, obvious simplicity, when we know how to look.

How we look predetermines what we see. The context or assumptions we hold about many concepts such as consciousness are defining. A paradigm is a way of seeing, a point of view. For a long time the earth appeared flat until someone observed it was not. With that change in perspective, we and the world changed. So it is with Krishnamurti or any realized being who experiences directly what Rinpoche described as *absolute truth*.

A problem cannot be solved at the level of the problem. A new frame of reference is needed. Suddenly, from this new perspective our normal state of mind looks different. We can't experience this new way of understanding when the very act of looking is defined by old patterns. Having an insight often implies a bursting into awareness of a fresh way of seeing that changes everything we see.

Rinpoche's context, his culture, training, his way of seeing and understanding this bursting insight, along with the nature of our very old patterns, is very different than ours. This different way of looking is the rare and tremendous value of his sharing. Just as the Arctic Inuit has fifty words to describe snow, Rinpoche's culture has as many or more ways to describe what takes place in our mind. His inner world is rich and three-dimensional, whereas ours is somewhat flat. When we seek to understand and look through a flat model, what we see is often one-dimensional or if we are lucky, two. Being invited to look though a more refined and precise lens renders what we see in greater depth, detail, and clarity. One dimension suddenly becomes three-dimensional. That was Rinpoche's gift to me.

Years ago, when Rinpoche described how he saw no difference between the Buddha's description of the absolute truth and Krishnamurti teachings, I was moved, but how obvious this was, from his point of view, remained elusive. There are only two states—enlightened and unenlightened—with no gradation in between. Anyone who negates the source of the unenlightened state sees that same thing. How they describe the difference between the two will vary wildly. This is so simple but life- and world-changing.

Another key is to understand how our word-based reality flattens, compresses and transforms (Rinpoche used the word *converts*) a three-dimensional, living, moving experience into our flat, comfortable reality—what we already know. "The word is not the thing," as Krishnamurti said so often. We only see what we see, no matter in how many ways it is described. As the great ones say, "We have to see the truth for ourselves." No one can do it for us. And this different way of seeing, this new paradigm or insight, happens in a flash. We can prepare the soil but cannot predict or invite the lightning to strike. Krishnamurti called this *choiceless awareness*.

The need and utility of the three distinct types of meditation or practices Rinpoche described was part of the simplifying and distilling that took place in my understanding. The very first media program I produced from Krishnamurti's works was a talk to parents titled "The Quality of Attention." How many times did Krishnamurti emphasize quiet, intense, sensitive attention? How we use our attention defines our life and all of our relationships. Everything begins and ends with the nature and quality of our attention, which is the first essential step in Rinpoche's model—to cultivate attention.

The next step or practice in preparing the soil that Rinpoche described, which is dependent on being able to hold undistracted attention, is the use of a particular quality of thought, incisive analysis and logic to burst and reveal as false the countless images, beliefs, and emotions thought produces about itself and others. Looking over the landscape of what is called *Krishnamurti's teachings*, this is exactly what he did. I suggest this is what Krishnamurti did best. He relentlessly challenged the way thought reifies; how it mistakenly treats the abstractions it creates as if they had concrete or material existence.

Imagine cultivating vast, sensitive attention and not diffusing, distorting, and wasting this most precious and rare evolutionary resource pandering to a thousand-and-one false idols, images, systems, theories, and beliefs. Moses descending from the mountain with his new insights only to find people worshiping idols and images comes to mind. As Rinpoche said, the ego exploiting the ego is the root of all our problems—the image, idol, and ego all being variations of the same root, the old patterns.

What would you see and how would you behave differently if this image-making and exploitation ended? You would have no choice but to express insight, innate intelligence, and compassion in creative new ways moment by moment. If this were the common state of human consciousness, the world and everything in it would be quite different. The third practice Rinpoche described was this blending of vibrant, clear attention with insight, passion, and compassion in action. Krishnamurti called this *a different way of living.*

I rarely quote the Bible but I will again. The irony implied in Luke 23:34 (Jesus dying on the crucifix, having demonstrated that miraculous life- and world-changing power—that insight, innate intelligence, and compassion in action—saying, "Father, forgive them, for they know not what they do," while the soldiers tossed dice for his clothes) is appropriate. We are the soldiers playing games of chance with this unique consciousness we have been given, chasing our own tails, often violently, imagining all sorts of fantastic things and, as Krishnamurti said, we don't see our own tragedy. The metaphors of Moses witnessing from his enlightened perspective what we are doing and Jesus uttering his last words are archetypes. Not much has changed.

The power and value of what I understand of Buddhism and Krishnamurti's teachings begin with our having our own insight: "Forgive us, for we know not what we do." This opens the door to inquiry, as did Krishnamurti's relentless challenging. Insight, challenging and questioning assumptions bring us back to the state of wonder and curiosity we knew as children before *the known* closed that door. Thought, the known, is dull compared to this childlike state that is always fresh. Here is where our true nature is. *Freedom from the known* implies always awakening.

Michael Mendizza

NOTES

In Hinduism, ignorance of one's true self *(avidya)*, leads to ego-consciousness of the body and the phenomenal world. This grounds one in *karma* (desire) and the perpetual chain of *karma* and reincarnation. Through egotism and desire, one creates the causes for future becoming. The state of illusion that gives rise to this false becoming is called *maya*, a false mental image that appears to be true.

Within Buddhism, *samsara* is defined as the continual repetitive cycle of birth, death, and an intermediate *bardo* state that arises from ordinary beings' generating and fixating on a mistaken concept of self and experiences. *Samsara* arises out of wrong knowledge about reality *(avidya)* and is characterized by *dukkha* (failure, suffering, anxiety, dissatisfaction). Buddhists believe that liberation from *samsara* is possible by following the Buddhist eight-fold path.

With Krishnamurti, true intelligence is universal and unconditioned, not a material process, not generated by the body-brain. Thought, knowledge, and the false perception of time they produce is a material, body-brain centered process, therefore limited and therefore not true intelligence. Implicit in thought-knowledge-time is the false perception of a thinker or ego separate from thought. The exploitation of one false thinker or ego by other false egos is the root cause of disorder and conflict throughout the world (suffering). The thinker being a fragment of thought, not independent from thought, disappears when thought is silent, implying complete attention no longer fragmented by conditioned thought or distorted by thought-as-ego, effectively negating the root cause of disorder. Complete attention also and simultaneously invites insight, the direct perception of true intelligence and the flowering of goodness in all aspects of human life.

Michael Mendizza

GLOSSARY

Always Awakening *is intended for a wide audience. Samdhong Rinpoche noted how important it is to be precise when discussing abstract philosophical notions such as mind and consciousness. A slight misinterpretation of a word or phrase can have a profound influence on what is understood. At the same time, scholars have been known to nitpick for centuries. Our intent is to navigate the middle way. With this in mind, Rinpoche was kind enough to provide brief descriptions for a number of Sanskrit (S) and Tibetan (T) words.*

Ātmagrāha (S): self-grasping, ego-grasping; clinging onto the soul or clinging to the wrong view that things exist by their own nature.

Abhi (S): manifest; thorough; an adjective that has various contextual meanings: manifest, thorough, etc.

Abhidharma (S): manifest phenomena; teachings by Buddha on phenomena pertaining to training on wisdom.

Abhyudaya (S): high rebirth (high status); rebirth in the two higher mundane realms: the human or celestial realm.

Ācārya (Acharya) (S): teacher or a spiritual guide.

Adhi (S): superior, higher; an adjective denoting superiority, such as, in the phrase: "the three higher trainings," indicating they are distinct to the three trainings of other systems.

Adhigama (S): realized; as, for instance, in this expression: "Kondniya realized the four truths."

Adhiprajñā (S): higher wisdom, exalted wisdom; the wisdom that is based on the broader realization of reality, which is with the foundation of training in altruistic morality.

Adhiśil-Adhisamādhi-Adhiprajñā (S): Higher morality, ~meditative-concentration, ~wisdom; the three trainings on the path towards liberation and full enlightenment: the higher training in morality, meditative concentration and wisdom.

Āgama (S): spoken teachings, teachings transmitted; the spoken words of the Buddha.

Arha (S): Foe-destroyed being; a practitioner who has realized the reality and through that realization has destroyed all mental defilements (the actual foes).

Asaṅga (Asanga) (S): the name of the Buddhist teacher who pioneered the understanding of the Mind Only perspective. Born in Gandharva region. Asanga presented the five texts of Maitreya. The name literally means The Unobstructed One, Thogs-med (T).

Atīśa (Atisha) (S): the great Buddhist teacher of India who was invited to Tibet in 1040 AD and who, for the next seventeen years, taught in Tibet, greatly reviving the correct elucidation of the teachings.

Bhavacakra (Bhavachakra) (S): The cycle of [the mundane] existence; a depiction in painting of how a sentient being circles through the twelve dependent-links in the mundane realms, wandering from one mundane rebirth to the next, in a continuous cycle of sufferings.

Bodhgaya (S): the place in present-day India where Buddha Śākyamuni attained full enlightenment; the holiest pilgrimage site for Buddhists.

Bodhicitta (Bodhichitta) (S): Enlightenment Mind; the trained perfected thought in altruism, which aspires to achieve enlightenment, so as to be able to help all beings.

Bodhisattva (S): a Heroic Enlightenment Aspirant; a trainee on the Great Vehicle path who has taken the Enlightenment Mind vow to benefit all sentient beings, and towards that goal aspires to achieve full enlightenment.

Bodhisattva-caryā (bodhisattva-charyā) (S): bodhisattva conducts, bodhisattva practices; the practices ("conducts") a bodhisattva trains on to achieve full enlightenment for the welfare of all sentient beings. They comprise of the practices such as, the six perfections, the four means for drawing others, in the service of others, etc.

Bon (T): the religion prevalent in Tibet prior to the advent of Buddhism in the country.

Brahmā (S): the chaste; the Hindu God of creation.

Buddha Amitābha (S): the Buddha Limitless Light; the manifestation in physical form of the purity of speech of all enlightened beings.

Buddha (S): the Awakened-Advanced One; the source of Buddhism. Etymologically: One who has awakened from the stupor of defilements, and whose realization on all phenomena has fully developed.

Buddha Nature: the basic pure and cognitive nature of the mind present with all beings, thus having the potential to become enlightened. Known also as "Tathāgatha-garbha" (the essence of Those Thus Gone, Buddha essence).

Cakra (Chakra) (S): wheel; in general context, wheel symbolizes continuity, passing on from one to another.

Carvāka (Charvaaka), or Lokātaya (S): Rejector of the Conventional Distant; an ancient nihilist tenet that rejects the existence of all that are beyond this life; thus they do not believe in the existence of former and next lives, nor do they believe in the law of karma.

Citta (Chitta) (S): mind; an entity that is clear and cognitive.

Denma Tongpon Rinpoche (ldan-ma ston-dpon-rin-po-che) (T): one of great masters of Tibet (1889–1949).

Dharma (S): teachings; teachings of the Buddha; methods, the path, the law or doctrine of Buddhism. This term has, according to the teacher Vasubhandu, some ten varying contextual meanings.

Dharmakāya (S): Reality Body; the state of enlightenment. It is the purity of the enlightened mind in having all realizations.

Dharma Protectors: realized beings who have made the pledge to help guard the teachings and the practitioners of the teachings. The supramundane, or the beyond-worldly, category of Dharma Protectors were often manifestations, in their respective Dharma Protector aspect, of enlightened beings.

Drepung (hbras-spuns) (T): Established in 1416, it is the largest Tibetan monastic university, with many thousands of resident ordained scholar-practitioners.

Duḥkha (S): suffering; unpleasant feeling/experience, produced by non-virtuous action, action that directly or indirectly harms others.

Eight-Fold Path (ārya-asta-angiki-mārga) (S): The practices, along with the remainder of the thirty-seven attributes corresponding to enlightenment, a person who has realized the reality (a superior being) focuses on. The eight are: correct view, correct realization (~conceptuality), correct speech, correct action, correct livelihood, correct effort, correct mindfulness, and correct single-pointedness.

Four Formless Absorptions (catur-ārupā-samā-patti) (S): The four meditative absorption states in the formless realms of: limitless space, limitless consciousness, nothingness, and of neither recognitionlessness nor non-recognitionlessness.

Guru (S): teacher, a spiritual teacher. Etymologically, the term means "weighty," one who has the weight of virtues. Also, the term has the meaning as "the sublime," that there is none other who surpasses in terms of knowledge, compassion and abilities.

Gyan (jñāna) (S): pristine wisdom; the mind of a Buddha.

Gyu-ma (sgyuma) (T): illusion; Illusion is a metaphor of something unreal, that which appears to exist but is not to be found so.

Indra (S): A God, also known as Śakra, who rules over devas, the celestial beings.

Iśvara (S): the powerful one; an epithet for God. (See Iśvaravādin)

Iśvaravādin (S): Iśvara proponents; the creationist proponents who assert that the world was created by the God Iśvara.

Jain (S): the followers of Jainism; a spiritual faith in India founded by Jina Mahāvīr, circa fourth century (BCE).

Jātaka (S): chronicles of former lives; the stories of previous lives of the Buddha.

Kālacakra (Kalachakra) (S): a Deity of the highest yoga tantra path to enlightenment; the word literally means Time Wheel.

Kālacakra Tantra (S): the teachings on the practice of Kālacakra, taught by the Buddha manifested as the Deity Kālacakra.

Kaliyuga (S): degenerate times; times when the five degenerations are on the rise: degenerate lifespan (short lifespan), degenerate views (distorted views), degenerate defilements (intense and many defilements), degenerate sentient beings (becoming of unruly nature), and degenerate time.

Kalon Tripa (T): Prime Minister; the Chairperson of the Council of Ministers in the Tibetan government. (in Introduction)

Karma (S): action; action of body, speech and mind. Action is the cause, and the experiences of pleasure and suffering are the results of action. A virtuous action is the cause of happiness, a non-virtuous action the cause of suffering. The law of causality, or in another words, the karmic causality system, is explained in terms of the nature of the action (cause), bringing about the corresponding similar effect (result) for the person.

Karu☐a (S): compassion; the altruistic thought wishing others to be freed of their sufferings and the causes of sufferings. It is not just a mere wish; rather such an altruistic thought is generated through a sequence of thought-transformation training in meditations.

Kleśa (S): defilements (afflictions); the impure state of an ordinary being's mind. The main mental defilements are ignorance, attachment and hatred, known as "the three root defilements." Etymologically, they are called "afflictions," or "disturbed" (not at peace), because they make the person become as such.

Kleśavara☐a (S): afflictive obscuration; the imprints of the mental defilements; the strong, subtle residues of defilements with the ordinary mind.

Kundalini (S): "the fierce" (inner heat); the inner heat inside the body generated through certain meditational practices.

Lalitavistara Sūtra (S): the Extensive Manifestations Discourse. Comprised of twenty-seven chapters, this discourse (Sūtra) narrates the biography and benevolent deeds of the Buddha.

Lama (bla-ma) (T): teacher; a spiritual teacher.

Lhagthong (lhag-mthon) (T): vipaśyana (S): transcendent insight (special insight); the direct, not conceptual, realization of the reality of all phenomena.

Madhyamik Philosophers: the Buddhist tenets of the highest level who do not fall into the fallacies of the two extremes of nihilism and eternalism. It is comprised of two schools: the Autonomous Tenet (Svāntantrika) and the Consequentialist Tenet (Prāsaṅgika), the latter being the highest Buddhist tenet.

Māhaparinirvā☐a Sūtra (S): the Discourse on the great Sorrow Transcendence; a discourse on the physical demise of the Buddha. Comprising ten chapters, it explains such subjects as the adamantine body, vajra kāya, etc.

Maitreya (S): the next Buddha to appear in this world. Lit: The Kind One.

Manas (S): that which has the capacity to think; a word synonymous with citta (chitta), mind.

Ma☐☐ala (S): centric; Lit: circle, centric, round. In the context of tantric practices, mandala refers to the entire domain of the deity's enlightened presence and retinues.

Manovijñāna (manovigyan) (S): mental consciousness; In the Buddhist perspective, the mind at the gross level is of six kinds: the five sensory consciousnesses (of eyes/sight, ear/

hearing, nose/smell, tongue/taste, body/touch) and mental consciousness, which is not dependent on the senses.

Māyā (maya) (S): illusion; an appearance that actually does not exist; a metaphor for falsity.

Mig-ḥkhrul (migtrul) (T): visual confusion; an illusion to the eye.

Nāgārjuna (Nagarjuna) (S): the Buddhist teacher revered as the foremost pioneer of the Middle Way view, devoid of the two extremes, who wrote, besides many other texts, the six principal texts on the correct understanding of the view. The name literally means "Serpentine Accomplished One," klu-sgrub (T).

Nālanda (Nalanda) (S): the ancient Buddhist monastic university in India, renowned as the leading great Indian center of learning, where the classical great Buddhist teachers taught.

Nirmāṇakāya (S): emanation body; a physical manifestation in visible conventional forms, out of Dharmakāya, the enlightened state.

Nirvāṇa (S): Sorrow Transcendence; the achieved state of mental purity where all defilements, and their imprints, have been gotten rid of; thus there is no suffering and no causes of suffering (sorrows) with the mind. It is the state synonymous with liberation.

Oracle (State Oracle): the deity consulted on important matters of the nation. Oracle deities make their presence through a human medium in a trance. Tibet's state oracle is Nechung.

Pāramitā (S): perfection; to go beyond the ordinary limit. A bodhisattva's practices comprise mainly the six major perfections of: generosity, morality, patience, diligence, meditative concentration, and wisdom. The mark of perfection in the training is that once perfected, these attributes are always with the mind, requiring no further effort to generate them.

Paramārthasatya (S): the ultimate truth. It refers to the ultimate reality of all phenomena, which is that things do not exist inherently; rather they are of a dependent arising nature and undeniably exist conventionally.

Pāramitāyana (S): the perfection vehicle; the Great Vehicle path that is not of the speedy tantric category.

Panchen Lama (Pan-chen-bla-ma) (T): revered as the human emanation of Buddha Amitābha, whose monastic seat is Tashilhunpo Monastery, in central-west Tibet.

Prajñāpāramitā (S): perfection of wisdom; one of the six perfections (see Pāramitā) a bodhisattva trains on.

Prāṇa (prana) (S): wind (inner energy); the subtle air/energy in the body moving through the channels.

Prāṇayāma (S): exercise of breath that circulates in the body.

Ramagang (T): a village in Tibet.

Ratna (S): jewel, precious; an epithet for the three sublime fields of Refuge.

Rinpoche (rin-po-che) (T): the Precious One; an appellation for teachers who have chosen to be reborn in the human form to help sentient beings; a reincarnated lama.

Rūpakāya (S): Form Body; the visible physical appearance of an enlightened being. These are of two kinds: Emanation Body (Nirmānakāya), visible even to an ordinary being of karmic purity; and Complete Enjoyment Body (Sambhogakāya, Requisites of Riches Complete Body), visible only to bodhisattvas on the tenth ground.

Śakti (shakti) (S): Energy, power.

Śākyamuni Buddha (Shakyamuni ~) (S): the historical Buddha, who is the fourth Buddha (Enlightened Being) of a thousand Buddhas to appear within the period known as the Fortunate Era.

Samādhi (S): meditative concentration; single-pointed concentration of the mind.

Śamatha (shamatha) (S): calm, abiding; perfection in the training of meditative single-pointed concentration of the mind. The mind at this stage is free of the faults of mental scattering and mental sinking; they are "calmed" (pacified), and the mind abides single-pointedly for as long as one wants to.

Sambhogakāya (S): Enjoyment Body (see Rūpakāya)

Sāṃkhya (S): the Enumerators; one of the earliest ancient non-Buddhist tenets. They list, enumerate, fields of knowledge into twenty-five categories.

Saṃsāra (Samsara) (S): the cycle, cyclic existence; the mundane existence of the repeating cycle of birth and death, with the accompanying resultant sufferings. Such an existence is caused primarily by the three primary mental defilements: attachment, hatred and ignorance.

Saṃvṛttisatya (S): the conventional truth, the deceptive "truth"; the truth at the conventional level, not the ultimate.

Saṃgha (sangha) (S): the ordained community, ~congregation; the ordained practitioners of the Buddha's teachings.

Shambhala (S): a kingdom associated with Kālacakra Tantra. Its exact location is not known; rather it is believed to be a realm that is accessible in spiritual purity.

Sherab kyi pharol tu chyinpa (T): Transcendent insight.

Shunyata (Śūnyatā) (S): emptiness, voidness; the ultimate reality of all phenomena, that they are devoid of (empty of) the two extremes: absolutely existent, the extreme of permanence; and absolutely non-existent, the extreme of nothingness, nihilism.

Takṣaśilā (Taxila; Takshila) (S): a great ancient Buddhist monastic university located to the west of central India.

Tan (S): body.

Tantra (S): "continuity"; the advanced altruistic path towards enlightenment, the method where one utilizes the present ordinary place, body, riches and deeds into pure-outlook, transformative means for achieving enlightenment to benefit all beings. It is often used synonymously with the word mantra to mean the entire tantric path and practices.

The Three Refuges: Buddha, the enlightened being, who has shown the path; Dharma, the teachings, which are the actual means of achieving refuge from misery and its causes; Sangha, the realized practitioners who are of assistance on one's path towards achieving enlightenment. They are also known as "The Three Jewels," the Three Rare Supreme.

Three-Fold Training: the three trainings in morality, meditative concentration, and wisdom.

Tra (S): protect.

Tulku (sprul-sku) (T): a re-emanated teacher, a lama-reincarnate. It refers to teachers who have willingly chosen to be reborn again in human form to help sentient beings. (see Nirmāṇakāya)

Tulpa (sprul-pa) (T): an imagined being, a magical creation generated by a powerful concentration of thought.

Tushita (Tusita) (S): the Joyful [Realm]. One referent of Tushita is a celestial realm that is within Samsara, the cyclic existence. Located in solitude away from this celestial realm is the Tushita Holding Delightful Attributes where Buddha Maitreya resides.

Uniśvaravādin (an-īśvaravādin) (S): those who do not believe in a creator; those who do not assert the view that Iśvar created the world.

Upādhyāya (S): "abbot," preceptor; one who inducts a novice into the monastic community; also, head of a monastery.

Vēsākh (vesakh) month: the fourth lunar month in a year. The month is regarded as the holiest month in the Buddhist calendar, as it was on the full moon of the month of vesakh (vēsākh) when Buddha was born, become enlightened, and passed away into parinirvana.

Vijñāna (vigyan) (S): consciousness; to know directly, to perceive things. This includes not only the realm of thought, but through sensory perceptions as well.

Vikramshila (Vikramaśila) (S): the ancient Buddhist monastic university where the great Teacher Atisha (eleventh century) served as the abbot.

Vipaśyanā (vipashyana) (S): special insight, transcendent insight. (see Lhagthong)

APPENDIX

Going Beyond Self As Image

Michael Mendizza in conversation with Keith A. Buzzell, AB, DO

Our exploration began and is centered on the simple observation that "we are not what or who we think we are.'" This fact begs two questions: What is the nature and structure of the feelings, images and beliefs we "think" we are, and if we are not that, what are we?

The second question, what then are we?, is beyond measure, beyond definition. Recall as Alan Watts described, "We can't catch the wind in a paper sack." Or Krishnamurti, "The word is not the thing."

This leaves the easier challenge: What is the nature and structure of the feelings, images, and beliefs we "think" we are? What follows is the exploration in a unique way of just that question.

Keith, what led to your interest in human development, health and the central role the brain plays in our continued evolution?

I have always asked questions. At the age of seven, I recall being asked not to come back to Sunday school, because of the questions I asked. They made my teachers and the church very uncomfortable.

In the 1950s, I found the works of Gurdjieff, who had introduced the concept that human beings have not one but three brains. This was 50 to 60 years before Paul MacLean began his work on the "Triune Brain." Gurdjieff developed a sophisticated view of three-brained beings, and talked about many of the issues to which Paul has given a neuro-anatomical foundation. As a physician, when I came across MacLean's work, it created an explosion of connectedness between Gurdjieff's views and modern neuro-physiology.

What do you mean by human beings having three brains?

Over 600 million years ago, with the appearance of the cold-blooded vertebrates, there appeared sensory systems that could construct a resonant representation, or image, of some portion of the external world. The life of cold-blooded vertebrates—what I call one-brain creatures—is determined by the spectrum of sensors and imaging capacity of this basic core brain. The primary function of this reptilian brain is survival, focused around the triad of food, reproduction, and defense.

What is your definition of a brain?

A brain really should be called a brain when it has developed the capacity to take a slice through all of the variable forms and energies "out there" and build a resonant representation or an image of the external world; and then, within the confines of that creature, act upon these images for survival. Then you have a brain.

The world is defined by the range of sensitivity of its sensors emanating from the brain. Once the first brain becomes well-established as a whole sensory/motor instrument, which occurred about 200 million years ago, elements of what MacLean refers to as the "Limbic Brain," or the "Second Brain," began to appear.

Actually elements of this second brain begin to appear long before that second brain could be called a whole brain. The critical difference is that the world that the second brain opens to is not the world "out there" beyond the bounding membrane, but the inner world of dynamic metabolism and motions.

For instance, lizards and crocodiles have all the various muscle groups, but they have a rather gross muscular control. This begins to become more refined as the muscles themselves become interpenetrated by extensions of the second brain. Muscle spindles begin to measure the state of affairs of smaller and smaller groups of muscle fibers, which send information back to the spinal cord and up to the second brain. This increasingly complex monitoring and imaging of inner states is the hallmark of the second brain. With this feedback, we develop a feeling or image of what the body is doing, inside and out.

Self-perception, when limited to the first brain, is a representation only of the body surface. Certainly a lizard has receptors that will tell it to some degree the amount of pressure it's putting on one of its fore limbs. But it doesn't relate the internal dynamic state of the limb itself, the muscles, the blood flow, etc. This capacity evolved with the second brain.

With the development of the second brain, we also see a transition from a two-chambered heart to a four-chambered heart. We see the evolution of the diaphragm, the uterus, and the support for intra-body development of the embryo. In addition, all of the neural controls and the monitoring of all of the blood vessels, of all of the other fluids, of the so-called lymphatic system of the body, and we have the appearance of more and more sophistication in the immune system.

A crocodile has an immune system but it is elemental and primarily related again to the body surface and the outside world. With the limbic system, or second brain, we see an incredible diversification of internal defenses via the immune system. The core brain senses and represents an image of the external world. The second or limbic brain monitors and images inner bodily states. When we take all of the states of both brains, the resonate representations or images that are formed from those states, including feelings, this is what MacLean very appropriately calls the emergence of the "Sense of Self."

What kind of image is created from these inner states?

We subjectively experience our inner world in a totally different way than we do external sensations. There is a blending between these two in perception or consciousness. Both, however, are sensations. We flip from a state of sensation into a state of feeling—when you stub your toe and then you kick the dog, for example. There is pain and suddenly we are angry because we have been in pain. The states of sensation at one level will blend into the other and it can be very difficult to differentiate the two. A more clear-cut sense of self appears with the *cingulate gyrus*, the highest part of the second brain. It is interesting that no cellular precursor of the *cingulate gyrus* has been discovered in one-brained beings. Here we see the centers for nurturing, audio vocal communication between parent and child, and play. MacLean calls this great triad of functions the "Family Triad." He feels that as we study the biological cellular evolution of this area of the Second Brain, we will be studying the history of the family. It's a lovely way to put that, although it is certainly controversial in some circles.

We have been raised to believe that human life was somehow different, shall I say superior, to that of other animals. How does this hold up under current research?

Many traditions place an absolute separation between what we as three-brained or human beings experience and what other creatures experience. The neuro-chemicals inside a chimpanzee are exactly the same as inside of us. Their facial expressions are the same, their play behavior is very similar, etc. It is increasingly difficult to deny that they are living a world of great, rich feeling. This is one of the most essential insights; that all mammalian life has a rich experience.

Our world is far more complex and subtle, however, because we've got a neural system hundreds of times larger. Fundamentally, all mammals, because we all share this second brain, have similar subjective experiences, which are just as real and just as whole and just as important in the life of that creature as is our inner experience. We should be eminently respectful of that, because that's what we come from and are part of.

Traditions would have us believe; due to our superior nature, that humanity holds dominion over all of nature.

The word "dominion" has been misunderstood. Etymologically, the word "dominion" is not power over, it is responsibility toward, recognizing that everything in creation is inside of us. When we are disrespectful or abuse aspects of the outside world, other life forms, we are abusing ourselves.

Back to the brain. I can close my eyes and see an image of what my room looks like, which I assume is a function of the core or first brain. When we start talking about the image of emotions or the image of inner states, it's a different experience. Help me with that.

All sensory instruments are an extension of a brain, whether it's the core brain looking into the outside world or the second brain interfacing with the inside world, or the third brain, which interfaces with both of those brains.

In each case, a system of sensors feedback data, which the brain uses to construct a resonant representation of the energies and forms that that particular sensory system opens to. They are all images.

First brain images, because they are created via data from a world beyond the boundary of the creature, are relatively concrete. They are, you could say, literal images. When we come to the second, emotional or Limbic brain, it's much more difficult for most people to see the image.

Perhaps it would be helpful to introduce the term, self-image. What do we mean by self-image?

We are looking at pride, vanity, a presumption of honesty, of strength, of purpose, and anger. Externally we see these states expressed as postures, gestures, tones of voice and facial expressions. We can see anger and hostility, suspicion and fear. We see satisfaction, constancy or hesitation. We see maternal love expressed between many mammalian forms. We are looking at the external image reflected through this interpenetration of the first brain muscular system by the second brain. That inside state is an image because it is not a material "whole" of anything. The organism has sampled a variable range of energies, which reflect the internal state. We experience that reflection or image as "self."

So we now have two brains.

With the evolution of the second brain special chemicals, called neuro peptides, report to the brain the inner state of the body. Candice Pert, formerly of the National Institute of Health, calls them the "chemicals of emotion."

The important differentiation is that the world of the second brain is a world of both neural and chemical formation and function. It isn't just the nervous system alone. Now there's an interplay of inner and outer images.

It is important to keep in mind that our emotional world is very rarely composed of one feeling. Each moment may be filled with a kaleidoscope of emotional images. We can be happy, sad, depressed, and joyful simultaneously. We can be happy and sad at the same time. When your child goes off to school for the first time, you're standing there with a big smile on your face. But she's also begun to separate and enter the "outside" world, so you get tears coming down your face. All this is happening at once. How we feel, our emotional state, can be a complex flow of multiple experiences.

Is the core or maintenance brain completely different in form and function from the emotional or second brain?

MacLean never said that the three brains are separate. The primary structures have evolved over long periods of time. They are fundamentally different in their function and can, relatively speaking, function independently. Do they all the time? No. They should function as a tightly integrated whole.

There's a great deal of misunderstanding about the third brain. What is the third brain and what does it really do?

As we move up the evolutionary ladder, over the last 200 billion years we see increasingly dense neural structures, which begin to open capacities and functions that look like the third brain. Cleverness, a monkey digging with a stick for food. We see the emergence of curiosity, not for food, not for survival, but curiosity for its own sake. All this requires the neural matrix of a third brain. As this third brain develops, we naturally see in the life of many mammalian forms, aspects that appear surprisingly similar to those that emerge with the full human brain. But the third brain isn't complete.

When it is complete it will have the capacity to create various types of abstract images—of letters, words, numbers; of comparisons, analogies, similarities; of spatial and sound forms. It will "image" logical sequences, and "play" with symbols, words, colors, sounds, and forms. This is the world of the third brain.

This third brain, being the latest evolutionary structure, might be considered immature. We described how the core and mid-brains have developed feedback systems that create images of what is happening outside and inside (proprioception). David Bohm suggested, however, that the new brain, the neocortex, has not evolved such a feedback system to keep track of thought, and that this is a major source of confusion and conflict. We lose track of what the third brain is doing.

This is a recurring theme in Mac Lean's monumental work, *The Triune Brain in Evolution*. There are far fewer paths connecting the second brain to the third brain than those that connect the first brain to the third brain. This makes the new brain much more vulnerable to data from the outside than information coming from the sensors of the second brain, which monitor inside states.

We have a strong neural prejudice from the outside world and fail to give equal attention to what is going on inside. There also seems to be a clear difference between generic males and females in this regard.

Males tend to emphasize the outside world. Women, because they are the source of nurture, the source of life and continuity, are more aware of the inner world. The connections between the second brain and the third brain of females, especially the right side of the third brain, are much more pronounced than males. As a result, they can be more attentive to the reality of their second brain inner world. You can see this principal in the arrogance, the plundering and the domination that has often emerged from the male-dominated third brain.

More important, so far as the emergence of the third brain is what it does in terms of perspective. Lizards live in a one-dimensional world. They have fixed habit patterns that react and respond only to the present. They have very poor memories. Two brain creatures develop an enormous tail into the past. Memory develops and becomes longer and longer and immensely dense. But the second brain has little capacity to reach into the future.

With the appearance of the third brain, there is a sudden extension into the future, built upon the second brain's past and the first brain's present. With that extension, life takes on a three-dimensional perspective. I can't emphasize that too much.

Another way of looking at our three-brained nature is to see that we have the outside world represented by the first brain, the inside world imaged by the second brain, and the third brain emerges as the third point of a triad, receiving input from both. Adding this third dimension alters the first brain's sense of the outside world and the second brain's sense of self/other. Now we get a three-dimensional perspective that gives rise to the inner representation, or the subjective experience, of an independent "I".

We talk about having a body. We talk about having feelings. This third brain subjective experience of "I" is unique and enormously powerful. It is an instrument of infinite separation, as well as an instrument of infinite unification. It can cut both ways.

Bohm described how we could look at our image of self as being made up of three completely different representations, "Me", "Myself" and "I". In light of what we have been exploring, "Me" might be the image created by the first brain; "Myself", the resonate representation of the limbic or emotional brain; and "I" a representation of self generated by the new brain.

All three are images, however. If you penetrate to the core of the great traditions, you always find this differentiation. There "lawfully" appears in all humans a sense of "I", a sense of singularity, but that is still an image. There is a possibility of moving beyond the image to what may be called "Real I"…to a perception of participation and relationship which is not an "I" independent and separate from, but an "I" that is completely integrated in and through everything.

To "consciously" go beyond the images created by our triune brain presents extraordinary challenges. We each have imbedded in the neural matrix of our first and second brains a hardwired imperative to accept and respond to the created images as if they were real and whole. Hundreds of millions of years underpin these physical and social survival patterns. Clearly the first and second brains cannot question themselves. The third brain has that capacity, if it applies reasoning, logical analysis, comparison, etc.

The awareness that it is an image and not the reality is, however, a very tenuous state, one that we very quickly fall out of view, especially when highly evocative images are presented by the first or second brain. For instance, when a phone call from the IRS occurs, or when we are cut off on a superhighway while traveling at 70 miles an hour.

In those instances and thousands like them, the immediacy of the image as being real is both appropriate (in survival terms) and undeniably potent. Because of the way in which our first and second brains function, we are equally vulnerable to the facial expression or tone of voice of the boss, and to mistaking a tree root for a snake. A moment later, when the brains have processed more data and the image is understood as non-threatening, we may "feel" foolish. However, our heart and breathing-rate muscle tension, and circulation of adrenalin, betray that our first and second brain is continuing to react to the imaged threat.

As difficult as it is to sustain our impartiality to first and second brain images, it is more difficult yet with regard to third brain images. The sense-of-"I" naturally created by the neural imaging of the third brain brings a potent sense of singularity that is both real and imaginary. Real because of the physical and subjective feelings that we are a separate individual. Imaginary in that this image artificially separates us from everything. It also creates a subjective "specialness" that is the germ of a false and intrinsically malevolent egoism. It is this imaginary "false I" that results in monsters like Idi Amin, Pol Pot, and Hitler, as well as in abusive parents and arrogant corporate CEOs.

Is possible to go beyond the three images of the Outside, the Self and "I"?

There have been many approaches to this question over the past 5,000 years. In our time, however, the challenge has been made considerably greater because of the extraordinary and positive insights of modern science and the unparalleled negative impact of technology.

There is overwhelming evidence that the third brain's use of technological power, radio, TV, computers—to industrial conglomerates, managed health care, and the unending stream of toys and trivia—has confused and greatly diminished the attention needed to go beyond our embedment in the image, to true relationship, to "Real I".

It has fractured our personal and community life, and now seriously threatens the continuity of life on the planet. The origin of this gross imbalance is not out there in the outside world, it is inside, in the images created by the third brain of each of us. All of that represents a great obstacle in discovering what may lie beyond the image, what I call "Real I". That is why David Bohm's dialogue process and his conception of the explicate, implicate, and super-implicate order is of such value.

They help make the implicit image explicit. This going beyond the limited images of the three brains is also at the core of the deep ecology of nature and of childhood. For myself, it is why I have unmeasured respect and value for Gurdjieff, Bohm, and many others who explore the path that reaches beyond image.

> Dr. Buzzell is currently Founder and Medical Director of Hospice of Western Maine, Medical Director, of Fryeburg Health Care Center, and Founder of Wyllaned, an educational, research and developmental community.

ABOUT THE AUTHORS

Professor Samdhong Rinpoche

Name: Professor Samdhong Rinpoche (Lobsang Tenzin)
Date of Birth: 5 November 1939
Place of Birth: Nagdug, Kham Province, Eastern Tibet
Social Status: Fully Ordained Monk (Bhikkhu Mahathero)

At the age of five, Rinpoche was recognized as the reincarnation of the 4th Samdhong Rinpoche. Two years later, Lobsang Tenzin took vows as a monk and started his education at the feet of the great Teacher, Reverend Ngawang Jinpa, and other teachers. At the age of 12, he entered the great monastic university Drepung. After the Chinese invasion of Tibet, along with His Holiness, the 14th Dalai Lama, Tenzin Gyatso, Rinpoche was forced into exile, and sought political asylum in India.

At age 21, Samdhong Rinpoche taught the Tibetan language to the ordained scholars of the three great monasteries at Dalhousie. At age 26, Rinpoche became Principal of the Central School for Tibetans at Dalhousie. At age 38, he became Director of the Central Institute of Higher Tibetan Studies at Sarnath. Recognized early as detailed, clear and wise, one who has a precise understanding of the origins of terms, names, labels, and the reasons behind them, in 1960 Rinpoche was advised by His Holiness the Dalai Lama to work for the Tibetan Administration in Dharamsala. In 2001 he became the first democratically elected Prime Minister (officially Kalon Tripa, or Chairman of the Cabinet) of the Central Tibetan Administration, or the Tibetan Government in Exile, based in Dharamsala, India, with 84 percent of votes cast.

From helping to draft the new constitution for the Tibetan Government in Exile, education and economic reforms, enhancing Tibetan unity, a renowned Buddhist scholar and student of Gandhi, Rinpoche ensured that actions and policies were nonviolent, transparent, not harmful to the environment, benefitted the poorest, and were sustainable. Working closest to His Holiness the Dalai Lama, Rinpoche served by negotiating with the Chinese and was one of the very few Buddhists in the world with this depth, experience and clarity who for many years spent time exploring directly with J. Krishnamurti.

Michael Mendizza

Michael is an author, educator, documentary filmmaker, stage and screenwriter, and founder of Touch the Future, a nonprofit learning design center. He is the author of four books: *Playful Wisdom: A Father's Adventure*; *Magical Parent–Magical Child: The Art of Joyful Parenting*; *Always Awakening: Buddha's Realization Krishnamurti's Insight* with Samdhong Rinpoche, a close advisor to His Holiness the Dalai Lama; and *Flowering*, a collection of Michael's floral and seascape images with quotes by Krishnamurti, edited by Evelyne Blau. Michael and his wife share several art galleries that feature designer jewelry, Czech art glass, and Michael's photography.
Contact: michael@ttfuture.org

Bibliography

PERMISSIONS AND SOURCES

All texts by Jiddu Krishnamurti are copyright Krishnamurti Foundation of America and/or Krishnamurti Foundation Trust Ltd. All extracts are quoted with permission from the publishers and/or the copyright holders.

J. KRISHNAMURTI

pp. 54, 74, 80, 82, 94, 98, 104, 106, 112, 114, 116, 130, 170, 194, 204, 206, 224, 246
Krishnamurti, Jiddu. 1970. *The Only Revolution*. HarperCollins Publishers Ltd.

pp. 32, 142, 168, 240, 242, 250
——. 2003 (2nd ed.). *Krishnamurti's Notebook*, 1976. Krishnamurti Foundation Trust Ltd.

p. 28
——. 1978. Brockwood Park, UK, 2nd Public Dialogue, 31 August 1978. Krishnamurti Foundation Trust Ltd.

p. 34
——. 1973. *The Awakening of Intelligence*. 1st Dialogue with Alain Naudé, Malibu, 27 March 1971. HarperCollins Publishers Ltd.

p. 38
——. 1983. 4th Public Talk, 22 May 1983, Ojai, California. Krishnamurti Foundation Trust Ltd.

p. 42
——. 1991. *A Wholly Different Way of Living*. 13th Dialogue with Allan W. Anderson. Victor Gollancz Ltd.

p. 48
——. 1970. Australian Broadcasting Company Interview with Krishnamurti. Foundation Bulletin, No. 11, Autumn 1971, p. 8. Krishnamurti Foundation Trust Ltd.

p. 56
——. 1966. PBS Broadcast, Ojai, California, 1966, published in *The Collected Works of J. Krishnamurti*, Vol. 17, 1966–1967. Kendall/Hunt Publishing Company.

p. 70
——. 1979. 3rd Public Dialogue, Chennai (Madras), India, 1 January 1979. Krishnamurti Foundation Trust Ltd.

p. 78
———. 1978. *Can Humanity Change? J. Krishnamurti in Dialogue with Buddhists.* Shambhala Publications Inc.

p. 90
———. 1927. *Who Brings the Truth?* Talk at Castle Eerde, The Netherlands, 2 August 1927. Star Publishing Trust.

p. 96
———. 1977. *The Wholeness of Life.* Saanen, Switzerland, 4th Public Talk, 17 July 1977. Krishnamurti Foundation Trust Ltd.

p. 100
———. 1977. *Truth and Actuality.* Saanen, Switzerland, 7th Public Talk, 25 July 1976. Krishnamurti Foundation Trust Ltd.

p. 120
———. 1984. Saanen, Switzerland, 22 July 1984, 1st Question & Answer. Krishnamurti Foundation Trust Ltd.

p. 122
———. 1991. *The Collected Works of J. Krishnamurti*, Vol. 15, 1964–1965. Bombay, India, 6th Public Talk, 28 February 1965. Kendall/Hunt Publishing Company.

p. 126
———. 1972. *The Impossible Question.* Saanen, Switzerland, 8th Public Dialogue, 9 August 1970. Krishnamurti Foundation Trust Ltd.

p. 136
———. Brockwood Park, UK, 3rd Public Talk, 11 September 1971. Krishnamurti Foundation Trust Ltd.

p. 150
———. 1956 (1967 ed.). *Commentaries on Living: Series I.* Quest Books.

p. 154
———. 1981. Ojai, California, 6th Public Talk, 17 May 1981. Krishnamurti Foundation Trust Ltd.

p. 156
———. 1991. *The Collected Works of J. Krishnamurti*, Vol. 9, 1955–1956. Benaras, India, 1st Public Talk, 11 December 1955. Kendall/Hunt Publishing Company.

p. 160
———. 1972. *The Impossible Question.* Saanen, Switzerland, 8th Public Dialogue, 9 August 1970. Krishnamurti Foundation Trust Ltd.

p. 164
———. 1991. *The Collected Works of J. Krishnamurti*, Vol. 4, 1945–1948. Ojai, California, 1st Public Talk, 1946. Kendall/Hunt Publishing Company.

p. 166
———. 1980. *From Darkness to Light*: "The Search." HarperCollins Publishers Ltd.

p. 176
———. 1991. *The Collected Works of J. Krishnamurti*, Vol. 5, 1948–1949. Poona, India, 6th Public Talk, 3 October 1948. Kendall/Hunt Publishing Company.

p. 178
———. 1997. *The Perfume of the Teachings: A Dialogue with Trustees.* Krishnamurti Foundation Trust Ltd.

p. 180
———. 1991. *The Collected Works of J. Krishnamurti*, Vol. 1, 1933–1934. Adyar, India, 6th Public Talk, 3 January 1934. Kendall/Hunt Publishing Company.

p. 196
———. 1970. *The Urgency of Change:* "Conditioning." HarperCollins.

p. 198
——. 1991. *The Collected Works of J. Krishnamurti*, Vol. 13, 1962–1963. Varanasi, India, 6th Public Talk, 12 January 1962. Kendall/Hunt Publishing Company.

p. 200
——. 1991. *The Collected Works of J. Krishnamurti*, Vol. 10, 1956–1957. Stockholm, Sweden, 3rd Public Talk, 21 May 1956. Kendall/Hunt Publishing Company.

p. 210
——. 1997. *The Ending of Time* (1st ed.). HarperCollins.

p. 216
——. 1928. *Let Understanding Be the Law*, Castle Eerde, The Netherlands, 2 August 1928. Star Publishing Trust.

p. 226
——. 1958 (1971 ed.). *Commentaries On Living: Series II*. Quest Books.

p. 228
——. 1991. *A Wholly Different Way of Living.* San Diego, California, 3rd Conversation with Allan W. Anderson, 1972. Victor Gollancz Ltd.

p. 230
——. 1991. *The Collected Works of J. Krishnamurti*, Vol. 9, 1955–1956. Benaras, India, 2nd Public Talk, 18 December 1955. Kendall/Hunt Publishing Company.

p. 232
——. 1991. *A Wholly Different Way of Living.* 1st Dialogue with Allan W. Anderson. Victor Gollancz Ltd.

p. 236
——. 1984. *The Challenge of Change*. Krishnamurti Foundation of America.

p. 244
——. 2009. *The Krishnamurti Reader*. Ojai, California, 4th Public Talk, 10 April 1977. Shambhala Publications Inc.

p. 248
——. 1972. Saanen, Switzerland, 3rd Public Dialogue, 4 August 1972. Krishnamurti Foundation Trust Ltd.

p. 252
——. 1981. Ojai, California, 1st Public Question and Answer Meeting, 5 May 1981. Krishnamurti Foundation Trust Ltd.

p. 262
——. 1929. *Truth Is a Pathless Land*. Ommen, The Netherlands, 3 August 1929. Quoted in Lutyens, Mary, 1975 (1997), *Krishnamurti: The Years of Awakening*. Shambhala Publications Inc.

pp. 265–272
——. 1972. Krishnamurti Speaking to a Small Group of Trustees. Unpublished.

pp. 214, 269
——. Letters to Annie Besant, quoted in Lutyens, Mary, 1975 (1997), *Krishnamurti: The Years of Awakening*. Shambhala Publications Inc.

pp. 266–267
Clark, R. 1978. Interview with Evelyne Blau and Michael Mendizza. Krishnamurti Foundation of America.

p. 269
Nitya's account to A. Besant and C. W. Leadbeater (1922), quoted in Lutyens, Mary, 1975 (1997), *Krishnamurti: The Years of Awakening*. Shambhala Publications Inc.

pp. 266–272
Lutyens, Mary. 1990. *The Life and Death of J. Krishnamurti*. Rider.

BUDDHISM / HIS HOLINESS THE DALAI LAMA

pp. 40, 108, 172, 174
His Holiness the Dalai Lama. 2000. *Transforming the Mind*. HarperCollins Publishers Ltd.

p. 124
——. 2011. *Beyond Religion: Ethics for a Whole World*. Houghton Mifflin Hardcore Publishing Company.

pp. 26, 50, 66, 98, 132, 140, 148, 192, 204, 254
——. 1966. *The Opening of the Wisdom-Eye*. Quest Books.

pp. 36, 44, 68, 72
——. 2006. *How to See Yourself as You Really Are: A Practical Guide to Self-Knowledge*. Atra Books/Simon & Schuster.

pp. 110, 146
Ross Komito, David. 1987. *Nagarjuna's "Seventy Stanzas": A Buddhist Psychology of Emptiness*. The Permissions Company Inc., on behalf of Shambhala Publications Inc.

pp. 19, 24, 102, 118
Sogyal Rinpoche and Gaffnely P. and Harvey A (eds.). 1993. *The Tibetan Book of Living and Dying*. HarperCollins Publishers Ltd.

p. 72
Patrul Rinpoche. 1998. *The Words of My Perfect Teacher: A Complete Translation of a Classic Introduction to Tibetan Buddhism*. Shambhala Publications Inc.

pp. 20, 32, 86, 116, 138, 144
David-Néel, Alexandra and Lama Yongden. 1967. *The Secret Oral Teachings in Tibetan Buddhist Sects*. City Lights Publishers.

OTHER

p. 202
Chilton Pearce, Joseph. 1992. *Evolution's End*. HarperCollins Publishers Ltd.

pp. 134, 246
Anderson, Allan W. 2012. *Practical Wisdom: Reflections on the Teaching of J. Krishnamurti*. Karina Library Press.

pp. 120, 208
Lee, R. E. Mark. 2015. *Knocking at the Open Door: My Years with J. Krishnamurti*. Hay House Publishers, India.

pp. 88, 92
Krishna, Padmanabhan. 2016. *A Jewel on a Silver Platter: Remembering Jiddu Krishnamurti*. Peepal Leaves Publishing, India.

Photographic Credits

Photographs on pages 158, 212, 250 by Michael Mendizza; page 25 by Chandmal; pages 54, 90, 190 by Ziegler; page 168 by Garwand; page 260 © Rameshwar Das, used with permission; all photographs of Samdhong Rinpoche are reproduced with his permission. All other photographs are by unknown photographers; every attempt has been made to find their sources.

BUDDHISM / HIS HOLINESS THE DALAI LAMA

pp. 40, 108, 172, 174
His Holiness the Dalai Lama. 2000. *Transforming the Mind*. HarperCollins Publishers Ltd.

p. 124
——. 2011. *Beyond Religion: Ethics for a Whole World*. Houghton Mifflin Hardcore Publishing Company.

pp. 26, 50, 66, 98, 132, 140, 148, 192, 204, 254
——. 1966. *The Opening of the Wisdom Eye*. Quest Books.

pp. 36, 44, 68, 72
——. 2006. *How to See Yourself as You Really Are: A Practical Guide to Self-Knowledge*. Atra Books/Simon & Schuster.

pp. 110, 146
Ross Komito, David. 1987. *Nagarjuna's "Seventy Stanzas": A Buddhist Psychology of Emptiness*. The Permissions Company Inc., on behalf of Shambhala Publications Inc.

pp. 19, 24, 102, 118
Sogyal Rinpoche and Gaffnely P. and Harvey A (eds.). 1993. *The Tibetan Book of Living and Dying*. HarperCollins Publishers Ltd.

p. 72
Patrul Rinpoche. 1998. *The Words of My Perfect Teacher: A Complete Translation of a Classic Introduction to Tibetan Buddhism*. Shambhala Publications Inc.

pp. 20, 32, 86, 116, 138, 144
David-Néel, Alexandra and Lama Yongden. 1967. *The Secret Oral Teachings in Tibetan Buddhist Sects*. City Lights Publishers.

OTHER

p. 202
Chilton Pearce, Joseph. 1992. *Evolution's End*. HarperCollins Publishers Ltd.

pp. 134, 246
Anderson, Allan W. 2012. *Practical Wisdom: Reflections on the Teaching of J. Krishnamurti*. Karina Library Press.

pp. 120, 208
Lee, R. E. Mark. 2015. *Knocking at the Open Door: My Years with J. Krishnamurti*. Hay House Publishers, India.

pp. 88, 92
Krishna, Padmanabhan. 2016. *A Jewel on a Silver Platter: Remembering Jiddu Krishnamurti*. Peepal Leaves Publishing, India.

Photographic Credits

Photographs on pages 158, 212, 250 by Michael Mendizza; page 25 by Chandmal; pages 54, 90, 190 by Ziegler; page 168 by Garwand; page 260 © Rameshwar Das, used with permission; all photographs of Samdhong Rinpoche are reproduced with his permission. All other photographs are by unknown photographers; every attempt has been made to find their sources.